Laboratory Manual

Darrel Hess
City College of San Francisco

Physical Geography

Ninth Edition

A Landscape Appreciation

Tom L. McKnight • Darrel Hess

PEARSON

Prentice
Hall

Upper Saddle River, NJ 07458

Editor-in-Chief, Science: Nicole Folchetti
Publisher: Dan Kaveney
Associate Editor: Amanda Brown
Executive Managing Editor: Kathleen Schiaparelli
Assistant Managing Editor: Gina M. Cheselka
Managing Editor, Art Programs: Abigail Bass
AV Production Editor: Rhonda Aversa
Production Editor: Jessica Barna
Copyeditor: Marcia Youngman
Supplement Cover Manager: Paul Gourhan
Supplement Cover Designer: Victoria Colotta
Associate Director of Operations: Alexis Heydt-Long
Manufacturing Buyer: Ilene Kahn
Cover Image: Grand Canyon, South Rim © TIM FITZHARRIS / Minden Pictures

© 2008 Pearson Education, Inc.
Pearson Prentice Hall
Pearson Education, Inc.
Upper Saddle River, NJ 07458

Printed in the United States of America

10 9 8 7 6 5 4

ISBN 13:   978-0-13-238113-0
ISBN 10:   0-13-238113-3

Pearson Education Ltd., *London*
Pearson Education Australia Pty. Ltd., *Sydney*
Pearson Education Singapore, Pte. Ltd.
Pearson Education North Asia Ltd., *Hong Kong*
Pearson Education Canada, Inc., *Toronto*
Pearson Educación de Mexico, S.A. de C.V.
Pearson Education—Japan, *Tokyo*
Pearson Education Malaysia, Pte. Ltd.

CONTENTS

INTRODUCTION

TO THE STUDENT

The exercises in this Laboratory Manual give you the opportunity to apply many of the concepts studied in your physical geography course. The emphasis of the first half of the manual is understanding basic meteorological processes, and the interpretation of weather maps, weather satellite images and climate data. The emphasis of the second half is understanding the development of landforms, and the interpretation of topographic maps and stereo aerial photographs.

Each exercise begins with a brief introductory section that reviews key concepts and provides background information for the exercise problems. A reference to relevant pages in the textbook, *Physical Geography: A Landscape Appreciation*, 9th edition, by McKnight and Hess, is provided at the beginning of most exercises. Key terms are marked in bold type, and a glossary is found at the back of the Laboratory Manual in Appendix III. It is likely that your instructor will assign several exercise problem sets to you each week. The length and relative difficulty of the problems vary from exercise to exercise.

Few supplies are needed to complete the exercises. A ruler (about six inches long; graduated to at least 1/16"; scaled in both inches and centimeters), a three-foot length of string, and blue, green, and red pencils will be useful. An inexpensive magnifying glass (about 5×) may be helpful in some map reading exercises. For a few of the exercises you will need access to a 25-centimeter (10-inch) diameter or larger globe and a small atlas with an index.

Several of the exercises include stereo aerial photographs ("stereograms"). To view the aerial photographs in stereo, you can use the simple lens stereoscope included at the back of this Lab Manual (your instructor may make more sophisticated lens stereoscopes available to you in class). It is possible to complete the exercises that include stereo aerial photographs even if you have difficulty using a lens stereoscope.

Sixteen topographic maps are reproduced in color in the back of the Lab Manual. These maps are referred to in the exercises as "Map T-1," "Map T-2," and so on. A series of graphic map scales and a color map showing global climate distribution is found inside the front cover of the Lab Manual. Charts showing standard symbols used on topographic maps and metric system conversion formulas are found on the inside of the back cover.

Ten of the exercises in the Lab Manual have problems based on satellite images, maps, photographs or weather data you can access over the Internet. A Web page for the Lab Manual is available to simplify accessing the recommended Web sites (see the description of the Lab Manual Web site below).

Unless otherwise directed by your instructor or the exercise problems, you should round off numbers in your answers to one decimal place. For example, round off 12.437 to 12.4.

LAB MANUAL WEB SITE

A Web site has been established for this Lab Manual. The Lab Manual Web site contains maps, images, photographs, and satellite movie loops you will need to complete several of the exercise problem sets. The Web page also has links to Internet sites you can use to complete several of the exercise problem sets (Exercises 16, 17, 18, 20, 21, and 24).

To access the Lab Manual Web site:

- Go to the McKnight and Hess textbook Web site:
  <http://www.prenhall.com/mcknight>

- Then select *Lab Manual* on the textbook Web page. From the Lab Manual Web page, simply click on the exercise you are completing.

The URLs (Internet "addresses") of the recommended Internet sites are provided for each Internet exercise, but since the World Wide Web can change quickly, the URLs printed in the Lab Manual may become out of date or better sites might become available in the future. The Lab Manual Web page Internet links will be kept up to date to ensure that the exercises can be completed.

Even if you are not using the Internet links from the Lab Manual Web page, you might want to check the Web page periodically for any updated suggestions on completing the exercises in the Lab Manual.

TO THE INSTRUCTOR

This new edition of the Lab Manual retains the basic organization of previous editions. The most important changes include a new exercise on Doppler radar, as well as revised or expanded exercises on hurricanes, topographic maps, volcanoes, mass wasting, stream rejuvenation, and alpine glaciation. Two new stereograms have been added to accompany the topographic maps (in the exercises on Floodplains and Sand Dunes). Questions based on photographs posted on the Lab Manual Web site have been added for the exercises on Volcanoes, Mass Wasting, and Alpine Glaciation. A glossary of key terms (shown in bold type in the Lab Manual text) has been added as Appendix III.

Although either English units or S.I. units may be used to complete many of the exercises, the emphasis in the first half of the manual is on S.I. units. Since the topographic maps used in the second half of the manual are based on English units, most of the topographic map interpretation exercises retain their emphasis on English units.

All of the exercises that include stereo aerial photographs have matching topographic maps. A simple lens stereoscope is included in the back of the Lab Manual; however, if higher quality stereoscopes are available they will be useful, especially when students are first learning to use stereo aerial photographs. As in earlier editions of the Lab Manual, if students are unable to see the images in stereo, it is still possible to complete the exercise problems.

For greater flexibility, some major topics are covered over several exercises, and the problems for most exercises are divided into two or more parts. The length and difficulty of the exercise problem sets vary greatly from exercise to exercise. While most exercises are designed to stand alone, in a few cases one exercise builds upon the previous one. For example, the exercise on the adiabatic processes assumes an understanding of relative humidity.

An answer key for the exercises in the Lab Manual is available. The Answer Key also includes a sample course syllabus as well as suggestions on supplementing Lab Manual exercises. Contact your local Prentice Hall representative to receive a copy of the Answer Key.

Students will be called upon to use several key skills repeatedly. For example, the interpretation of various kinds of isolines will be required throughout the first half of the manual, and the interpretation of contour lines and the construction of topographic profiles will be required in the second half. These skills should be emphasized early on.

If the materials are available, instructors are encouraged to supplement the maps and stereo aerial photographs in this manual with additional topographic maps and aerial photographs. Also, feel free to recommend different, or additional, Internet sites to your students. Even if you are not having students use the Lab Manual Web site to access Internet sites, you may want to check the Lab Manual Web page periodically for any updates or suggestions on completing the exercises.

ACKNOWLEDGMENTS

I would like to thank the instructors who offered suggestions for improving this and earlier editions of the Lab Manual, including Peter Combs, Hunter College-CUNY; James E. Court, City College of San Francisco; Purba Fernandez, DeAnza College; W. Franklin Long, Coastal Carolina Community College; Robert Manlove, City College of San Francisco and Contra Costa College; Deborah A. Salazar, Oklahoma State University; Janet Valenza, Austin Community College; and Craig ZumBrunnen, University of Washington. Many of their suggestions are incorporated into the present manual. Of course, any errors remaining are my responsibility alone.

The staff of the U.S. Geological Survey Earth Sciences Information Center in Menlo Park, California, provided valuable assistance in obtaining many of the maps and photographs used in this manual, as did the USGS/EROS Data Center in Sioux Falls, South Dakota. Special thanks go to Brendan Kelly and Greg Durocher of the U.S.G.S. in Anchorage, Alaska, for their help selecting aerial photographs from that part of the country. Ed Shelden, Jr., provided much appreciated help with the processing of some of the digital images used in the Lab Manual.

Many thanks to all at Prentice Hall, especially to Associate Editor Amanda Brown, Media Editor Andrew Sobel, Production Editor Jessica Barna, Copy Editor Marcia Youngman, Editorial Assistant Jessica Neumann, and Geosciences Publisher Dan Kaveney for guiding me through the process of completing this Lab Manual. Thanks also go to my longtime City College of San Francisco Earth Sciences Department colleagues, Katryn Wiese, Joyce Lucas-Clark, and Wanda Simpson-Baczek, for their ongoing help and support.

Most of all, I wish to thank my students who, often without knowing it, helped me develop and improve the exercises for this Lab Manual.

If students or instructors have any comments, please address them to:

Darrel Hess
Earth Sciences Department
City College of San Francisco
50 Phelan Avenue
San Francisco, CA 94112
email: *dhess@ccsf.edu*

EXERCISE 1
METRIC CONVERSIONS

Objective:	To practice making unit conversions between the English system and the metric (S.I.) system of measurement.
Reference:	McKnight and Hess, *Physical Geography*, 9th ed., pp. 4 and A1–A2.

METRIC CONVERSIONS

Although the general public in the United States still uses the so-called "English" system of measurement (e.g., feet, miles), most of the rest of the world—and the entire scientific community—use the metric system (e.g., meters, kilometers). Today, the metric system has been incorporated into what is formally known as the ***Système International*** or ***S.I.*** system of measurement. In this Lab Manual you will encounter both English units and S.I. units of measure. It is useful for you to be comfortable using both systems, and for you to be able to convert units from one system into the other.

There are two levels of conversion precision that may be useful to you. First, it is helpful to have a rough idea of the equivalents—the kind of conversion you can do quickly in your head without a calculator. For example, it is useful to know that one kilometer is about 2/3 of a mile. The second kind of conversion is a precise equivalent—for example, one kilometer = 0.621 mile. These exact conversions are necessary if a precise measurement in one system must be duplicated in the other system. Some commonly used conversions are given below (to an accuracy of 3 decimal places). Additional conversions factors are found on the back cover of the Lab Manual.

Conversions: *S.I. to English*

	Approximate Conversions	**Exact Conversions**
Distance:	1 centimeter = a little less than $\frac{1}{2}$ inch 1 meter = a little more than 3 feet 1 kilometer = about 2/3 mile	cm × 0.394 = inches m × 3.281 = feet km × 0.621 = miles
	1 cm (centimeter) = 10 mm (millimeters) *1 m (meter) = 100 cm* *1 km (kilometer) = 1000 m*	
Volume:	1 liter = about 1 quart	liters × 1.057 = quarts
Mass (Weight):	1 gram = about 1/30 ounce 1 kilogram = about 2 pounds	g × 0.035 = ounces kg × 2.205 = pounds
	1 kg (kilogram) = 1000 g (grams)	
Temperature:	1°C change = 1.8°F change	(°C × 1.8) + 32 = °F

Conversions: *English to S.I.*

	Approximate Conversions			**Exact Conversions**			
Distance:	1 inch	=	about $2\frac{1}{2}$ cm	inches	$\times$	2.540	= centimeters
	1 foot	=	about 1/3 m	feet	$\times$	0.305	= meters
	1 yard	=	about 1 m	yards	$\times$	0.914	= meters
	1 mile	=	about $1\frac{1}{2}$ km	miles	$\times$	1.609	= kilometers

$$1'(foot) = 12''(inches)$$
$$1\ yard = 3'$$
$$1\ statute\ mile = 5280'$$

Volume:	1 quart	=	about 1 liter	quarts	$\times$	0.946	= liters
	1 gallon	=	about 4 liters	gallons	$\times$	3.785	= liters

$$1\ gallon = 4\ quarts$$

Mass (Weight):	1 ounce	=	about 30 g	ounces	$\times$	28.350	= g
	1 pound	=	about 1/2 kg	pounds	$\times$	0.454	= kg

$$1\ lb.\ (pound) = 16\ oz\ (ounces)$$

Temperature:	1°F change	=	about 0.6°C change	$(°F - 32) \div 1.8 = °C$

Rounding

In scientific work many of the numbers used are measured quantities and so are not exact—they are limited by the precision of the instrument used in the measurement. Further, calculations based on measured quantities can be no more precise than the original measurements themselves. Therefore, measurements and the results of calculations should be recorded in a way that shows the degree of measurement precision. For example, if you use an electronic calculator to divide the following two measured quantities, you would get:

$$5.7 \text{ centimeters} \div 1.75 \text{ minutes} = 3.2571429 \text{ cm/min.}$$

But is 3.2571429 cm/min. a truly correct answer? Not really. In general, the greater the number of digits in a measurement or calculation answer, the greater the implied precision of measurement. A mathematical operation cannot make your measurements more precise. In the example above, our distance measurement is only accurate to tenths of centimeters (perhaps limited by the measuring device we used), and our final answer can be no more precise than this. So:

$$5.7 \text{ centimeters} \div 1.75 \text{ minutes} = 3.3 \text{ cm/min.}$$

When rounding off numbers, if the first digit to be dropped is less than 5, leave the preceding digit unchanged; if the first digit to be dropped is 5 or greater, increase the preceding digit by one. So: 6.74 becomes 6.7, while 6.75 becomes 6.8.

Your instructor may introduce the concept of *significant digits* to you. This will further extend your understanding of the proper rounding of measured quantities.

Name _____   Section _____

EXERCISE 1 PROBLEMS—PART I

1. Complete the following conversions using exact conversion factors (round your answers to one decimal place):

	S.I. Units	English System Units
(a)	14 centimeters	_____ inches
(b)	29 meters	_____ feet
(c)	175 kilometers	_____ miles
(d)	42 liters	_____ quarts
(e)	57 grams	_____ ounces
(f)	65 kilograms	_____ pounds
(g)	37°C	_____ °F

2. Complete the following conversions using exact conversion factors (round your answers to one decimal place):

	English System Units	S.I. Units
(a)	3 inches	_____ centimeters
(b)	4.3 feet	_____ meters
(c)	18 yards	_____ meters
(d)	73 miles	_____ kilometers
(e)	6.2 quarts	_____ liters
(f)	10 gallons	_____ liters
(g)	14 ounces	_____ grams
(h)	155 pounds	_____ kilograms
(i)	47°F	_____ °C

EXERCISE 1 PROBLEMS—PART II

1. Complete the following conversions using exact conversion factors (round your answers to one decimal place):

	S.I. Units	English System Units
(a)	72 centimeters	_____ inches
(b)	24 meters	_____ feet
(c)	1,300 kilometers	_____ miles
(d)	4.5 liters	_____ quarts
(e)	144 grams	_____ ounces
(f)	228 kilograms	_____ pounds
(g)	12°C	_____ °F

2. Complete the following conversions using exact conversion factors (round your answers to one decimal place):

	English System Units	S.I. Units
(a)	55 inches	_____ centimeters
(b)	1,774 feet	_____ meters
(c)	220 yards	_____ meters
(d)	23,900 miles	_____ kilometers
(e)	24 quarts	_____ liters
(f)	300 gallons	_____ liters
(g)	26 ounces	_____ grams
(h)	4,500 pounds	_____ kilograms
(i)	88°F	_____ °C

EXERCISE 2
LOCATION

Objective: To review the system of latitude and longitude, and provide experience using atlases and globes.

Materials: 25 cm (10 inch) or larger diameter globe. World atlas (with index).

Reference: McKnight and Hess, *Physical Geography*, 9th ed., pp. 10–15.

LATITUDE AND LONGITUDE

Any location on Earth can be described using the grid system of **latitude** and **longitude**. Latitudes and longitudes are angular measures, with latitude describing north-south location, and longitude describing east-west location.

Lines of latitude on a map or globe are called **parallels** since they are all parallel to each other (Figure 2-1a). Latitude ranges from 0° at the equator, to 90° north latitude at the North Pole, and 90° south latitude at the South Pole.

Lines of longitude are known as **meridians** (Figure 2-1b). The meridians are farthest apart at the equator and converge at the poles.

The starting point for measuring longitude is the **prime meridian**, which runs through the Royal Observatory at Greenwich, England (just outside London). Locations east of the prime meridian are described in degrees east longitude, and locations west of the prime meridian in degrees west longitude. Longitude ranges from 0° at the prime meridian to 180° (on the opposite side of the Earth from the prime meridian).

When more exact descriptions of location are required (as when using detailed maps of a region), fractions of degrees of latitude and longitude are used. One degree is divided into 60

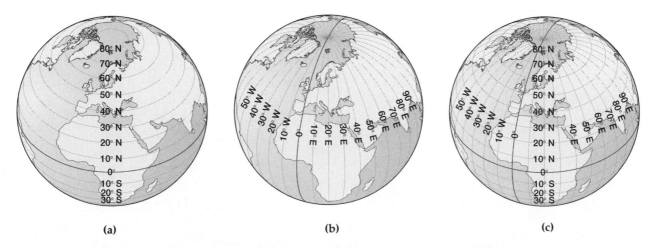

(a) (b) (c)

Figure 2-1: The geographic grid: (a) Parallels of latitude. (b) Meridians of longitude. (c) Complete grid system. (From McKnight and Hess, *Physical Geography*, 9th ed.)

"minutes" (often written 60') and each minute can be further divided into 60 "seconds" (60"). Therefore: $1° = 60'$, and $1' = 60"$. When describing angular measures such as latitude and longitude, minutes and seconds are *not* referring to time, but to fractions of degrees.

As an example, the precise location of the crater of Mount St. Helens in Washington is 46°11'55" north latitude, 122°11°15" west longitude.

With the increasing use of **Global Positioning System (GPS)** satellite technology to determine location, it has become common in some circumstances to indicate fractions of degrees in decimal units. For example, 45°35' N can be written 45.583° N, while 32°23'55" N can be written 32°23.917' N.

GLOBES AND ATLASES

Parallels and meridians are typically marked on globes in 10° or 15° increments. If the parallels and meridians are not marked on the globe, latitude and longitude are determined by using the degree markings on the arms or rings supporting the globe.

When searching for a location in an atlas, take advantage of the atlas index. The index will often comprise more than one-third of the pages in an atlas. In the index, cities, rivers, mountains, and other features are listed alphabetically. For each location, the index will typically provide the page number of the best map to use, the country, and often its latitude and longitude. Some atlases provide a pronunciation guide as well.

Some atlases do not refer to places in the index by latitude and longitude. Instead they provide a coordinate (such as "F7") that refers to a simplified grid system marked along the margins of each map in the atlas.

EXERCISE 2 PROBLEMS—PART I

1.   Using a globe, determine the latitude and longitude (to the nearest degree) of the following cities. Be sure to indicate if the location is north or south latitude, and east or west longitude.

	City	Latitude	Longitude
(a)	Chicago, Illinois	_____	_____
(b)	Tokyo, Japan	_____	_____
(c)	Sydney, Australia	_____	_____
(d)	Singapore	_____	_____
(e)	Buenos Aires, Argentina	_____	_____

2.   Using a globe, determine which major city is located at the following coordinates:

	Latitude	Longitude	City
(a)	14° N	100° E	_____
(b)	56° N	38° E	_____
(c)	19° N	99° W	_____
(d)	1° S	37° E	_____
(e)	37° S	175° E	_____

EXERCISE 2 PROBLEMS—PART II

1.   On the diagram at right, plot the following coordinates with a dot. Then label each dot with its corresponding letter:

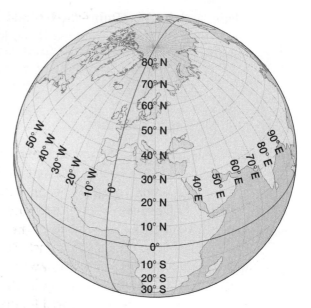

    (a)   10° N, 40° W

    (b)   50° N, 40° E

    (c)   40° N, 25° W

    (d)   5° S, 10° W

    (e)   65° N, 70° E

2.   Use the index of an atlas to find the following places. Determine the latitude and longitude to the nearest degree:

Place	Latitude	Longitude
(a) Pusan	_____	_____
(b) Reykjavik (Reikjavik)	_____	_____
(c) Walvis Bay	_____	_____
(d) Tuvalu (Ellice Islands)	_____	_____

3.   If you start at the equator and travel to 10° N latitude, approximately how many kilometers (or miles) north of the equator will you be? Take the circumference of the Earth to be 40,000 kilometers (24,900 miles). Show your calculations.

4.   If you travel west through 10° of longitude along the equator, the distance traveled will be very different from the distance traveled through 10° of longitude at 60° N latitude. Why?

EXERCISE 3
TIME

Objective: To learn to calculate time and day differences around the world.

Reference: McKnight and Hess, *Physical Geography*, 9th ed., pp. 23–26.

LOCAL SUN TIME

Although few people today are concerned with the local **Sun time**, it is a useful starting point for a discussion of time. Local Sun time is based on the position of the Sun in the sky. The local Sun time "noon" for a given location is the moment in the day when the Sun reaches its highest point in the sky. However, at the same moment that it is local Sun time noon at our location, at locations east or west of us the local Sun time is different.

The Earth rotates from west to east (looking down at the North Pole on a globe, the Earth would appear to be spinning counterclockwise). This means that at the same moment the Sun is low in the morning sky in Honolulu, it is high in the sky at noon in Denver, and low in the afternoon sky in New York. In other words, as we travel to the east, the time becomes progressively later.

STANDARD TIME

Rather than having people continually adjusting clocks to local Sun time when moving east or west, 24 **standard time zones** have been established by international agreement. Each time zone is a band of longitude, within which it is the same standard time (although, of course, the local Sun time varies slightly within the time zone). When moving from one time zone to the next, we adjust our watches by 1 hour.

The time zones are based on **central meridians** spaced 15° of longitude apart. The Earth rotates through 360° of longitude in 24 hours, and so rotates through 15° of longitude in one hour (360° ÷ 24 = 15°). While a standard time zone is 15° of longitude wide, the actual time zone boundaries have been adjusted over most inhabited areas of the Earth (Figure 3-1).

TIME ZONE CALCULATIONS

The map in Figure 3-1 shows standard time zones around the world. If we remember that it is always later in New York than in San Francisco, it is easy to calculate time differences. It becomes one hour later for each time zone we cross moving from west to east (from San Francisco toward New York), and 1 hour earlier for each time zone we cross moving from east to west. New York is 3 time zones to the east of San Francisco, so New York time is 3 hours later than San Francisco time.

To avoid confusion, it is usually best to refer to "12:00 midnight" and "12:00 noon" rather than to 12:00 A.M. and 12:00 P.M. respectively.

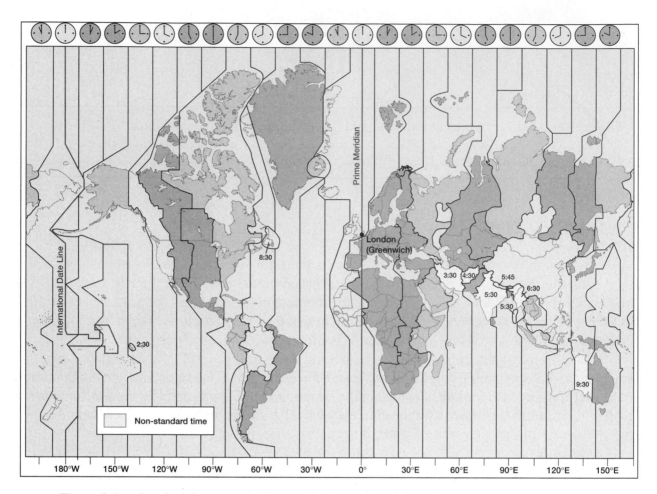

Figure 3-1: Standard time zones of the world. (From McKnight and Hess, *Physical Geography*, 9th ed.)

Notice that a few time zones are based on the half-hour (such as for Newfoundland and India), but the same logic applies. For example, India is 5 1/2 hours later than Greenwich, England.

In 1884, **Greenwich Mean Time (GMT)** was established as the world reference for standard time (the Greenwich time zone is based on the prime meridian). Today, Greenwich time is known as **Universal Time Coordinated (UTC)** or **Zulu** time (Zulu time uses a 24-hour clock, so that "1530Z" would be 3:30 P.M. Greenwich time).

If you know the central meridians, it is also possible to calculate time differences mathematically by determining the number of degrees of longitude between two locations. For example, Tokyo time is based on the 135° E central meridian and Rome is based on the 15° E meridian, a difference in longitude of 120°:

$$135° - 15° = 120° \text{ difference between Tokyo and Rome}$$

Fifteen degrees of longitude represents 1 hour of time, so:

$$120° \div 15° = 8 \text{ hours difference between Tokyo and Rome.}$$

Since Tokyo is east of Rome, the time will be 8 hours later in Tokyo than in Rome.

10

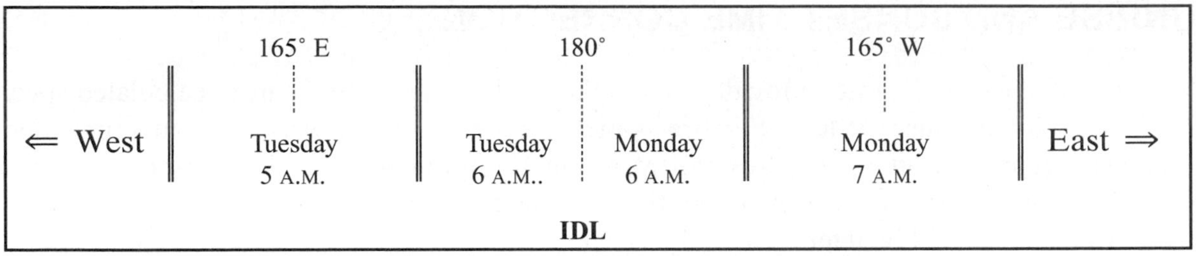

```
         165° E              180°              165° W

⟸ West    Tuesday    Tuesday │ Monday    Monday    East ⟹
          5 A.M.      6 A.M.. │ 6 A.M.    7 A.M.

                         IDL
```

Figure 3-2: International Date Line (IDL) and bordering time zones, shown here with their central meridians along with sample days and times.

INTERNATIONAL DATE LINE

When determining time differences between two places around the world, remember that the day may also be different. The day changes under two circumstances. First, the day changes at midnight. When traveling from west to east, when we cross into the time zone where it is midnight, it becomes the next day. Conversely, when traveling from east to west, when we cross into the 11 P.M. time zone it becomes the previous day.

The day also changes at the **International Date Line** (IDL), which generally follows the 180° meridian down the middle of the Pacific Ocean. When crossing the IDL going from west to east (from Japan toward Hawaii), it becomes the previous day. When crossing the IDL going from east to west (from Hawaii toward Japan), it becomes the next day.

The International Date Line runs down the middle of a time zone. When first entering into this time zone, the hour changes, but the day remains the same until crossing the IDL (at which point only the day changes, not the time). Figure 3-2 shows the International Date Line and the bordering time zone boundaries. Sample times and days are shown in the diagram.

DAYLIGHT-SAVING TIME

A variation of standard time is **daylight-saving time**. Daylight-saving time is used throughout most of the United States during part of the year. In the summer, the days are longer than in the winter, and so there is a period of daylight that is "wasted" in the morning before people go to work. By shifting time ahead by 1 hour, there is, in effect, an "extra" hour of daylight in the afternoon after people come home from work. For many years, most of the United States went on daylight-saving time on the first Sunday of April, and went back to standard time on the last Sunday of October. Beginning in 2007, daylight-saving time is scheduled to begin on the second Sunday in March and end on the first Sunday in November.

Daylight-saving time calculations are easy. Simply remember the saying: "spring forward, and fall back." In other words, in the spring when going on daylight-saving time, we "spring forward" by adding 1 hour. When returning to standard time in the fall, we "fall back" by subtracting 1 hour.

When calculating time differences around the world, if both cities are observing daylight-saving time, you need not change your calculation procedure. If, for example, only the first city is observing daylight-saving time, convert that city back to standard time (by subtracting 1 hour), then proceed with your calculations as before.

SUNRISE AND SUNSET TIME CORRECTION

Local news media often provide us with the time of sunrise and sunset calculated specifically for our city. Because the local Sun time varies if we move east or west, the actual time of sunrise and sunset at locations east or west will vary slightly from that stated for our city. In locations to the east of our city, the exact time of sunrise and sunset will be earlier, while in locations to the west, the exact time will be later.

The sunrise/sunset time correction for different longitudes is easy to calculate. The Earth rotates through 15° of longitude in 1 hour. Therefore, the Earth rotates through 1° of longitude in 4 minutes (60 minutes ÷ 15° = 4 minutes per 1°). Locations to the east of us will experience sunrise/sunset 4 minutes earlier for each degree of longitude. Locations to the west will experience sunrise/sunset 4 minutes later for each degree of longitude. Note: this ignores differences in latitude which may also affect the sunrise/sunset time.

For example, if the stated sunset time for 75° W is 6:15 P.M., at 73° W, sunset will occur 8 minutes earlier (at 6:07 P.M.), while at 78° W, sunset will occur 12 minutes later (at 6:27 P.M.).

EXERCISE 3 PROBLEMS—PART I

Using the longitude of a time zone's central meridian (which has been provided for you), answer the following questions. Be sure to indicate if the time is A.M. or P.M.; however, refer to "noon" or "midnight" rather than to 12:00 P.M. or 12:00 A.M. It may be helpful to draw a simple diagram, such as Figure 3-2, when making your calculations.

1. If it is 10:00 A.M. Monday in Denver (based on 105° W), what time and day is it in New York City (75° W)?

2. If it is 11:00 A.M. Thursday in Seattle (120° W), what time and day is it in Seoul, South Korea (135° E)?

3. A satellite image of the United States was taken at "0900Z." What was the local standard time in Chicago (90° W)?

4. If it is Friday at 3:00 P.M. daylight-saving time in Kansas City (90° W), what is the day and time in Quito, Ecuador (75° W), where daylight-saving time is not being observed?

EXERCISE 3 PROBLEMS—PART II

1. (a) Your plane leaves Boston (75° W) at 7:00 A.M. on Saturday, bound for Los Angeles (120° W). The flight takes 5 hours. What is the time and day when you arrive in Los Angeles?

    (b) Your connecting flight to Taipei (120° E) leaves Los Angeles at 1:00 P.M. on that same day. The flight takes 11 hours. What is the time and day when you arrive in Taipei?

2. For a given latitude, if the stated time of sunset is 6:45 P.M. at 90° W, what is the time of sunset at 91° W?

3. For a given latitude, if the stated time of sunrise is 6:10 A.M. at 120°00' W, what is the time of sunrise at 117°30' W?

EXERCISE 4
MAP SCALE

Objective: To review the concept of map scale, and to practice determining distances on a map using graphic and fractional scales.

Reference: McKnight and Hess, *Physical Geography*, 9th ed., pp. 30–32.

MAP SCALE

The **scale** of a map indicates how much the Earth has been reduced for reproduction on that map. In practical terms, scale is the relationship between the distance shown on a map and the actual distance that this represents on the Earth. There are two common ways to indicate the scale of a map.

Graphic Scales: The graphic scale for a map is a bar graph, graduated by distance. For example, Figure 4-1 shows the graphic map scales from a U.S. Geological Survey topographic map. To use a graphic scale, simply measure a distance on the map (or mark off the distance along the edge of a piece of paper), then compare the measured distance to the bar graph to determine the actual distance represented. On some graphic scales, "zero" is not at the far left. Graphic scales are useful since they remain accurate even if the map is enlarged or reduced in size.

In some cases, one graphic scale may not be accurate for all parts of the map. Some maps have several different graphic scales that are to be used for specified latitudes.

Fractional Scales: The fractional scale (also called the **representative fraction**) expresses the scale of a map as a fraction or ratio: 1/24,000 or 1:24,000.

This scale (read "one to twenty-four thousand"), says that one unit of measurement on the map represents 24,000 units of measurement on the Earth. At this scale, one centimeter on the map represents an actual distance of 24,000 centimeters on the Earth, while 1 inch on the map represents an actual distance of 24,000 inches on the Earth. Note that the units of measurement must be the same in both the numerator and the denominator.

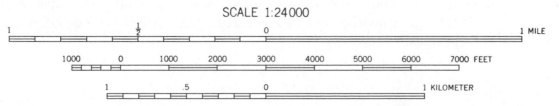

Figure 4-1: Graphic scales from a map with a fractional scale of 1:24,000. (From U.S. Geological Survey)

15

COMPUTING DISTANCES WITH FRACTIONAL SCALES

In addition to using the graphic scale, it is possible to determine distances represented on a map by using the fractional scale:

1. Use a ruler to measure the distance on the map in centimeters (or inches). This is the *measured distance*.
2. Multiply the *measured distance* by the map's fractional scale denominator. This will give you the *actual distance* in centimeters (or inches).
3. To convert your *actual distances* in centimeters (or inches) to other units, use the following formulas:

To determine the distance in *meters*:   *Actual Distance* in centimeters $\div$ 100
To determine the distance in *kilometers*:   *Actual Distance* in centimeters $\div$ 100,000

To determine the distance in *feet*:   *Actual Distance* in inches $\div$ 12
To determine the distance in *miles*:   *Actual Distance* in inches $\div$ 63,360

For example, if we have a map with a scale of 1/50,000, a measured distance of 22 centimeters on the map represents an actual distance of 1,100,000 centimeters:

$$22 \text{ cm} \times 50,000 = 1,100,000 \text{ cm}$$

To calculate the actual distance in meters and kilometers:

$$1,100,000 \text{ cm} \div 100 \quad = 11,000 \text{ meters}$$

$$1,100,000 \text{ cm} \div 100,000 = 11 \text{ kilometers}$$

If we have a map with a scale of 1/24,000, a measured distance of 8.25 inches on the map represents an actual distance of 198,000 inches (8.25" $\times$ 24,000 = 198,000 inches). So:

$$198,000" \div 12 \quad = 16,500 \text{ feet}$$

$$198,000" \div 63,360 = 3.1 \text{ miles}$$

LARGE VERSUS SMALL SCALE MAPS

Large scale maps refer to maps with a relatively large representative fraction (such as 1/10,000), while **small scale maps** refer to maps with a relatively small representative fraction (such as 1/1,000,000). Large scale maps show a small area of the Earth in great detail, while small scale maps show large areas in less detail.

EXERCISE 4 PROBLEMS—PART I

For questions 1 through 4, calculate the following distances using the fractional map scale. (Your instructor may ask you to show your work in the space provided.)

1. On a map with a scale of 1:24,000, a measured distance of
    one inch represents an actual distance of: _____ feet

2. On a map with a scale of 1:62,500, a measured distance of
    4.5 inches represents an actual distance of: _____ miles

3. On a map with a scale of 1:250,000, a measured distance of
    4.5 inches represents an actual distance of: _____ miles

4. On a map with a scale of 1:50,000, a measured distance of
    7.5 centimeters represents an actual distance of: _____ kilometers

5. Map T-1 (in the back of the Lab Manual) shows part of the island of Hawaii at a scale of 1:250,000. Using the appropriate graphic scale found inside the front cover of the Lab Manual, determine the distance from the "Patrol Cabin" (at the summit of Mauna Loa) to the "Rest House" (northeast of the summit of Mauna Loa):

    _____ statute miles

    _____ kilometers

6. Map T-9 shows an area near Park City, Kentucky, at a scale of 1:24,000. Using the appropriate graphic scale, determine the distance from the "Fairview Church" (in the southwest corner of the map) to the "X" marked "BM 585" along the Louisville and Nashville railway:

    _____ feet

    _____ miles

    _____ kilometers

EXERCISE 4 PROBLEMS—PART II

1. If a measured distance of 10 inches on a map represents an actual distance of 5 miles, what is the fractional scale of the map?

Questions 2 through 3 are based on this set of graphic scales for a map with a fractional scale of 1:50,000:

1000	500	0	1000	2000	3000	4000	5000 Meters
1000	500	0	1000	2000	3000	4000	5000 Yards
1	½	0		1		2	3 Statute Miles

2. Why isn't "0" at the far left of the scales?

3. If a map with these graphic scales is enlarged along with the scales (such as by using a photocopy machine):

    (a) Will the fractional scale of the map change? Why?

    (b) Will the graphic scales (shown above) still be usable? Why?

EXERCISE 5
MAP PROJECTIONS

Objective:	To examine the characteristics of different map projections.
Materials:	25 centimeter (10 inch) or larger diameter globe.
Reference:	McKnight and Hess, *Physical Geography*, 9th ed., pp. 33–38.

CONFORMAL VERSUS EQUIVALENT MAPS

Only a globe can show the true area, shape, direction, and distance relationships of the spherical surface of the Earth. It is impossible to show all of these relationships on a map without distortion.

Of the many different properties of maps, **equivalence** and **conformality** are perhaps the most important. An **equivalent map** (also called an **equal area map**) shows correct area relationships over the entire map. With an equivalent map, the area of one region on the map can be directly compared with the area of any other region. In contrast, a conformal map shows the correct angular relationships over the entire map. In practical terms, a conformal map shows the correct shapes of features in a limited area, although the true shapes of the continents can only be shown with a globe.

Figure 5-1 compares a conformal map (a) with an equivalent map (b). When compared with a globe, you will notice that the conformal map maintains the basic shapes of the continents, but the areas of the continents are severely distorted near the poles. On the other hand, the equivalent map shows the areas of the continents accurately, but the shapes are severely distorted in the high latitudes. It is impossible for a map to be both equivalent and conformal, and many maps are neither,

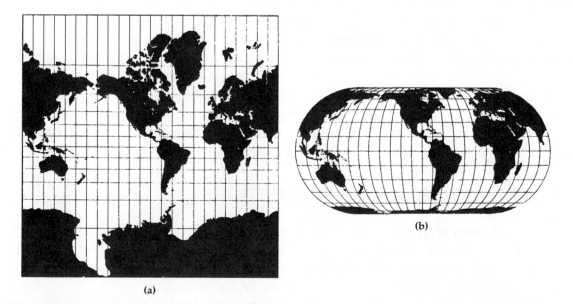

(a)

(b)

Figure 5-1: (a) Conformal projection—the Mercator. (b) Equivalent projection—the Eckert. (From McKnight, *Physical Geography*, 4th ed.)

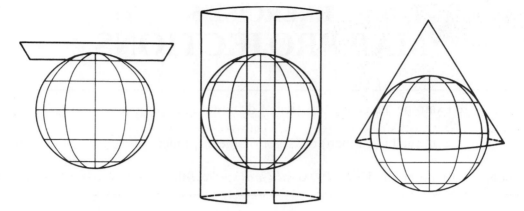

Figure 5-2: Three common families of map projections: plane, cylindrical, and conic. (From McKnight, *Physical Geography*, 4th ed.)

but are instead a compromise. (Note that these distortions are most pronounced on world maps—on large scale maps showing limited areas, these distortions may not be a serious problem.)

Properties other than equivalence and conformality may also be maintained on a map. For example, true direction can be retained in some projections, and true distances can be shown on *equidistant maps,* but only from the center of the projection or along a specific set of lines.

MAP PROJECTIONS

Cartographers transfer the surface features of the Earth to a map by mathematically "projecting" the **graticule** (the grid of latitude and longitude) out from the sphere onto a flat surface. Three common families of map projections are shown in Figure 5-2. In each case, there is one latitude or one point at which the map is tangent to ("touches") the Earth. These latitudes are called *standard parallels* and represent the location of least distortion on the final map.

In the example shown, the **plane projection** (also called an *azimuthal projection*) is tangent to the North Pole, and so would be suitable for maps of polar regions. The **cylindrical projection** is tangent to the equator, and would produce a map with low distortion in the equatorial regions. The **conic projection** is tangent to a parallel in the midlatitudes, making it a good choice for the midlatitude regions. Some cylindrical and conic projections are based on more than one standard parallel.

A fourth family of map projection is called **pseudocylindrical**. Pseudocylindrical projections are mathematically based on a cylinder, tangent to the equator, but the cylinder "curves back" down toward the poles so that the projection gives a sense of the curvature of the Earth. The Eckert (Figure 5-1b) is based on a pseudocylindrical projection.

CHARACTERISTICS OF MAP PROJECTIONS

No single map projection is ideal for all purposes. Different kinds of projections produce maps that are suitable for different uses. For example, the conformal Mercator (Figure 5-1a) is based on a cylindrical projection. On the Mercator, any straight line is a **rhumb line** (a *loxodrome* or line of constant direction), making these maps useful for navigation.

The Robinson (Figure 5-3) is a pseudocylindrical projection that has become a standard compromise projection used for wall maps of the world. It is neither conformal nor equivalent, but offers a good balance between correct shape and correct area.

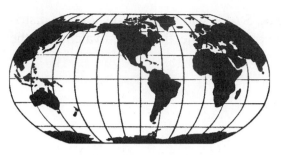

Figure 5-3: Robinson projection. (From U.S. Geological Survey *Map Projections* poster)

The Lambert Conformal Conic projection (Figure 5-4) uses two standard parallels, and is often used by the U.S. Geological Survey for large-scale topographic maps.

Orthographic projections (Figure 5-5a) are known as perspective maps. They make the Earth appear as it would from space. On **gnomonic maps** (Figure 5-5b), a straight line represents a path along a **great circle** (the largest circle that can be drawn on a sphere) and shows the shortest path between two points. Both orthographic and gnomonic maps are based on plane projections.

An interesting type of cylindrical projection is the "Transverse Mercator" (Figure 5-5c). Instead of being tangent to the equator, the Transverse Mercator is tangent to a standard meridian (the 90° W/90° E meridian in the example shown). The Transverse Mercator is conformal, and is used on many U.S. Geological Survey topographic maps.

Figure 5-4: Lambert Conformal Conic. (From U.S. Geological Survey *Map Projections* poster)

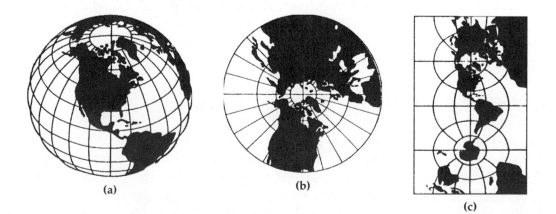

(a) (b) (c)

Figure 5-5: (a) Orthographic. (b) Gnomonic. (c) Transverse Mercator. (From U.S. Geological Survey *Map Projections* poster)

21

Goode's Interrupted Homolosine projection (Figure 5-6) is widely used to show the distribution of phenomena on the continents. The Goode's Interrupted projection is equivalent, yet the shapes of the land masses are also very well maintained.

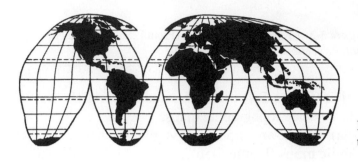

Figure 5-6: Goode's Interrupted Homolosine Projection. (From McKnight, *Physical Geography*, 4th ed.)

EXERCISE 5 PROBLEMS—PART I

1. Compare the Mercator projection (Figure 5-1a) to a globe.

    (a) Are all of the lines of latitude parallel to each other on both the globe and the Mercator projection?

    (b) Do all of the parallels and meridians cross each other at right angles on both the globe and the Mercator?

    (c) On a globe, the meridians converge toward the poles. Describe the pattern of meridians on the Mercator.

    (d) Is north always straight toward the top of the Mercator projection?

    (e) How would the North Pole be represented on the Mercator?

    (f) Could a single graphic scale be used to measure distances on a Mercator projection? Explain.

2. Study the Eckert projection (Figure 5-1b).

    (a) Do all of the parallels and meridians cross each other at right angles? _____

    (b) How does the Eckert maintain equivalence in the high latitudes (what happens to the meridians)?

    (c) What happens to the shape of Greenland?

    (d) Is north always straight toward the top of the Eckert? Explain.

EXERCISE 5 PROBLEMS—PART II

1.   Study the Goode's Interrupted projection (Figure 5-6):

    (a)   Are ocean areas "left off" this map? Explain.

    (b)   The Goode's is based on two different projections, one for the low latitudes, and one for the high latitudes. At approximately what latitude does the projection change? (Hint: look for the change in the shape of the map margins in the South Pacific.)

2.   On a globe, use a piece of string to find the shortest path between Yokohama, Japan (near Tokyo) and San Francisco. This path is a "great circle" path. Two maps are shown below, a Gnomonic (i) and a Mercator (ii).

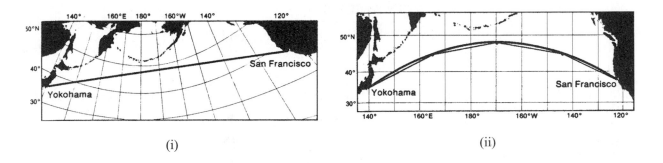

            (i)   (ii)

    (a)   Is the path of the string on your globe the same as the heavy line shown on just one of these maps, or on both of these maps?

    (b)   In terms of a navigator trying to maintain a compass heading, why would the great circle path shown above be difficult to follow exactly?

    (c)   How would both a Mercator and a Gnomonic map be used together in navigation?

EXERCISE 6
ISOLINES

Objective:	To practice interpreting and drawing isolines.
Reference:	McKnight and Hess, *Physical Geography*, 9th ed., pp. 39–41.

ISOLINES

Often in geography we are interested in mapping particular characteristics of an area, such as the elevation, the amount of rainfall, or the temperature. A common and very useful method of showing varying levels or concentrations of some phenomenon is with **isolines**. An isoline is a line on a map that connects points of equal value.

For example, **contour lines** on topographic maps are isolines that show elevation (contour lines are discussed in Exercise 23). In our study of weather and climate we will use several kinds of isolines, such as **isotherms**, to show temperature, and **isobars** to show atmospheric pressure. There are just a few basic rules pertaining to all isolines:

(a) An isoline connects points on a map where the value of some phenomenon is the same.

(b) Isolines are drawn at regular intervals (for example, for every 5° of temperature difference).

(c) Isolines are always closed lines, although they often close beyond the margins of a map.

(d) Isolines never cross each other.

(e) Where isolines are close together, they show a rapid horizontal change in the phenomenon; where they are far apart, they show a gradual horizontal change.

(f) Values inside a closed isoline are either higher or lower than those outside the closed isoline (it is usually clear which is the case based on the pattern of adjacent isolines).

The following example will help illustrate how isotherms are drawn. Figure 6-1 shows a simple map with temperatures plotted for 17 different cities.

We will draw isotherms at 5° intervals (15°, 20°, 25°, etc.). An isotherm will pass through any point with the same value as the isotherm, but between higher and lower values. On one side of the line, the temperatures will be higher than the value of the isotherm, while on the other side, temperatures will be lower.

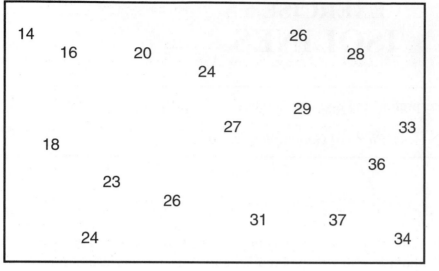

Figure 6-1: Map showing the temperatures in 17 cities.

Drawing isolines involves interpolation. For example, the 15° isotherm passes between the 14° and 16° locations, while the 27° location is about half way between the 25° and 30° isotherms. Figure 6-2 shows the completed isotherm map. Notice that isotherms show the spatial pattern of temperature more clearly than the temperatures of the cities alone.

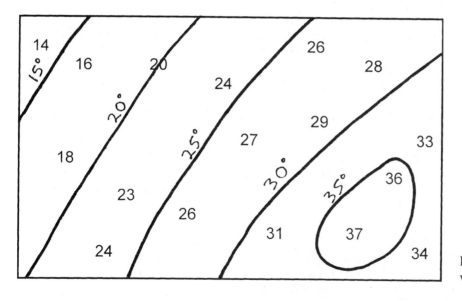

Figure 6-2: Temperature map with isotherms drawn.

EXERCISE 6 PROBLEMS—PART I

The following questions are based on the isotherm map below, showing average January sea-level temperatures in °C and °F. Eight lettered points (labeled "A" to "H") are shown on the map.

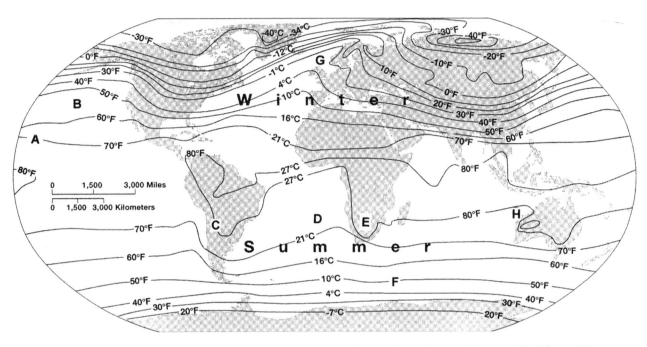

Figure 6-3: Average January sea-level temperatures (°C and °F). (Adapted from McKnight and Hess, *Physical Geography*, 7th ed.)

Determine the average January sea-level temperature at the following eight lettered points. Indicate if your answers are in °C or °F:

°C or °F (circle scale used)

A _____   E _____

B _____   F _____

C _____   G _____

D _____   H _____

EXERCISE 6 PROBLEMS—PART II

The map below shows the location of 52 cities. The temperature of each city is given in degrees. Draw isotherms at 5° intervals, beginning with the 0° isotherm in the upper right corner. Label each isotherm.

```
                        11        4                    -2
              17              8              3
    21
                    15                            2

              20          13          6               0
                                   5
                                        4                  -1
        23          19          10              1

              22                        9

      25          21      16                       4
                              14
    27                              10        6

                    26              12
              30
        32                    20              11        9

              35                      14
                    31
      34      37                  17
                  32      26                      13
          36                              15
                          24
    33              29              19
```

EXERCISE 7
EARTH–SUN RELATIONS

Objective:	To review Earth–Sun relations, and the reasons for the change of seasons.
Reference:	McKnight and Hess, *Physical Geography*, 9th ed., pp. 15–23.

THE CHANGE OF SEASONS

The changes brought by the annual march of the seasons are due to four characteristics of the Earth in its relationship to the Sun.

Rotation: The Earth completes one rotation on its axis every 24 hours. The most obvious consequence of this rotation is the daily change from day to night.

Revolution: The Earth orbits around the Sun, completing one revolution every 365 1/4 days. The orbit of the Earth is not a perfect circle. The distance averages about 150 million kilometers (93 million miles), but the Earth is 3.3 percent nearer to the Sun on about January 3rd at its closest point (known as **perihelion**), than it is on about July 4 at its farthest point (**aphelion**).

Inclination: The Earth's axis is tilted relative to the **plane of the ecliptic**, the Earth's orbital path. The Earth's axis maintains an inclination of 23.5° from the vertical throughout the year.

Polarity (Parallelism):   The Earth's axis is always pointing in the same direction (toward the North Star, *Polaris*). Notice in Figure 7-1 that because of polarity, in June the North Pole is leaning most directly toward the Sun, while in December it is leaning most directly away from the Sun.

Earth–Sun relations on four special days of the year, the **March equinox** (about March 20), the **June solstice** (about June 21), the **September equinox** (about September 22), and the **December solstice** (about December 21), are shown in Figure 7-1.

On the equinoxes (Figure 7-2), the **vertical rays of the Sun** are striking the equator. In other words, on an equinox, at the equator the Sun would be directly overhead in the sky at noon. The **tangent rays of the Sun** (those just skimming past the Earth) are striking the North and South Poles. Notice also that the **circle of illumination** (the dividing line between night and day) is bisecting all parallels. This means that all latitudes experience 12 hours of daylight and 12 hours of darkness on this day.

On the solstices, the situation is quite different. On the June solstice (Figure 7-3), the North Pole is leaning most directly toward the Sun, and the vertical rays of the Sun are striking the Tropic of Cancer at 23.5° N latitude. On the December solstice, six months later, the North Pole is leaning most directly away from the Sun, and the vertical rays of the Sun are striking the Tropic of Capricorn at 23.5° S latitude.

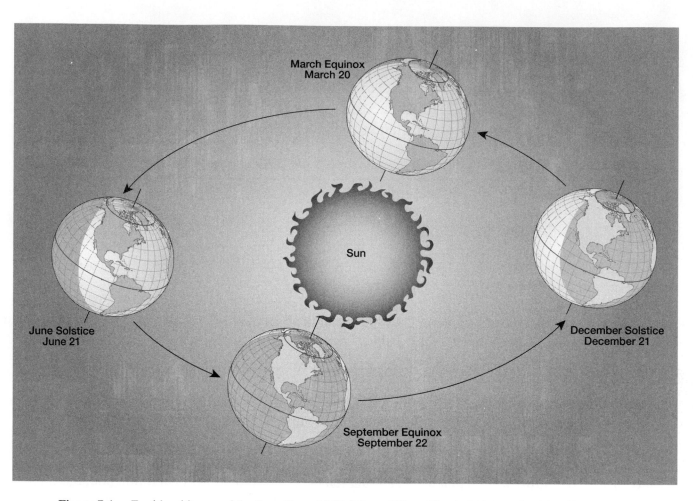

Figure 7-1: Earth's orbit around the Sun. (From McKnight and Hess, *Physical Geography*, 9th ed.)

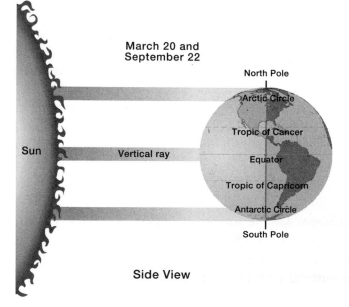

Side View

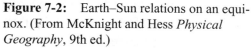

Figure 7-2: Earth–Sun relations on an equinox. (From McKnight and Hess *Physical Geography*, 9th ed.)

30

EXERCISE 7 PROBLEMS—PART I

The following questions are based on Figure 7-3 at right, showing Earth–Sun relations on June 21:

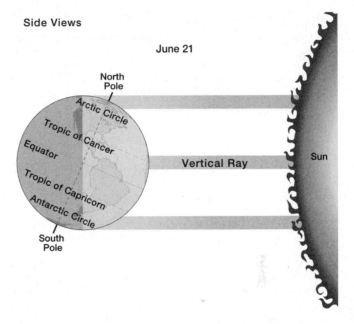

Figure 7-3: Earth–Sun relations on June solstice. (From McKnight and Hess, *Physical Geography*, 9th ed.)

1. What is the latitude of the vertical (direct) rays of the Sun?   _____

2. (a) What is the latitude of the tangent rays in the Northern Hemisphere?   _____

    (b) What is the latitude of the tangent rays in the Southern Hemisphere?   _____

3. Why is the June solstice associated with the Southern Hemisphere winter?

4. Noting the orientation of the circle of illumination on June 21, explain the following:

    (a) Why does the equator receive equal day and night?

    (b) Why does the length of day become longer as you move north of the equator?

    (c) Within which range of latitudes in the Northern Hemisphere is 24 hours of daylight experienced?

EXERCISE 7 PROBLEMS—PART II

Using the diagram below, draw in and label the following as they would appear on the December solstice. You are encouraged to use a straight edge and protractor to increase the accuracy of your diagram.

1.   North and South Poles.

2.   The equator.

3.   Tropic of Cancer.

4.   Tropic of Capricorn.

5.   Circle of illumination.

6.   Arctic Circle.

7.   Antarctic Circle.

Using arrows to represent incoming sunlight, show the latitudes of the following:

8.   Vertical rays of the Sun.

9.   Tangent rays of the Sun.

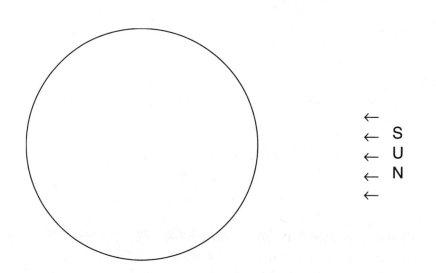

EXERCISE 8
SOLAR ANGLE

Objective:	To use the analemma to determine the latitude of the vertical rays of the Sun throughout the year, and to learn to calculate the altitude of the noon Sun at different times of the year.
Reference:	McKnight and Hess, *Physical Geography*, 9th ed., pp. 21–22.

DECLINATION OF THE SUN

The **vertical rays of the Sun** at noon (rays coming in perpendicular to the surface; sometimes called the "direct" rays) will strike the Earth at the Tropic of Cancer on the June solstice, at the equator on the equinoxes, and at the Tropic of Capricorn on the December solstice. The latitude of the vertical rays of the Sun is known as the **declination of the Sun**.

The changing declination of the Sun throughout the year is shown graphically with the **analemma** (Figure 8-1). On the analemma, the days of the year are shown on the "figure-eight" pattern. The declination of the Sun is read along the vertical axis. The latitudes shown range from 24° N at the top, to 24° S at the bottom, with the equator (0°) in the center. (The horizontal scale showing the "equation of time" will not be dealt with here.)

On the analemma, notice that the declination of the Sun is 0° on about September 22 and March 20, 23.5° N on about June 21, and 23.5° S on about December 21. The declination of the Sun on other days of the year is also easy to determine with the analemma. For example, on October 15, the declination is about 8° S. This means that on October 15, the noon Sun is directly overhead at a latitude of 8° S.

SOLAR ALTITUDE

The **solar altitude** refers to the apparent elevation of the noon Sun in the sky. In other words, the solar altitude is the angle of the noon Sun above the horizon. You can calculate the solar altitude for any latitude on any day of the year with the equation:

$$SA = 90° - AD$$

"SA" is the solar altitude, and "AD" is the "arc distance." The arc distance is the number of degrees of latitude between the latitude in question and the declination of the Sun.

For example, we can calculate the solar altitude at 40° N on the September equinox. On September 22 the declination of the Sun is 0° (as shown on the analemma). The arc distance between the declination of the Sun (0°) and the latitude in question (40°) is 40° (Figure 8-2). The solar altitude is: 90° − 40° = 50°. This means that on September 22, at a latitude of 40° N, the noon Sun will be 50° above the southern horizon.

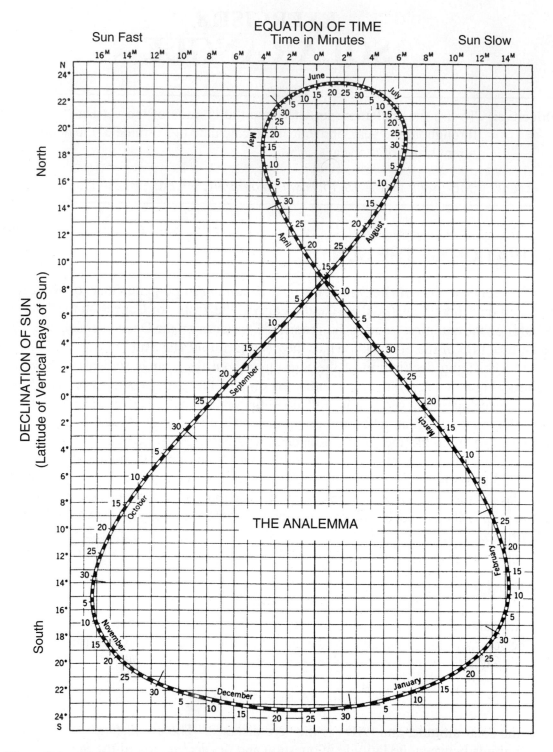

Figure 8-1: The analemma shows the declination of the Sun and the difference in time between clock noon and sundial noon for each day of the year. (Adapted from U.S. Coast and Geodetic Survey)

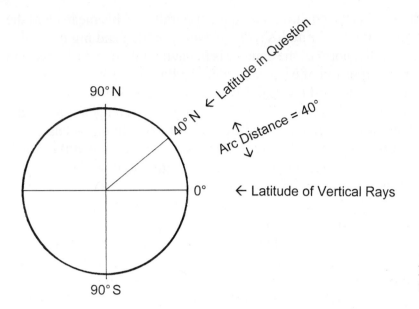

Figure 8-2: Earth–Sun relations on September 22.

Now, let's calculate the solar altitude at 40° N on February 9. The declination of the Sun is 15° S (as shown on the analemma). The arc distance is 55° (40° + 15° = 55°; Figure 8-3). The solar altitude is 90° − 55° = 35°. So, on February 9, at a latitude of 40° N, the noon Sun will be just 35° above the southern horizon.

LENGTH OF DAY

In Exercise 7 (Earth–Sun Relations) we discussed the changes in the length of day throughout the year, focusing on the circumstances during the equinoxes and solstices. With our understanding of the analemma we can now begin to describe the situation on other dates.

Figure 8-4 shows the Earth–Sun relationship on April 23. On this date the declination of the Sun is 12° N (as determined with the analemma). Notice that the **circle of illumination** (the

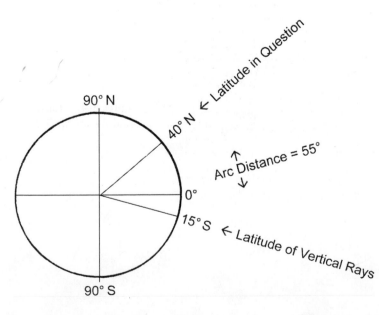

Figure 8-3: Earth–Sun relations on February 9.

dividing line between day and night) bisects the equator, but no other parallels. This means that the equator will have equal day and night, but other latitudes will have *unequal* day and night.

A greater proportion of each parallel north of the equator is in daylight than in darkness, and as we move toward the North Pole, the proportion of each parallel in daylight increases. This means that the length of day increases as we move toward the North Pole. Also notice that we can reach a latitude at which *no* portion of a parallel is in darkness. This is the latitude of the tangent rays of the Sun at midnight—north of this latitude, we would experience 24 hours of daylight on this day.

Looking in the Southern Hemisphere, the opposite is true, as we move toward the South Pole, the length of day becomes shorter and shorter, until we reach the latitude of the tangent rays of the Sun at noon—south of this latitude, we would experience 24 hours of darkness.

For any day of the year it is possible to calculate the latitude of the tangent rays of the Sun at midnight in the summer hemisphere, and the latitude of the tangent rays of the Sun at noon in the winter hemisphere, and therefore, the lowest latitude (the latitude closest to the equator) that would experience 24 hours of daylight or darkness. Notice in Figure 8-4 that the circle of illumination extends 90° to the north of the declination of the Sun, and 90° to the south of the declination of the Sun (which is 12° N in our example). This means that the tangent rays of the Sun will strike 12° beyond the North Pole at a latitude of 78° N. Therefore, on April 23, all latitudes north of 78° N will experience 24 hours of daylight. Conversely, all latitudes south of 78° S will experience 24 hours of darkness.

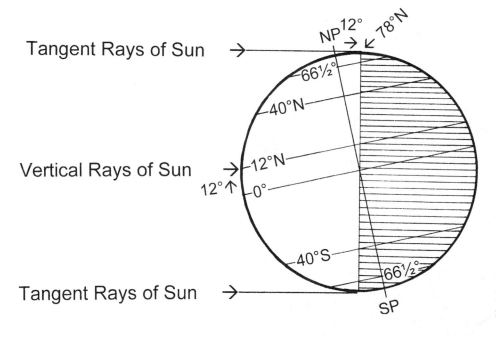

Figure 8-4: Earth–Sun relations on April 23.

36

EXERCISE 8 PROBLEMS—PART I

1. Using the analemma (Figure 8-1), find the declination of the Sun on the following dates; indicate whether the declination is north latitude or south latitude:

	Date	Declination		Date	Declination
(a)	January 10	_____	(c)	May 9	_____
(b)	March 6	_____	(d)	November 18	_____

2. Using the analemma and the equation SA = 90° − AD, calculate the solar altitude at the following latitudes on the dates given:

	Date	Latitude	Declination of Sun	Arc Distance	Solar Altitude
(a)	January 10	0°			
(b)	March 6	38° N			
(c)	May 9	70° S			

3. In your own words, explain what you have calculated in problem 2c above (explain what the answer tells us, not how it was calculated). Be as specific as possible:

4. Determine the latitude of the tangent rays of the Sun in the Northern Hemisphere on the following days of the year, then indicate if latitudes north of the tangent rays in the Northern Hemisphere are receiving 24 hours of daylight or 24 hours of darkness.

Date	Declination of Sun	Latitude of Tangent Rays of Sun (and the circle of illumination) in Northern Hemisphere	Are latitudes north of the tangent rays receiving 24 hours of daylight or 24 hours of darkness? (Choose either "daylight" or "darkness")
March 29			
July 3			
October 14			

EXERCISE 8 PROBLEMS—PART II

Using the analemma, answer the following questions:

1. Determine the rate of change of the declination of the Sun during the following 10-day periods. Since the angular change will be relatively small, convert the number of degrees of declination change into the number of "minutes" of change (remember, there are 60 minutes in one degree). Keep in mind that you are calculating angular change, not time change.

Period	Beginning Declination (to nearest $\frac{1}{2}°$)	Ending Declination (to nearest $\frac{1}{2}°$)	Total Change in Degrees (°)	Total Change in Minutes (')	Minutes of Change Per Day
12/12–12/22					
1/15–1/25					
3/20–3/30					

2. Based on your calculations in Problem #1 above, as well as your general observations from the analemma, answer the following questions:

   (a) During which two times (or months) of the year (six months apart) is the declination of the Sun changing most rapidly from one day to the next?

   (b) During which two times (or months) of the year (six months apart) is the declination of the Sun changing most slowly?

   (c) Since solar altitude and length of day are related to the declination of the Sun, during which two times of the year (six months apart) should the solar altitude and length of day be changing most rapidly from one day to the next?

   (d) During which two times of the year (six months apart) should the solar altitude and length of day be changing most slowly?

EXERCISE 9
INSOLATION

Objective:	To study how insolation patterns are influenced by the angle of incidence of the Sun's rays, variations in the length of day, and the obstruction of the atmosphere.
Reference:	McKnight and Hess, *Physical Geography*, 9th ed., pp. 89–92.

INSOLATION

In previous exercises, we saw how the changing relationship of the Earth to the Sun produces differences in the angle of the incoming solar rays and in the length of day at different latitudes. In this exercise we will explore how these differences influence the average daily **insolation** (*in*coming *sol*ar radi*ation*) patterns at the surface of the Earth.

In this exercise, insolation is defined as the rate at which solar energy strikes a surface (this is defining insolation in terms of intensity—the amount of energy received during a given period of time, in a given area). **Average daily insolation** refers to the average of this rate over a 24-hour period.

One common way to describe insolation is in watts per square meter (W/m^2). One watt is equivalent to 0.239 calories per second (one calorie is the amount of energy required to raise the temperature of one gram of water by 1°C).

The insolation at the Earth's upper atmosphere is about 1372 W/m^2 (this is known as the **solar constant** and assumes that the radiation is striking perpendicularly). However, the average daily insolation at the Earth's surface is less than this. Three factors—the angle of incidence of the incoming radiation, the length of day, and the obstruction of the atmosphere—determine the actual daily insolation at the surface.

ANGLE OF INCIDENCE

There is a direct relationship between the **angle of incidence** (the angle at which the Sun's rays strike the surface) and the intensity of radiation that reaches the ground. Figure 9-1 shows that a beam of incoming solar radiation will be spread out over an increasingly larger surface area as the angle of incidence decreases from 90° (directly overhead) to lower angles of incidence (when the Sun is close to the horizon). A high angle of incidence, in essence, concentrates the solar energy in a small area, while a low angle of incidence spreads this energy out over a greater area.

Figure 9-2 is a chart showing the angle of incidence (the **solar altitude** of the noon Sun) at the equator, 45° N, and the North Pole on the 22nd day of each month (these solar altitudes were calculated using the method described in Exercise 8). The 22nd day of each month was chosen so that the solstices and equinoxes would fall on a day shown in the table.

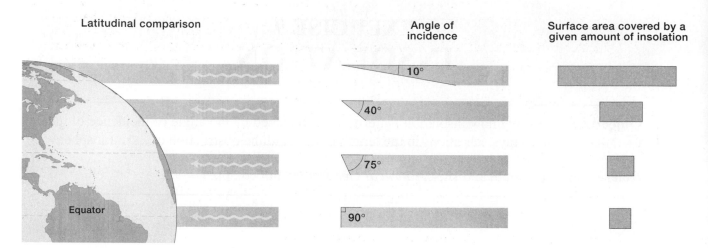

Figure 9-1: Comparative angles of the Sun's rays. (From McKnight and Hess, *Physical Geography*, 9th ed.)

	J	F	M	A	M	J	J	A	S	O	N	D
Equator	70°	80°	90°	78°	70°	66.5°	70°	78°	90°	79°	70°	66.5°
45° N	25°	35°	45°	57°	65°	68.5°	65°	57°	45°	34°	25°	21.5°
90° N	−20°	−10°	0°	12°	20°	23.5°	20°	12°	0°	−11°	−20°	−23.5°

Figure 9-2: Angle of noon Sun above the horizon (solar altitude) on the 22nd day of each month. Negative angles indicate the Sun is below the horizon at noon.

LENGTH OF DAY

The length of day is the second important factor that influences the amount of solar energy received at the surface. Even if the intensity of radiation is low, long hours of daylight significantly increase the total energy received. Figure 9-3 is a chart showing the approximate hours of

	J	F	M	A	M	J	J	A	S	O	N	D
Equator	12	12	12	12	12	12	12	12	12	12	12	12
45° N	9.5	10.5	12	14	15	15.5	15	14	12	10.5	9	8.5
90° N	0	0	12*	24	24	24	24	24	12*	0	0	0

Figure 9-3: Approximate hours of daylight (to the nearest half-hour) on the 22nd day of each month. (*The North Pole receives 12 hours of daylight only on the two equinoxes, *not* for the entire months of March and September.)

	J	F	M	A	M	J	J	A	S	O	N	D
Equator	420	430	440	420	405	395	410	425	440	430	420	410
45° N	150	230	305	405	460	475	455	400	300	200	140	120
90° N	0	0	0*	300	480	520	450	250	0*	0	0	0

Figure 9-4: Average daily insolation at the top of the atmosphere on 22nd day of each month in W/m^2. (*The North Pole receives no insolation in March during the days preceding the equinox, but increasing amounts of insolation following the equinox; in September the North Pole receives decreasing amounts of insolation preceding the equinox, but no insolation following the equinox.)

daylight at the equator, 45° N, and the North Pole on the 22nd day of each month. Notice that the equator receives 12 hours of daylight throughout the year, and the midlatitudes show moderate variation in the length of day from winter to summer. And the North Pole receives either 24 hours of darkness or 24 hours of daylight (with the exception of the two equinoxes—the North Pole receives 12 hours of daylight on March 22 and September 22, but *not* for the entire months of March and September).

Figure 9-4 is a chart showing the average daily insolation at the top of the atmosphere (in W/m^2) at the equator, 45° N, and the North Pole on the 22nd day of each month. These data take into account variations in the angle of incidence and the length of day, but do not take into account the travel of radiation through the atmosphere to the surface. Note that the North Pole *does* receive insolation in March *following* the equinox, and in September *preceding* the equinox.

ATMOSPHERIC OBSTRUCTION

The atmosphere exerts a strong influence over the intensity of radiation received at the surface. Because of processes such as absorption and scattering, when the Sun's rays travel a great distance through the atmosphere, the intensity of radiation reaching the surface will be less than if the rays travel a short distance through the atmosphere.

The length of travel through the atmosphere is determined primarily by the angle of incidence. When the Sun's rays strike perpendicular to Earth's surface (an angle of incidence of 90°), the radiation has the shortest possible travel through the atmosphere, and this results in relatively little decrease in intensity. In contrast, when the Sun's rays strike the Earth at a lower angle of incidence, the radiation reaching the surface will be less intense since it must travel through much more atmosphere (Figure 9-5).

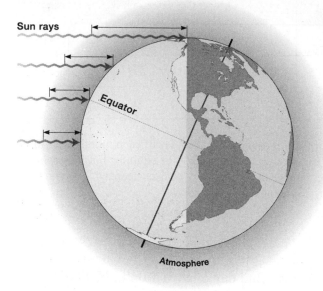

Figure 9-5: Atmospheric obstruction of sunlight. Low-angle rays must pass through more atmosphere than high-angle rays; thus, low-angle rays are subject to more depletion through reflection, scattering, and absorption. The day shown in this diagram is the December solstice. (From Mcknight and Hess, *Physical Geography,* 9th ed.)

This relationship is shown in Figure 9-6. This table shows the approximate percentage of solar radiation reaching the surface for different angles of incidence. These figures are *highly* generalized. The actual effect of the atmosphere varies greatly from place to place, and from time to time, and these values can provide only a rough approximation of the attenuating effects of the atmosphere.

Sun's Angle of Incidence	Percentage of Radiation Reaching Surface
90°	75%
70°	74%
50°	69%
30°	56%
20°	43%
10°	20%
5°	5%
0°	0%

Figure 9-6: The approximate percentage of solar radiation reaching the surface through the atmosphere.

EXERCISE 9 PROBLEMS—PART I

1. On the chart below, use the data from Figure 9-2 to plot the altitude of the noon Sun on the 22nd day of each month for the equator, 45° N, and 90° N. Connect the values for each latitude with a labeled line (you may also use a red line for the equator, a green line for 45° N, and a blue line for 90° N). Plot negative angles as a solar altitude of 0°.

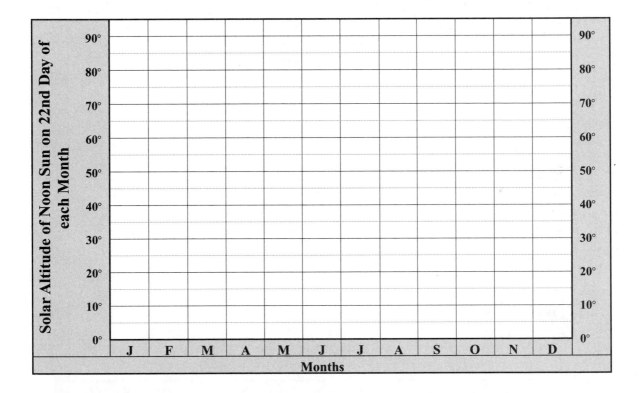

Using the completed chart from Problem #1 above, answer the following questions:

2. (a) On June 22, at which latitude (the equator or 45° N)
        is the noon Sun highest in the sky?   _____

    (b) At the North Pole is there any month of the year when the noon
        Sun is as high in the sky as it is on January 22 at 45° N?   _____

3. If the angle of incidence (based on the solar altitude at noon) were the **only** factor influencing average daily insolation at the surface:

    (a) Which of the three latitudes would receive the highest insolation on 6/22? _____

    (b) Which of the three latitudes would receive the lowest insolation on 6/22? _____

(c) Which of the three latitudes would receive the highest insolation on 12/22?_____

(d) Which of the three latitudes would receive the lowest insolation on 12/22? _____

4. On the chart below, use the data from Figure 9-4 to plot the average daily insolation at the top of the atmosphere (in W/m^2) for the 22nd day of each month at the equator, 45° N, and 90° N. Connect the values for each latitude with a labeled line (you may also use a red line for the equator, a green line for 45° N, and a blue line for 90° N).

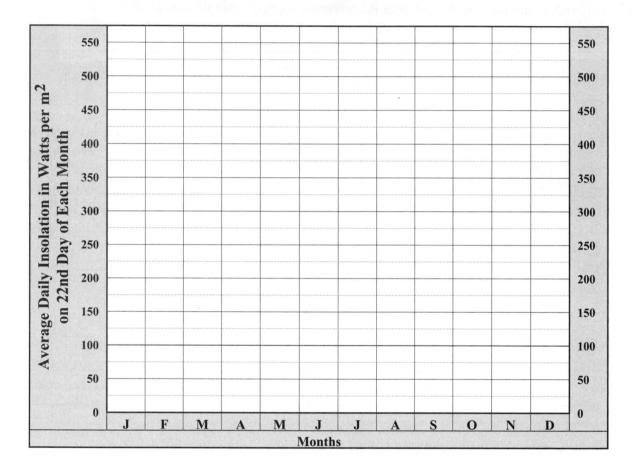

After completing the chart above, answer the following questions. Keep in mind that these data show the insolation at the top of the atmosphere—they take into account the angle of incidence of incoming radiation and the length of day, but ignore the effects of the atmosphere.

5. (a) During a year, which of the three latitudes experiences the least variation in average daily insolation at the top of the atmosphere? _____

(b) Why?

6. (a) During a year, which of the three latitudes experiences the greatest variation in average daily insolation at the top of the atmosphere? _____

   (b) Why?

7. (a) For how many months of the year does the North Pole receive no insolation? (Note: when answering this question you need to consider the *actual* period of time the North Pole goes without sunlight each year—interpret Figure 9-3 and your chart in Problem #4 carefully; you may want to determine the actual number of weeks each year that the North Pole receives no sunlight.)

      _____ months

   (b) Which dates mark the beginning and end of this period of zero insolation at the North Pole?

      Beginning: _____   End: _____

8. (a) In which month does the top of the atmosphere at 45° N receive its highest average daily insolation? _____

   (b) In that same month, does the top of the atmosphere at the equator receive higher or lower average daily insolation than at 45° N? _____

   (c) What explains this?

9. During the year, the equator experiences two periods (six months apart) of maximum average daily insolation and two periods (six months apart) of minimum average daily insolation.

   (a) When do the two maximums occur? _____

   (b) When do the two minimums occur? _____

   (c) Explain the reason(s) for this pattern:

Name _____   Section _____

EXERCISE 9 PROBLEMS—PART II

Answer the following questions after completing the problems in Part I:

10.   On the chart below, use the data from Figure 9-6 to plot the relationship between the angle of incidence of the incoming rays of the Sun and the approximate percentage of radiation reaching the surface through the atmosphere. Connect the values with a line.

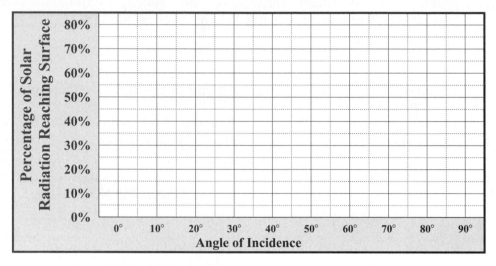

11.   (a)   Use the completed chart from Problem #10 above and Figure 9-2 (showing the angle of incidence of the noon Sun) to estimate the percentage of radiation passing through the atmosphere to the surface at noon on June 22nd at the following latitudes:

	Angle of Incidence on June 22	Percentage of Radiation Received at Surface on June 22
Equator		
45° N		
90° N		

(b)   If the effects of the atmosphere *are* taken into account, which of the three latitudes shown would exhibit the greatest overall **decrease** in average daily insolation at the surface in June from that shown in Problem #4? _____

(c)   Why?

46

EXERCISE 10
TEMPERATURE PATTERNS

Objective: To study global temperature patterns, and to explore the reasons for these patterns.

Reference: McKnight and Hess, *Physical Geography*, 9th ed., pp. 92–102.

FACTORS INFLUENCING TEMPERATURE PATTERNS

A number of factors influence the temperature regime of a location. The following factors are among the most important:

Latitude: Latitude is the most basic control of temperature. In general, because of the lower total insolation received at high latitudes compared with low latitudes, temperature decreases as we move away from the equator and toward the poles. In addition, the tropics generally show little temperature change during the year, while the mid- and high latitudes experience variation in temperature from summer to winter. These basic global patterns are apparent in Figure 10-1, showing average sea-level temperatures in January mapped with isotherms, and in Figure 10-2, showing average sea-level temperatures in July.

Were latitude the only control of temperature, the isotherms would run exactly east to west, parallel to the lines of latitude. However, this hypothetical pattern is altered by a number of additional factors.

Land-Water Contrasts: Land and water react differently to solar heating, and this exerts a strong influence on the atmosphere. In general, land heats up and cools off faster and to a greater extent than water. This means that the interiors of continents will be hotter in summer and colder in winter than maritime regions at the same latitude. The ocean also significantly moderates the temperatures of the coastal regions of a continent.

In addition to the lower annual temperature range associated with maritime regions, the ocean also exhibits a lag in reaching its coolest point in winter and its warmest point in summer. This means that coastal regions often reach their temperature extremes several months after interior regions.

Ocean Currents: The general circulation of the ocean is a significant mechanism of global heat transfer. Major surface ocean currents move warm water from the equatorial regions toward the poles, and bring cool water from the poles back toward the equator. In each of the main ocean basins, warm water is moving toward the poles off the east coasts of continents, while cool water is moving toward the equator off the west coasts of continents.

Wind Patterns and Air Masses: In many regions of the world, the dominant wind direction strongly influences local temperature patterns. For example, in the midlatitudes the dominant wind direction is from the west, meaning that air masses will tend to move from west to east. As a consequence, the temperature patterns of midlatitude locations along the east coast of a continent can be quite "continental"—the westerlies can bring the seasonal warmth or coldness of the interior of the continent all the way to the east coast.

Altitude: In general, temperature decreases with increased altitude. A high elevation station will have a very similar annual temperature pattern to a nearby lowland station, although the high elevation station will be consistently cooler throughout the year. On average, temperature in the **troposphere** decreases by approximately 6.5°C per 1000 meters of elevation increase (3.6°F/1000 feet)—this is known as the **average lapse rate**.

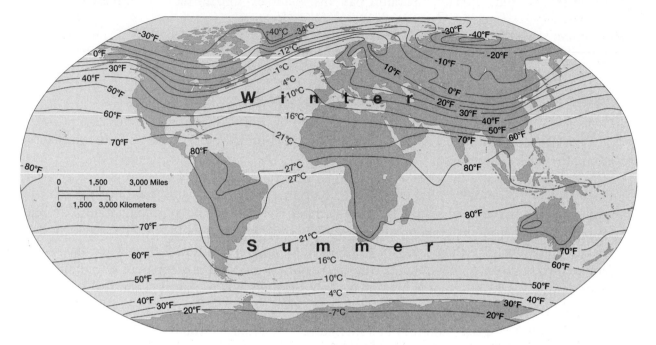

Figure 10-1: Average January sea-level temperatures. (From McKnight and Hess, *Physical Geography*, 9th ed.)

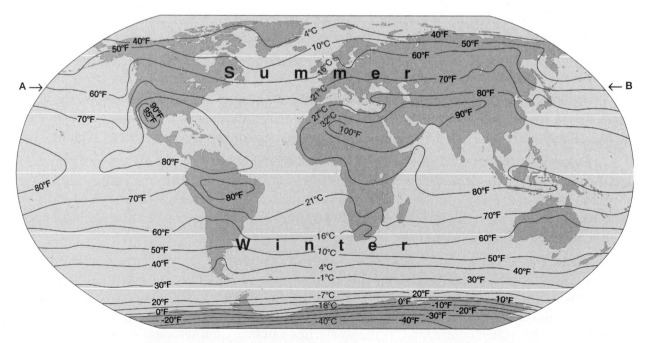

Figure 10-2: Average July sea-level temperatures. (Adapted from McKnight and Hess, *Physical Geography*, 9th ed.)

EXERCISE 10 PROBLEMS—PART I

The following questions are based on the maps of average January sea-level temperatures (Figure 10-1) and average July sea-level temperatures (Figure 10-2):

1.   Is the temperature contrast between the equator and the
      Arctic region greatest in the winter or summer?   _____

2.   (a)   Were latitude the only control of temperature, the isotherms would run straight
             across the maps from east to west. Describe one region of the world where this hy-
             pothetical isotherm pattern is actually observed:

      (b)   Why is the hypothetical pattern seen here?

3.   (a)   Is the influence of cool ocean currents on coastal
             temperatures more pronounced in summer or winter?   _____

      (b)   Why?

4.   (a)   Comparing the January map with the July map, describe one region of the world
             that exhibits a large annual temperature range (the difference between the January
             and July average temperatures):

      (b)   What explains this large annual temperature range?

      (c)   Describe one region of the world that exhibits a small annual temperature range.

      (d)   What explains this small annual temperature range?

EXERCISE 10 PROBLEMS—PART II

Using a straightedge, draw a line across the July temperature map (Figure 10-2) from point "A" to point "B." This reference line can be thought of as the "hypothetical" position of the 16°C (60°F) isotherm were there no land–water contrasts, ocean currents, and so on. Compare the actual 16°C isotherm, with the line you have just drawn. In places where the actual 16°C isotherm is south of the hypothetical line, temperatures are lower than expected; in places where the actual 16°C isotherm is north of the hypothetical line, temperatures are higher than expected.

Begin in the west and move across the map to the east, briefly explaining why the actual 16°C (60°F) isotherm deviates from the hypothetical:

EXERCISE 10 PROBLEMS—PART III

Six charts showing the average monthly temperature (in °C and °F) for seven U.S. cities are provided below. For each of the cities, the latitude and longitude, as well as the elevation, are provided.

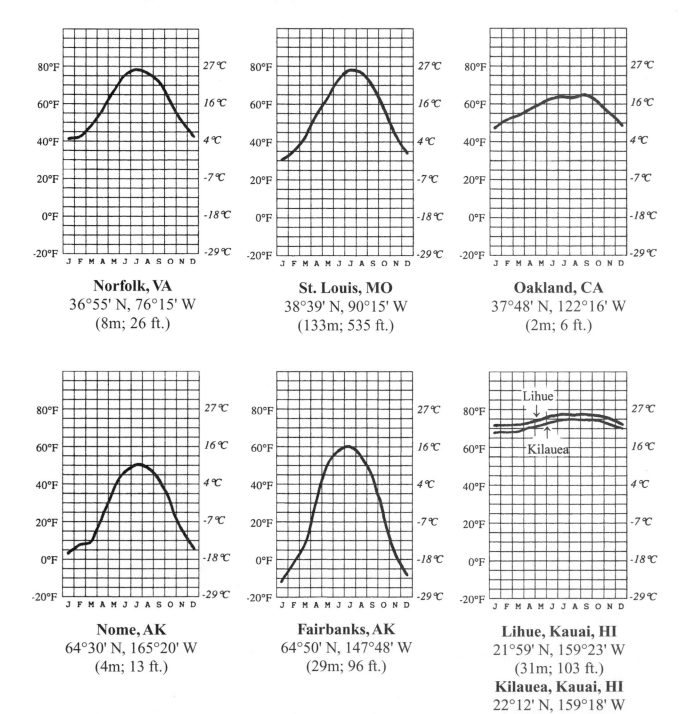

Norfolk, VA
36°55' N, 76°15' W
(8m; 26 ft.)

St. Louis, MO
38°39' N, 90°15' W
(133m; 535 ft.)

Oakland, CA
37°48' N, 122°16' W
(2m; 6 ft.)

Nome, AK
64°30' N, 165°20' W
(4m; 13 ft.)

Fairbanks, AK
64°50' N, 147°48' W
(29m; 96 ft.)

Lihue, Kauai, HI
21°59' N, 159°23' W
(31m; 103 ft.)
Kilauea, Kauai, HI
22°12' N, 159°18' W
(346m; 1134 ft.)

51

Answer the following questions by comparing the temperature charts on the previous page. In your answers, consider the *one* temperature control factor that is *most* responsible for the patterns shown (choose from latitude, land–water contrasts, wind patterns and air masses, or altitude). You may use the same answer for more than one question. You should locate each of the cities on a map before trying to answer the questions. If altitude is the main factor cited, calculate the expected temperature difference based on the average lapse rate.

1.   What explains the different temperature patterns of St. Louis and Oakland?

2.   Why is the warmest month of summer different in St. Louis and Oakland?

3.   Why does St. Louis have colder winters than Norfolk?

4.   Compared to Oakland, Norfolk has a very "continental" temperature pattern. Why?

5.   What explains the difference in temperature patterns between Fairbanks and St. Louis?

6.   What explains the difference in temperature patterns between Fairbanks and Nome?

7.   Why does Lihue have a smaller annual temperature range than Oakland?

8.   What explains the difference in temperature patterns between Lihue and Kilauea?

EXERCISE 11
AIR PRESSURE

Objective: To introduce the standard weather map station model, and to study pressure patterns shown on maps with isobars.

Reference: McKnight and Hess, *Physical Geography*, 9th ed., pp. 107–110.

AIR PRESSURE

The **pressure of air** is the force exerted by the atmosphere on a surface. Gravity pulls the gases of the atmosphere toward the surface of the Earth, and so atmospheric pressure is sometimes thought of as the "weight" of the air, but this is somewhat simplistic. Atmospheric pressure is a force exerted in all directions.

FACTORS INFLUENCING AIR PRESSURE

Many factors influence air pressure. The pressure, density, and temperature of the air are all closely interrelated. If one factor changes, the other two tend to change also. We can, however, make a few generalizations about the kinds of conditions that tend to produce either high or low pressure near the surface.

The following are generalizations and *not* absolute laws. In practice, however, most surface pressure cells can be explained by the dominance of one of these four conditions:

1. Ascending (rising) air tends to produce **low pressure** near the surface. Lows caused by strongly rising air are sometimes called **dynamic lows**.

2. Warm surface conditions tend to produce low pressure near the surface. Lows caused by warm surface conditions are sometimes called **thermal lows**.

3. Descending (subsiding) air tends to produce **high pressure** near the surface. Highs produced by strongly descending air are sometimes called **dynamic highs**.

4. Cold surface conditions tend to produce high pressure near the surface. Highs produced by cold surface conditions are sometimes called **thermal highs**.

MEASURING AIR PRESSURE

There are several measurement systems used to describe air pressure. While most television and newspaper weather reports use **inches of mercury** (the height of a column of mercury in a liquid barometer), the most common unit of pressure measurement used in meteorology is the **millibar**. The millibar (mb) is a measure of force per unit area. The definition of one millibar is the force of 1000 dynes per square centimeter (1 dyne is the force required to accelerate 1 gram of

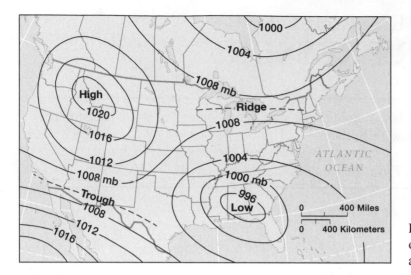

Figure 11-1: Isobar map showing areas of high and low pressure. (From McKnight and Hess, *Physical Geography*, 9th ed.)

mass 1 centimeter per second per second). (In some countries air pressure is described with the *kilopascal* [kPa; 1 kPa = 10 mb].)

For comparison, the average sea-level pressure is 29.92 inches of mercury, which is equivalent to 1013.25 mb. We are generally interested in relative differences in pressure. For example, at the surface, 1032 mb would usually represent relatively high pressure, while 984 mb would represent relatively low pressure (equivalent to 30.47 inches and 29.06 inches of mercury respectively).

ISOBARS

Differences in pressure can be mapped with isolines called **isobars**. Isobars are lines that connect points of equal atmospheric pressure. Figure 11-1 shows a region where areas of high and low pressure have been mapped with isobars. Note that a **ridge** is an elongated area of relatively high pressure, while a **trough** is an elongated area of relatively low pressure.

THE STATION MODEL

We are now going to introduce the **station model** and the standardized system of data presentation that is used on weather maps around the world. In its bare form, a station model is a circle on a map that shows the location of a weather station (in our scale of analysis, usually a city). Various weather data are then plotted in a specific form, and in a specific location, around (and within) this circle.

In this Lab Manual, we will be using an abbreviated form of the station model, introducing new elements in subsequent exercises. However, we will follow standard station model protocol in the placement of each data element.

Temperature: The current surface temperature of a station is written to the upper left of the circle. In the example below, the temperature is 65° Fahrenheit. Note that neither the degree symbol (°) nor an "F" (for Fahrenheit) is included:

65
○

Pressure: Current surface pressure is written to the upper right of the circle. In the example below, the surface pressure is 970.2 mb:

970.2
○

On standard weather maps, however, the notation for pressure is abbreviated. To save space, the first 9 or 10 is left off, and the decimal point is removed. So, in a standard station model, a pressure of 970.2 mb would be written:

702
○

While 1035.6 mb would be written:

356
○

To rewrite these pressures in their full form, simply add the decimal point, and then decide if adding a 9 or 10 makes more sense. Usually this is easy, since surface pressures typically range from about 960.0 mb to 1050.0 mb. For example, given the pressure shown on the following station model:

237
○

First add the decimal point: "_23.7"; then add a 10: "1023.7 mb." Adding a 9 usually would not make sense, because 923.7 mb is lower than expected for a typical surface pressure (a quick way to decide whether to add a 9 or a 10 is to choose the number that makes the pressure value closest to 1000 mb).

Occasionally, the pressure may be higher or lower than is typically encountered—the extremely low pressure associated with the eye of a hurricane is one example of this. In such cases, you will have to decide by the context of nearby stations if adding a 9 or a 10 makes more sense.

Name _____   Section _____

EXERCISE 11 PROBLEMS—PART I

1.   Encode the following data around the station model (using the standard abbreviated form for pressure):

	Temperature	Pressure	Station Model
(a)	42°F	1017.0 mb	○
(b)	101°F	1003.4 mb	○
(c)	23°F	1024.9 mb	○
(d)	54°F	998.2 mb	○

2.   Decode the following station models:

	Station Model	Temperature	Pressure
(a)	36 ○ 131		
(b)	76 ○ 768		
(c)	55 ○ 380		
(d)	81 ○ 997		

EXERCISE 11 PROBLEMS—PART II

The map below is a simplified weather map of the United States showing surface pressure conditions in millibars (here written out in full form). Draw in all of the appropriate isobars at 4 mb intervals. Your highest isobar value will be 1028 mb (the sequence of isobars will be 1028 mb, 1024 mb, 1020 mb, 1016 mb, etc.). Label each isobar. There is one high pressure center and one low pressure center on the map—label each appropriately ("H" or "L"). Begin by drawing your isobar lines lightly in pencil until you are certain of their location. For a review of drawing isolines in general, refer back to Exercise 6. Hint: first draw in the 1020 mb isobar that will run from northeast to southwest across the middle of the country.

EXERCISE 12
WIND

Objective:	To map and study winds associated with high and low pressure areas.
Reference:	McKnight and Hess, *Physical Geography*, 9th ed., pp. 110–125.

PRESSURE GRADIENTS

Air moves horizontally when there is a difference in pressure from one place to another. The change in pressure over a given distance is called the **pressure gradient**, and the force exerted by this difference in pressure is known as the **pressure gradient force**.

As we saw in Exercise 11, pressure patterns are mapped with **isobars** (lines of equal pressure). Closely spaced isobars indicate a great change in pressure over a short distance. A "steep" pressure gradient such as this produces a strong pressure gradient force, and so the resulting wind will be relatively strong. On the other hand, isobars spaced far apart indicate a small change in pressure over a given distance. A "gentle" pressure gradient such as this produces a weak pressure gradient force, and so the resulting wind will be relatively weak.

WIND DIRECTION

The initial propelling force behind wind is the pressure gradient force. Air begins to move "down" the pressure gradient, from high to low pressure, at right angles to the isobars (Figure 12-1a). However, the actual direction of the wind is influenced by two other factors: the Coriolis effect and friction.

At high elevations, above about 700 meters (about 2300 feet), the moving air encounters very little **friction**, but the **Coriolis effect** will deflect the path of the wind. The Coriolis effect (also referred to as the **Coriolis force**) deflects the path of free moving objects to the right in the Northern Hemisphere, and to the left in the Southern Hemisphere. Figure 12-1b shows that while the wind begins to blow down the pressure gradient, the Coriolis effect deflects the path of the wind about 90° to the right (in the Northern Hemisphere). In the upper atmosphere, the balance of the pressure gradient force and the Coriolis effect results in winds that blow approximately parallel to the isobars. These winds are called **geostrophic winds**.[1] In the Northern Hemisphere upper elevation winds tend to blow parallel to the isobars, clockwise around highs, and counterclockwise around lows.

In the lowest parts of the atmosphere, friction becomes important (Figure 12-1c). Friction from the surface slows the wind, and so the Coriolis effect deflection is reduced (rapidly moving objects are deflected more by the Coriolis effect than slowly moving objects).

Near the surface, the balance of the pressure gradient force, Coriolis effect, and friction results in winds that diverge clockwise out of **highs (anticyclones)** and converge counterclockwise

---

[1]Strictly speaking, geostrophic wind is only found in areas where the isobars are parallel and straight; the term *gradient wind* is a more general term used to describe wind flowing parallel to the isobars. In this Lab Manual we use the term geostrophic to mean all wind blowing parallel to the isobars.

(a) Pressure Gradient Force only:

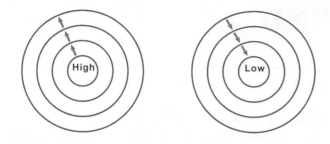

(b) Upper Atmosphere—Pressure Gradient Force and Coriolis Effect:

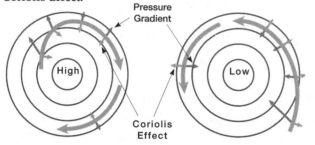

Pressure Gradient

Coriolis Effect

(c) Lower Atmosphere—Pressure Gradient Force, Coriolis Effect, and Friction:

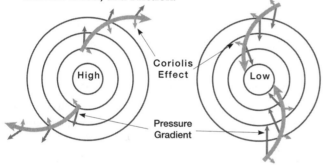

Coriolis Effect

Pressure Gradient

Figure 12-1: The direction of wind flow associated with high and low pressure cells in the Northern Hemisphere. (a) If pressure gradient force were the only factor influencing wind direction, air would flow down the pressure gradient away from high pressure and toward low pressure, crossing the isobars at right angles. (b) In the upper atmosphere (above about 700 meters [2300 feet]) an approximate balance develops between the pressure gradient force and the Coriolis effect deflection, resulting in geostrophic wind blowing parallel to the isobars. (c) Near the surface, friction slows the wind (which results in less Coriolis effect deflection) and so wind diverges clockwise out of a high and converges counterclockwise into a low. (From McKnight and Hess, *Physical Geography*, 9th ed.)

into **lows (cyclones)** in the Northern Hemisphere. In the Southern Hemisphere, winds are deflected in the opposite direction.

GENERAL CIRCULATION PATTERNS

At the global scale, the four most prominent components of the general circulation of the atmosphere are associated with the **Hadley cells** (Figure 12-2). This pair of large convection cells is driven by the warm surface conditions in equatorial latitudes. Warm air rises near the equator in the **intertropical convergence zone (ITCZ)**, an area of generally low pressure and cloudy conditions. This air descends at about 30° north and south latitude in the **subtropical highs** (STH), areas of high pressure and clear, dry conditions.

Two surface wind systems diverge from the STHs, the **westerlies** (blowing from the west) in the midlatitudes and the **trade winds** (blowing from the east) within the tropics. The

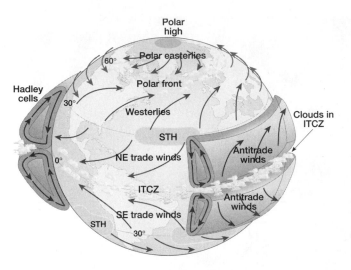

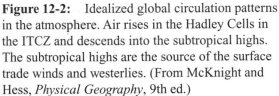

Figure 12-2: Idealized global circulation patterns in the atmosphere. Air rises in the Hadley Cells in the ITCZ and descends into the subtropical highs. The subtropical highs are the source of the surface trade winds and westerlies. (From McKnight and Hess, *Physical Geography*, 9th ed.)

upper atmosphere westerlies, including the high velocity **jet streams**, generally flow from west to east, as do the upper atmosphere trade winds (the **antitrade winds**).

INDICATING WIND ON WEATHER MAPS

Wind direction is indicated on weather map station models with a shaft that points *into* the wind. Wind direction is described as the direction *from* which the wind is blowing, so a "westerly" wind is blowing from the west, and an "easterly" wind is blowing from the east. Occasionally wind direction is described in terms of an **azimuth**—the number of degrees clockwise from north (so north = 000°; east = 090°; south = 180°; west = 270°; and so on).

The wind speed is shown with "feathers" on the wind direction shaft. The wind speed, in **knots**, is determined by adding up the number of feathers (a "knot" is one nautical mile per hour, which equals 1.15 statute mph or 1.85 km/hr). Each full feather represents an increase in wind speed of ten knots. Half-feathers are used to represent five knots, and a solid triangular flag is used to represent 50 knots. For example, the following station model indicates wind from the northwest at 25 knots:

When mapping upper atmosphere winds, wind direction shafts and feathers are often used without the rest of the station model (this is done occasionally when mapping surface wind patterns as well). Figure 12-3 shows a pair of satellite maps of the northeastern Pacific Ocean showing forecast surface and upper atmosphere winds. The centers of three pressure cells have been marked on the surface map. The 300 mb level is the elevation in the atmosphere where the pressure has decreased to 300 mb. This typically is at an elevation of around 9 kilometers (30,000 feet). The west coast of North America is visible along the right side of each image. The dark areas are ocean, and the white areas are clouds.

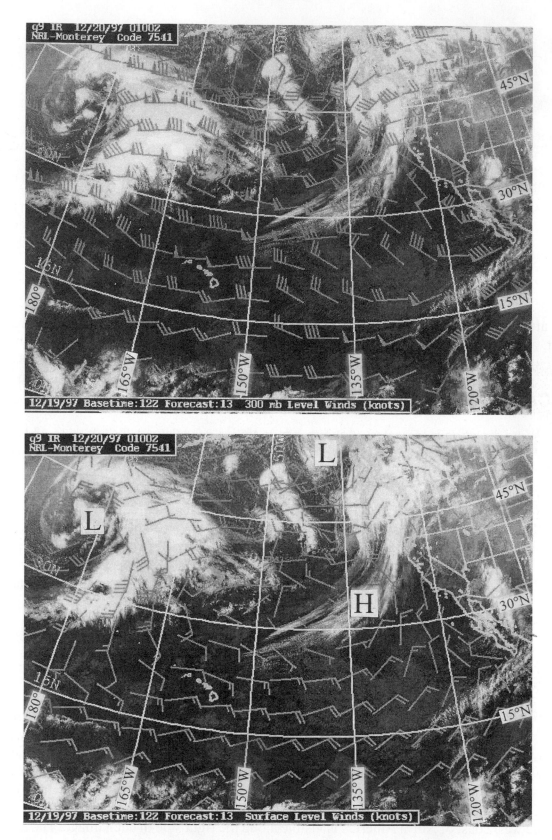

Figure 12-3: Forecast upper atmosphere wind at 300 mb level (top image) and surface wind (bottom image) in North Pacific on 12/20/97. (Images courtesy of Naval Research Laboratory, Marine Meteorology Division)

EXERCISE 12 PROBLEMS—PART I

The two maps below are pressure maps for the United States (pressure is shown in millibars). The top map (a) shows the isobars at an altitude of 2500 meters (8000 feet). The bottom map (b) shows the surface pressure.

On each map, use a colored pencil to draw 1 centimeter ($^1/_2$ inch) long arrows to show the wind pattern you would expect to observe. Align the arrows in their proper relationship to the isobars. Use 8 to 12 arrows for each map.

(a) Upper atmosphere
    pressure:

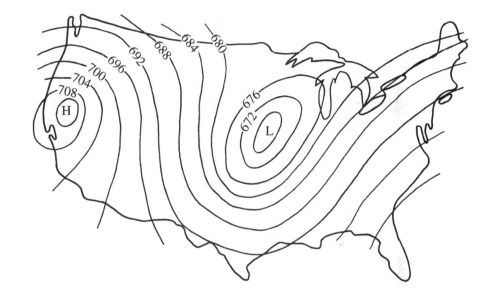

(b) Surface
    pressure:

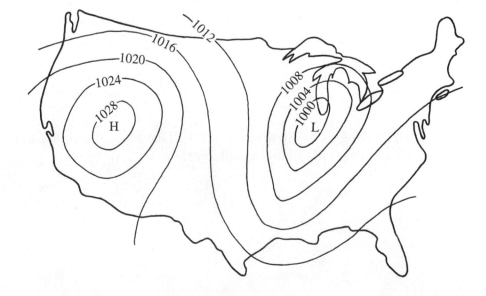

EXERCISE 12 PROBLEMS—PART II

Two satellite images are reproduced in Figure 12-3. They show the forecast surface and upper atmosphere winds (300 mb level) over the northeastern Pacific Ocean. The west coast of North America is visible along the right side of each image. The dark areas are ocean, and the white areas are clouds. The centers of three pressure cells have been marked on the surface map.

1. (a)   What is the surface wind direction off
          the coast of California (35° N, 125° W)?   From the _____

    (b)   What explains this wind direction?

2. (a)   What is the surface wind direction at
          latitude 30° N, longitude 175° W?   From the _____

    (b)   What explains this wind direction?

3. (a)   What is the surface wind direction in
          Hawaii (20° N, 160° W)?   From the _____

    (b)   What is the upper atmosphere wind
          direction over Hawaii?   From the _____

    (c)   What explains the difference in wind direction between the surface and the upper
          atmosphere over Hawaii?

    (d)   Suggest a reason why the surface wind speed and upper atmosphere wind speed
          over Hawaii are so different:

EXERCISE 13
HUMIDITY

Objective:	To study the relationship between the water vapor content of the air, temperature, and relative humidity.
Materials:	Sling Psychrometer (optional).
Reference:	McKnight and Hess, *Physical Geography*, 9th ed., pp. 149–151 and A8–A9.

HUMIDITY

In order to understand cloud formation and precipitation, we must begin by studying water vapor in the atmosphere. There are several ways to describe the **humidity**—the amount of **water vapor** in the air—but two are important for us here.

Mixing Ratio: The **mixing ratio** describes the actual amount of water vapor in the air. The mixing ratio is expressed as the mass ("weight") of water vapor in a given mass of dry air, described in grams of water vapor per kilogram of air (g/kg).

In addition to the mixing ratio, there are other ways to describe the actual amount of water vapor in the air. For example, the **specific humidity** is similar to the mixing ratio, except that it describes the number of grams of water vapor per kilogram of air, including water vapor. The **absolute humidity** describes the mass of water vapor in a given volume of air, expressed in grams of water vapor per cubic meter of air (g/m^3).

In many cases, the mixing ratio is more useful to meteorologists than the absolute humidity since the mixing ratio does not change as the volume of air changes (as happens when air rises). As a very rough comparison, at sea level one cubic meter of air at room temperature has a mass of about 1.4 kilograms.

Relative Humidity: **Relative humidity** does not describe the actual amount of water vapor in the air. Rather, it is a ratio that compares the actual amount of water vapor in the air (the mixing ratio) to the maximum amount of water vapor that can be in the air at a given temperature—also called the **capacity**:

$$\text{Relative Humidity} = \frac{\text{Actual water vapor content}}{\text{Water vapor capacity}}$$

The relative humidity (RH) expresses this degree of **saturation** as a percentage. For example, 50% RH means that the air contains half of the water vapor necessary for saturation; 75% RH means that the air has three-quarters of the water vapor necessary for saturation; 100% RH means that the air is saturated. When air is saturated, **condensation**, and therefore cloud formation, can take place.

The water vapor capacity of air at a given temperature is also called the **saturation mixing ratio**, since it is the mixing ratio of a saturated parcel of air. The water vapor capacity of air depends

Temperature		Saturation Mixing Ratio ("capacity") g/kg
°F	°C	
15°F	−9.4°C	1.9
20°F	−6.7°C	2.2
25°F	−3.9°C	2.8
30°F	−1.1°C	3.5
35°F	1.7°C	4.3
40°F	4.4°C	5.2
45°F	7.2°C	6.2
50°F	10.0°C	7.6
55°F	12.8°C	9.3
60°F	15.6°C	11.1
65°F	18.3°C	13.2
70°F	21.1°C	15.6
75°F	23.9°C	18.8
80°F	26.7°C	22.3
85°F	29.4°C	26.2
90°F	32.2°C	30.7
95°F	35.0°C	36.5
100°F	37.8°C	43.0

Figure 13-1: Approximate saturation mixing ratios in g/kg at various temperatures (°F and °C). (Note: at temperatures below freezing over ice, the saturation mixing ratios will be slightly lower than indicated here.)

almost entirely on temperature. As temperature increases, the water vapor capacity of the air also increases. Figure 13-1 shows the capacity (the saturation mixing ratio) of air at different temperatures.

In popular terms, it is said that warm air can "hold" more water vapor than cold air, but this is somewhat misleading. The air doesn't actually hold water vapor as if it were a sponge. Water vapor is simply one of the gaseous components of the atmosphere—the water vapor capacity of the air is determined by the temperature, which determines the rate of vaporization of water.

CALCULATING RELATIVE HUMIDITY

In this exercise, we will use the mixing ratio to describe the actual water vapor content of the air, and the saturation mixing ratio to describe the water vapor capacity of the air. Relative humidity is calculated with a simple formula:

$$RH = \frac{\text{Mixing Ratio}}{\text{Saturation Mixing Ratio}} \times 100$$

For example, if the mixing ratio is 13.5 g/kg and the saturation mixing ratio is 22.5 g/kg, the relative humidity is:

$$\frac{13.5 \text{ g/kg}}{22.5 \text{ g/kg}} \times 100 = 60\% \text{ RH}$$

The key to understanding relative humidity is recognizing the relationship between temperature and the water vapor capacity of air. When temperature changes, relative humidity changes. For example, as the temperature of the air decreases, water vapor capacity decreases. This means that as the temperature decreases, the relative humidity increases. If a parcel of air is cooled enough, its mixing ratio will match its capacity and the air will be saturated (100% relative humidity) and condensation can take place. If cooling continues after a parcel of air has become saturated, the relative humidity will tend to remain at 100%—as the capacity continues to decrease, more and more water vapor will condense out of the air, keeping the mixing ratio of the parcel the same as its capacity and so maintaining 100% relative humidity.[1]

THE DEW POINT TEMPERATURE

The temperature at which a parcel of air reaches 100% relative humidity is called the **dew point** (or dew point temperature). This is the temperature at which the water vapor capacity of the air (the saturation mixing ratio) is the same as the actual water vapor content of the air (the mixing ratio). Notice that the dew point is determined by the mixing ratio. For example, the dew point of a parcel of air with a mixing ratio of 11.1 g/kg is always 15.6°C (60°F). Conversely, a parcel of air with a dew point of 15.6°C has a mixing ratio of 11.1 g/kg. This relationship lets us use the table of saturation mixing ratios (Figure 13-1) in several ways:

(1)   If the temperature is known, you can determine the water vapor capacity of the air: read the "Saturation Mixing Ratio" directly from the table.

(2)   If the mixing ratio is known, you can determine the dew point temperature of the air: find the value of the mixing ratio in the "Saturation Mixing Ratio" column—the dew point is the "Temperature" (remember, at the dew point temperature the air is at 100% RH, so the mixing ratio and the saturation mixing ratio are the same).

(3)   If the dew point temperature is known, you can determine the mixing ratio of the air: find the value of the dew point in the "Temperature" column—the mixing ratio is the same as the "Saturation Mixing Ratio" (again, remember that at the dew point temperature, the mixing ratio and saturation mixing ratio are the same).

THE SLING PSYCHROMETER

One common method of determining relative humidity is with an instrument called a **sling psychrometer**. The sling psychrometer consists of two thermometers mounted next to each other. One of the thermometers is an ordinary one that is used to measure the air temperature, and is called

---

[1]It is possible for air have a relative humidity greater than 100% without condensation taking place. Such air is called "supersaturated." In this Lab Manual we make the simplifying assumption that condensation begins when air reaches 100% relative humidity.

the **dry-bulb thermometer**. The bulb of the other thermometer is wrapped in cloth that is saturated with room-temperature distilled water before use, and is called the **wet-bulb thermometer**.

The instrument is called a "sling" psychrometer since it has a handle that is used to whirl the apparatus around for several minutes. The whirling of the sling psychrometer promotes the evaporation of water from the wet-bulb thermometer. Since evaporation is a cooling process, the temperature of the wet-bulb will decrease. If the air is dry, there will be rapid evaporation and greater cooling, and the temperature of the wet-bulb thermometer will decline more than if the air is relatively moist. In other words, if the temperature of the wet-bulb thermometer is much lower than that of the dry-bulb thermometer, the relatively humidity is low. If the temperature of the wet-bulb thermometer is only slightly lower than that of the dry-bulb thermometer, the relatively humidity is high. If there is no difference in temperature, the air is saturated, since no net evaporation took place.

After using the sling psychrometer, the relative humidity is determined with a table, shown in Figure 13-2 (°C) or Figure 13-4 (°F). The dry-bulb temperature is the "Air Temperature" (read along the left side of the chart). The "Depression of Wet-Bulb Thermometer" is the difference (in degrees) between the dry-bulb and wet-bulb temperature. Match the "air temperature" with the appropriate wet-bulb depression to find the relative humidity, expressed as a percentage.

For example, after spinning the psychrometer, if the dry-bulb temperature is 20°C, and the wet-bulb temperature is 14°C, the wet-bulb depression is 6°C. From the chart in Figure 13-2, under an air temperature of 20° and a depression of 6°, you read that the relative humidity is 51 percent.

A sling psychrometer can also be used to determine the temperature of the dew point. The table in Figure 13-3 (°C) or Figure 13-5 (°F) provides the dew points for various "Dry-Bulb" and "Depression of the Wet-Bulb" readings from a psychrometer. For example, with an air temperature of 20°C and a wet-bulb depression of 6°, the temperature of the dew point is 10°C.

Tips On Using Sling Psychrometers: After moistening the wet bulb (and being careful not to spill any water on the dry bulb), whirl around the sling psychrometer for about one or two minutes. Stop briefly to check the wet-bulb temperature and begin whirling again. After another minute, stop again to check the wet-bulb temperature. If the temperature is the same as when you first checked, the wet-bulb temperature has stabilized and you can use the reading; if the temperature has continued to decrease, whirl again until the wet-bulb temperature stabilizes. Be sure that the wet bulb has not completely dried out in the process—if so, moisten again and take a new set of readings.

Air Temp. °C	Depression of Wet-Bulb Thermometer (°C)																					
	1	2	3	4	5	6	7	8	9	10	11	12	13	14	15	16	17	18	19	20	21	22
-4	77	54	32	11																		
-2	79	58	37	20	1																	
0	81	63	45	28	11																	
2	83	67	51	36	20	6			Relative Humidity (%)													
4	85	70	56	42	27	14																
6	86	72	59	46	35	22	10	0														
8	87	74	62	51	39	28	17	6														
10	88	76	65	54	43	33	24	13	4													
12	88	78	67	57	48	38	28	19	10	2												
14	89	79	69	60	50	41	33	25	16	8	1											
16	90	80	71	62	54	45	37	29	21	14	7	1										
18	91	81	72	64	56	48	40	33	26	19	12	6	0									
20	91	82	74	66	58	51	44	36	30	23	17	11	5									
22	92	83	75	68	60	53	46	40	33	27	21	15	10	4	0							
24	92	84	76	69	62	55	49	42	36	30	25	20	14	9	4	0						
26	92	85	77	70	64	57	51	45	39	34	28	23	18	13	9	5						
28	93	86	78	71	65	59	53	45	42	36	31	26	21	17	12	8	4					
30	93	86	79	72	66	61	55	49	44	39	34	29	25	20	16	12	8	4				
32	93	86	80	73	68	62	56	51	46	41	36	32	27	22	19	14	11	8	4			
34	93	86	81	74	69	63	58	52	48	43	38	34	30	26	22	18	14	11	8	5		
36	94	87	81	75	69	64	59	54	50	44	40	36	32	28	24	21	17	13	10	7	4	
38	94	87	82	76	70	66	60	55	51	46	42	38	34	30	26	23	20	16	13	10	7	5

Figure 13-2: Relative Humidity Psychrometer Tables (°C).

Air Temp. °C	Depression of Wet-Bulb Thermometer (°C)																					
	1	2	3	4	5	6	7	8	9	10	11	12	13	14	15	16	17	18	19	20	21	22
-4	-7	-17	-22	-29																		
-2	-5	-8	-13	-20																		
0	-3	-6	-9	-15	-24																	
2	-1	-3	-6	-11	-17				Dew Point (°C)													
4	1	-1	-4	-7	-11	-19																
6	4	1	-1	-4	-7	-13	-21															
8	6	3	1	-2	-5	-9	-14															
10	8	6	4	1	-2	-5	-9	-14	-28													
12	10	8	6	4	1	-2	-5	-9	-16													
14	12	11	9	6	4	1	-2	-5	-10	-17												
16	14	13	11	9	7	4	1	-1	-6	-10	-17											
18	16	15	13	11	9	7	4	2	-2	-5	-10	-19										
20	19	17	15	14	12	10	7	4	2	-2	-5	-10	-19									
22	21	19	17	16	14	12	10	8	5	3	-1	-5	-10	-19								
24	23	21	20	18	16	14	12	10	8	6	2	-1	-5	-10	-18							
26	25	23	22	20	18	17	15	13	11	9	6	3	0	-4	-9	-18						
28	27	25	24	22	21	19	17	16	14	11	9	7	4	1	-3	-9	-16					
30	29	27	26	24	23	21	19	18	16	14	12	10	8	5	1	-2	-8	-15				
32	31	29	28	27	25	24	22	21	19	17	15	13	11	8	5	2	-2	-7	-14			
34	33	31	30	29	27	26	24	23	21	20	18	16	14	12	9	6	3	-1	-5	-12	-29	
36	35	33	32	31	29	28	27	25	24	22	20	19	17	15	13	10	7	4	0	-4	-10	
38	37	35	34	33	32	30	29	28	26	25	23	21	19	17	15	13	11	8	5	1	-3	-9

Figure 13-3: Dew Point Psychrometer Tables (°C).

Depression of Wet-Bulb Thermometer (°F) — Relative Humidity (%)

Air Temp. °F	1	2	3	4	5	6	7	8	9	10	11	12	13	14	15	16	17	18	19	20	21	22	23	24	25	26	27	28	29	30
0	67	33	1																											
5	73	46	20																											
10	78	56	34	13	15																									
15	82	64	46	29	11																									
20	85	70	55	40	26	12																								
25	87	74	62	49	37	25	13	1																						
30	89	78	67	56	46	36	26	16	6																					
35	91	81	72	63	54	45	36	27	19	10	2																			
40	92	83	75	68	60	52	45	37	29	22	15	7																		
45	93	86	78	71	64	57	51	44	38	31	25	18	12	6																
50	93	87	74	67	61	55	49	43	38	32	27	21	16	10	5															
55	94	88	82	76	70	65	59	54	49	43	38	33	28	23	19	11	9	5												
60	94	89	83	78	73	68	63	58	53	48	43	39	34	30	26	21	17	13	9	5	1									
65	95	90	85	80	75	70	66	61	56	52	48	44	39	35	31	27	24	20	16	12	9	5	2							
70	95	90	86	81	77	72	68	64	59	55	51	48	44	40	36	33	29	25	22	19	15	12	9	6	3					
75	96	91	86	82	78	74	70	66	62	58	54	51	47	44	40	37	34	30	27	24	21	18	15	12	9	7	4	1		
80	96	91	87	83	79	75	72	68	64	61	57	54	50	47	44	41	38	35	32	29	26	23	20	18	15	12	10	7	5	3
85	96	92	88	84	81	77	73	70	66	63	59	57	53	50	47	44	41	38	36	33	30	27	25	22	20	17	15	13	10	8
90	96	92	89	85	81	78	74	71	68	65	61	58	55	52	49	47	44	41	39	36	34	31	29	26	24	22	19	17	15	13
95	96	93	89	86	82	79	76	73	69	66	63	61	58	55	52	50	47	44	42	39	37	34	32	30	28	25	23	21	19	17
100	96	93	89	86	83	80	77	73	70	68	65	62	59	56	54	51	49	46	44	41	39	37	35	33	30	28	26	24	22	21
105	97	93	90	87	84	81	78	75	72	69	66	64	61	58	56	53	51	49	46	44	42	40	38	36	34	32	30	28	26	24

Figure 13-4: Relative Humidity Psychrometer Tables (°F).

Depression of Wet-Bulb Thermometer (°F) — Dew Point (°F)

Air Temp. °F	1	2	3	4	5	6	7	8	9	10	11	12	13	14	15	16	17	18	19	20	21	22	23	24	25	26	27	28	29	30
0	-7	-20																												
5	-1	-9	-24																											
10	5	-2	-10	-27																										
15	11	6	0	-9	-26																									
20	16	12	8	2	-7	-21																								
25	22	19	15	10	5	-3	-15	-51																						
30	27	25	21	18	14	8	2	-7	-25																					
35	33	30	28	25	21	17	13	7	0	-11	-41																			
40	38	35	33	30	28	25	21	18	13	7	-1	-14																		
45	43	41	38	36	34	31	28	25	22	18	13	7	-1	-14																
50	48	46	44	42	40	37	34	32	29	26	22	18	13	8	0	-13														
55	53	51	50	48	45	43	41	38	36	33	30	27	24	20	15	9	1	-12	-59											
60	58	57	55	53	51	49	47	45	43	40	38	35	32	29	25	21	17	11	4	-8	-36									
65	63	62	60	59	57	55	53	51	49	47	45	42	40	37	34	31	27	24	19	14	7	-3	-22							
70	69	67	65	64	62	61	59	57	55	53	51	49	47	44	42	39	36	33	30	26	22	17	11	2	-11					
75	74	72	71	69	68	66	64	63	61	59	57	55	54	51	49	47	44	42	39	36	32	29	25	21	15	8	-2	-23		
80	79	77	76	74	73	72	70	68	67	65	63	62	60	58	56	54	52	50	47	44	42	39	36	32	28	24	20	13	6	-7
85	84	82	81	80	78	77	75	74	72	71	69	68	66	64	62	61	59	57	54	52	50	48	45	42	39	36	32	28	24	19
90	89	87	86	85	83	82	81	79	78	76	75	73	72	70	69	67	65	63	61	59	57	55	53	51	48	45	43	39	36	32
95	94	93	91	90	89	87	86	85	83	82	80	79	78	76	74	73	71	70	68	66	64	62	60	58	56	54	52	49	46	43
100	99	98	96	95	94	93	91	90	89	87	86	85	83	82	80	79	77	76	74	72	71	69	67	65	63	61	59	57	55	52
105	104	103	101	100	99	98	96	95	94	93	91	90	89	87	86	84	83	82	80	78	77	75	74	72	70	68	67	65	63	61

Figure 13-5: Dew Point Psychrometer Tables (°F).

EXERCISE 13 PROBLEMS—PART I *(S.I. Units)*

1.   Complete the following chart (round off relative humidity to the nearest percent):

	Mixing Ratio (g/kg)	Air Temperature (°C)	Saturation Mixing Ratio (g/kg)	Relative Humidity (%)
(a)	2.8	−1.1°C		
(b)	2.8	32.2°C		
(c)	11.1		13.2	
(d)	22.3		36.5	

2.   The air inside a room is at a temperature of 18.3°C and has a mixing ratio of 5.2 g/kg:

   (a)   What is the relative humidity?   _____ %

   (b)   What is the dew point?   _____ °C

   (c)   If the mixing ratio remains the same, but the temperature of
          the room increases to 26.7°C, what is the new relative humidity?   _____ %

3.   The air inside a room is at a temperature of 35°C and has a mixing ratio of 7.6 g/kg:

   (a)   What is the relative humidity?   _____ %

   (b)   What is the dew point?   _____ °C

   (c)   If the room temperature decreases by 5°C per hour, how many
          hours will it take for the air to reach saturation?   _____ hours

   (d)   After reaching saturation, if the temperature of the room
          continues to decrease for one more hour, approximately how
          many grams of water vapor (per kg of air) will have had to
          condense out of the air to maintain a relative humidity of 100%?   _____ g/kg

Name _____   Section _____

EXERCISE 13 PROBLEMS—PART II *(S.I. Units)*

Using the psychrometer tables (Figures 13-2 and 13-3) and the table of saturation mixing ratios (Figure 13-1), answer the following questions about determining relative humidity with a sling psychrometer:

1.   If the dry-bulb temperature is 32°C, and the wet-bulb temperature is 26°C:

    (a)   What is the relative humidity?   _____ %

    (b)   What is the dew point?   _____ °C

    (c)   What is the mixing ratio?
    (Estimate from Figure 13-1)   _____ g/kg

2.   If the dry-bulb temperature is 14°C, and the wet-bulb temperature is 12°C:

    (a)   What is the relative humidity?   _____ %

    (b)   What is the dew point?   _____ °C

    (c)   What is the mixing ratio?
    (Estimate from Figure 13-1)   _____ g/kg

OPTIONAL:

3.   If a sling psychrometer is available in class, determine the following both indoors (in the classroom) and outdoors:

	Indoors	Outdoors
Dry-Bulb Temperature		
Wet-Bulb Temperature		
Depression of Wet-Bulb Thermometer		
Relative Humidity		
Dew Point		
Mixing Ratio (Estimate from Figure 13-1)		

EXERCISE 13 PROBLEMS—PART III *(English Units)*

1. Complete the following chart (round off relative humidity to the nearest percent):

	Mixing Ratio (g/kg)	Air Temperature (°F)	Saturation Mixing Ratio (g/kg)	Relative Humidity (%)
(a)	2.8	30°F		
(b)	2.8	90°F		
(c)	11.1		13.2	
(d)	22.3		36.5	

2. The air inside a room is at a temperature of 65°F and has a mixing ratio of 5.2 g/kg:

   (a) What is the relative humidity?   _____ %

   (b) What is the dew point?   _____ °F

   (c) If the mixing ratio remains the same, but the temperature of
       the room increases to 80°F, what is the new relative humidity?   _____ %

3. The air inside a room is at a temperature of 70°F and has a mixing ratio of 7.6 g/kg:

   (a) What is the relative humidity?   _____ %

   (b) What is the dew point?   _____ °F

   (c) If the room temperature decreases by 10°F per hour, how many
       hours will it take for the air to reach saturation?   _____ hours

   (d) After reaching saturation, if the temperature of the room
       continues to decrease for one more hour, how many grams
       of water vapor (per kg of air) will have had to condense
       out of the air to maintain a relative humidity of 100%?   _____ g/kg

Name _____   Section _____

EXERCISE 13 PROBLEMS—PART IV *(English Units)*

Using the psychrometer tables (Figures 13-4 and 13-5) and the table of saturation mixing ratios (Figure 13-1), answer the following questions about determining relative humidity with a sling psychrometer:

1. If the dry-bulb temperature is 90°F, and the wet-bulb temperature is 79°F:

    (a)   What is the relative humidity?   _____ %

    (b)   What is the dew point?   _____ °F

    (c)   What is the mixing ratio?   _____ g/kg

2. If the dry-bulb temperature is 55°F, and the wet-bulb temperature is 52°F:

    (a)   What is the relative humidity?   _____ %

    (b)   What is the dew point?   _____ °F

    (c)   What is the mixing ratio?   _____ g/kg

OPTIONAL:

3. If a sling psychrometer is available in class, determine the following both indoors (in the classroom) and outdoors:

	Indoors	Outdoors
Dry-Bulb Temperature		
Wet-Bulb Temperature		
Depression of Wet-Bulb Thermometer		
Relative Humidity		
Dew Point		
Mixing Ratio (Estimate from Figure 13-1)		

EXERCISE 14
ADIABATIC PROCESSES

Objective: To study adiabatic processes in the atmosphere, and to calculate temperature and humidity changes in parcels of moving air.

Reference: McKnight and Hess, *Physical Geography*, 9th ed., pp. 153–155.

ADIABATIC PROCESSES

In Exercise 13 we looked at the relationship between temperature and **relative humidity**, noting that as the temperature of a parcel of air decreases, the relative humidity increases. When a parcel of air has cooled to the **dew point temperature**, it becomes saturated and **condensation** can take place. The most common way that a parcel of air is cooled enough to form clouds and precipitation is through **adiabatic cooling**.

As a parcel of air rises, it comes under lower pressure and expands. As the air expands, it cools adiabatically ("adiabatic" means without the gain or loss of heat). Rising air always cools adiabatically. Conversely, as air descends, it comes under higher pressure and compresses. As the air compresses, it warms adiabatically. Descending air always warms adiabatically.

If a parcel of rising air is unsaturated (the relative humidity is less than 100%) it will cool at the **dry adiabatic rate** (DAR; also called the "dry adiabatic lapse rate") of about 10°C per 1000 meters (5.5°F per 1000 feet). As the air rises and cools, its relative humidity increases. At some point, the parcel of air will have cooled enough to reach its dew point. The elevation at which a parcel of air reaches its dew point temperature is called the **lifting condensation level** (LCL), and at this point, condensation and cloud formation can begin.

If a parcel of air keeps rising while condensation is taking place, the air will continue to cool adiabatically, but at a slower rate. Saturated air cools at the **saturated adiabatic rate** (SAR; also called the "wet" or "saturated adiabatic lapse rate") of about 6°C per 1000 meters (3.3°F per 1000 feet). The SAR varies, however, and the rate of cooling may be as slow as 4°C per 1000 meters (2.0°F per 1000 feet).

Rising saturated air cools more slowly than rising unsaturated air because of the release of **latent heat** during condensation. **Evaporation** is, in effect, a cooling process since heat is stored when water changes from liquid to gas. When the water vapor condenses back to liquid water, this heat is released. As saturated air rises, it expands and cools adiabatically, but the latent heat released during condensation counteracts some of this cooling.

Figure 14-1 shows the temperature changes in a parcel of air as it rises up and over a 4000-meter-high mountain. In this hypothetical example, the dew point of the parcel is 5°C and the lifting condensation level is 2000 meters.

Figure 14-1: Temperature changes in a hypothetical parcel of air passing over a 4000-meter-high mountain (assuming no evaporation as the air descends down the lee side of the mountain). The lifting condensation level of the parcel is 2000 meters, the dry adiabatic rate is 10°C/1000 m, and the saturated adiabatic rate is 6°C/1000 m. Notice that because of the release of latent heat during condensation on the windward side of the mountain, by the time the air has descended back down to sea level on the leeward side, it is warmer than before it started up the windward side. (From McKnight and Hess, *Physical Geography,* 9th ed.)

Notice that the air descending down the lee side of the mountain warms at the DAR. Descending air generally warms at the DAR, because as air warms its capacity increases and so it cannot be saturated.[1]

Adiabatic temperature changes may lead to changes in both the relative humidity and the **water vapor** content—the **mixing ratio**—of a parcel of air. For example, as unsaturated air rises or descends (and the temperature decreases or increases), its capacity changes. Because of this, the relative humidity of the parcel will change.

On the other hand, as rising saturated air cools adiabatically, the relative humidity of the parcel generally remains at about 100% as condensation takes place. As the air continues to rise and water vapor is lost through condensation, the water vapor content (the mixing ratio) of the parcel will change.

[1]Although descending air usually warms at the dry adiabatic rate, there is a circumstance when this may not be the case. If air descends through a cloud, some water droplets may evaporate and the evaporative cooling will counteract some of the adiabatic warming. As a result, such descending air can warm at a rate very close to the saturated adiabatic rate. As soon as evaporation of water droplets ceases, this descending air will warm at the dry adiabatic rate as usual.

EXERCISE 14 PROBLEMS—PART I *(S.I. Units)*

Assume that a parcel of air is forced to rise up and over a 4000-meter-high mountain (shown below). The initial temperature of the parcel at sea level is 30°C, and the lifting condensation level (LCL) of the parcel is 2000 meters. The DAR is 10°C/1000 m and the SAR is 6°C/1000 m. Assume that condensation begins at 100% relative humidity and that no evaporation takes place as the parcel descends.

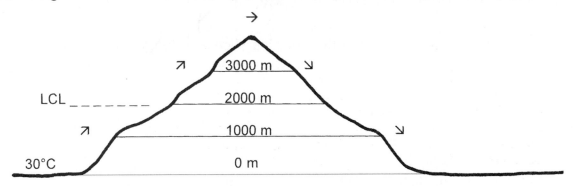

1.   Calculate the temperature of the parcel at the following elevations as it rises up the windward side of the mountain:

(a) 1000 m _____ °C   (b) 2000 m _____ °C   (c) 4000 m _____ °C

2.   (a)   After the parcel of air has descended down the lee side of the
             mountain to sea level, what is the temperature of the parcel?   _____ °C

      (b)   Why is the parcel now warmer than it was at sea level on the windward side (what
             is the source of the heat energy)?

3.   (a)   On the windward side of the mountain, is the relative
             humidity of the parcel increasing or decreasing as it
             rises from sea level to 2000 meters?   _____

      (b)   Why?

4.   (a)   On the lee side of the mountain, is the relative humidity
             of the parcel increasing or decreasing as it descends from
             4000 meters to sea level?   _____

      (b)   Why?

EXERCISE 14 PROBLEMS—PART II *(S.I. Units)*

Answer the following questions after completing the problems in Part I. You will also need to refer to the chart of Saturation Mixing Ratios in Figure 13-1; interpolate from the chart as needed. Assume that condensation begins at 100% relative humidity and that no evaporation takes place as the parcel descends.

5.   (a)   On the windward side of the mountain, should the relative
humidity of the parcel change as it rises from 2000 m to 4000 m? _____

       (b)   Why?

6.   As the air rises up the windward side of the mountain:

       (a)   What is the capacity (saturation mixing ratio) of the
rising air at 2000 meters?   _____ g/kg

       (b)   What is the capacity of the air at 4000 meters?   _____ g/kg

7.   What is the capacity of the air after it has descended back down to
sea level on the lee side of the mountain?   _____ g/kg

8.   (a)   Assuming that *no* water vapor is added as the parcel descends
down the lee side of the mountain to sea level, is the water vapor
content (the mixing ratio) of the parcel higher or lower than
before it began to rise over the mountain?   _____

       (b)   Why?

       (c)   What is the lifting condensation level of this parcel now?   _____ meters

EXERCISE 14 PROBLEMS—PART III *(English Units)*

Assume that a parcel of air is forced to rise up and over a 6000-foot-high mountain (shown below). The initial temperature of the parcel at sea level is 76.5°F, and the lifting condensation level (LCL) of the parcel is 3000 feet. The DAR is 5.5°F/1000' and the SAR is 3.3°F/1000'. Assume that condensation begins at 100% relative humidity and that no evaporation takes place as the parcel descends. Indicate calculated temperatures to one decimal place.

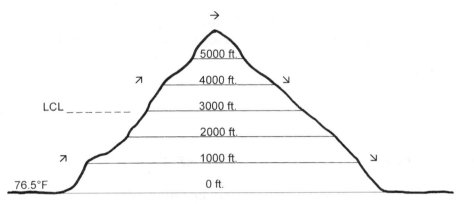

1.   Calculate the temperature of the parcel at the following elevations as it rises up the windward side of the mountain:

   (a) 1000' _____ °F   (b) 3000' _____ °F   (c) 6000' _____ °F

2.   (a)   After the parcel of air has descended down the lee side of the
           mountain to sea level, what is the temperature of the parcel?   _____ °F

   (b)   Why is the parcel now warmer than it was at sea level on the windward side (what
         is the source of the heat energy)?

3.   (a)   On the windward side of the mountain, is the relative humidity
           of the parcel increasing or decreasing as it rises from sea level
           to 3000 feet?   _____

   (b)   Why?

4.   (a)   On the lee side of the mountain, is the relative humidity
           of the parcel increasing or decreasing as it descends from
           6000 feet to sea level?   _____

   (b)   Why?

EXERCISE 14 PROBLEMS—PART IV *(English Units)*

Answer the following questions after completing the problems in Part III. You will also need to refer to the chart of Saturation Mixing Ratios in Figure 13-1; interpolate from the chart as needed. Assume that condensation begins at 100% relative humidity and that no evaporation takes place as the parcel descends.

5.   (a)   On the windward side of the mountain, should the relative humidity of the parcel change as it rises from 3000' to 6000'?   _____

     (b)   Why?

6.   As the air rises up the windward side of the mountain:

     (a)   What is the capacity (saturation mixing ratio) of the rising air at 3000 feet?   _____ g/kg

     (b)   What is the capacity of the air at 6000 feet?   _____ g/kg

7.   What is the capacity of the air after it has descended back down to sea level on the lee side of the mountain?   _____ g/kg

8.   (a)   Assuming that *no* water vapor is added as the parcel descends down the lee side of the mountain to sea level, is the water vapor content (the mixing ratio) of the parcel higher or lower than before it began to rise over the mountain?   _____

     (b)   Why?

     (c)   What is the lifting condensation level of this parcel now?   _____ feet

EXERCISE 15
STABILITY

Objective: To illustrate the concept of stability in the atmosphere.

Reference: McKnight and Hess, *Physical Geography*, 9th ed., pp. 159–162.

STABILITY

The stability of air is an important characteristic of the atmosphere. Air is **unstable** if it rises on its own. Air is **stable** if it resists vertical motion and will rise only when forced.

The temperature of a parcel of air, relative to the temperature of the surrounding air, determines stability for the most part. A parcel of air will be unstable if it is warmer than the surrounding air. A parcel of air will be stable if it is the same temperature, or cooler, than the surrounding air.

LAPSE RATES

In order to understand stability, we must distinguish between the "environmental" lapse rate and the "adiabatic" lapse rates.

The **environmental lapse rate** (ELR) reflects the temperature of the atmosphere at different altitudes—sometimes called the vertical temperature profile or vertical temperature gradient. The ELR averages about 6.5°C per 1000 meters (3.6°F per 1000 feet) within the troposphere (the lowest layer of the atmosphere)—this rate is called the **average lapse rate**. This means that, on average, as we move up through the troposphere, the temperature will be about 6.5°C cooler for each 1000 meters we climb. However, from day to day and from place to place, the ELR frequently deviates from this average rate. Changes in the ELR are also often observed from day to night. Further, there are times when the temperature will actually increase as we move up through the atmosphere—a situation known as a **temperature inversion**.

The **dry adiabatic rate** (DAR; also called the "dry adiabatic lapse rate") and the **saturated adiabatic rate** (SAR; also called the "saturated adiabatic lapse rate") reflect the temperature change within a specific parcel of moving air (see Exercise 14 for a discussion of adiabatic temperature changes). The DAR averages about 10°C per 1000 meters (5.5°F per 1000 feet), while the SAR averages about 6°C per 1000 meters (3.3°F per 1000 feet) but can vary significantly from this.

In the context of stability, we can think of the ELR as showing the temperature change of the surrounding air through which a parcel of air is moving and changing temperature adiabatically (following the DAR or SAR).

Figure 15-1 shows the temperature changes in a parcel of rising air. On the left, the temperature changes of the parcel relative to the temperature of the surrounding air are shown in diagram form, while on the right, these same changes are shown in graph form. In this hypothetical example, the ELR of the surrounding air is 8°C per 1000 meters. When the parcel rises, it cools first at the DAR of 10°C per 1000 meters, and after the **lifting condensation level** (LCL) of 2000 meters is reached, it cools at the SAR of 6°C per 1000 meters.

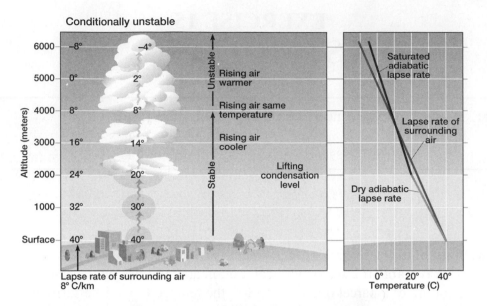

Figure 15-1: Temperature changes in a rising parcel of air (ELR = 8°C/1000 m; DAR = 10°C/1000 m; SAR = 6°C/1000 m; LCL = 2000 m). In this example the rising parcel of air is cooler than the surrounding air and is stable up to an elevation of 4000 meters; above that elevation, the release of latent heat during condensation warms the rising air enough to make it unstable—a circumstance known as conditional instability. (From McKnight and Hess, *Physical Geography*, 9th ed.)

Note that at elevations below 4000 meters, the parcel of air is stable (because it is cooler than the surrounding air) and must be forced to rise. However, if this parcel is lifted above 4000 meters, the temperature of the parcel will be warmer than the surrounding air. The parcel will then become unstable and will continue to rise on its own. This circumstance is known as **conditional instability**, since the parcel becomes unstable only after it begins to cool following the SAR.

EXERCISE 15 PROBLEMS—PART I *(S.I. Units)*

1. On the chart below, use the following sets of hypothetical data to plot the vertical temperature profile (the environmental lapse rate) of the atmosphere in two locations. Using a straightedge, connect the temperature points for Location A with a blue line, and for Location B with a green line (if you do not use colored lines, label each line clearly). After completing the temperature profiles, answer the questions on the following page.

Elevation	Temperature	
	Location A	Location B
5000 meters	−10°C	−8°C
3500 meters	−4°C	4°C
2500 meters	5°C	14°C
1500 meters	14°C	26°C
1000 meters	9°C	30°C
0 meters	15°C	35°C

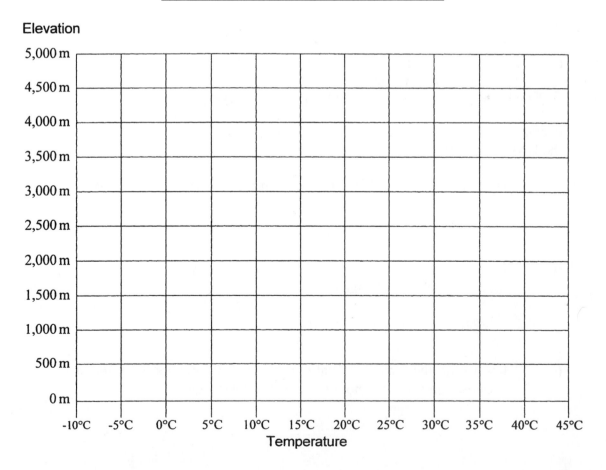

Remember, the vertical temperature profiles show the temperature of the surrounding air through which parcels of air can move. For the following questions, assume that the DAR is 10°C/1000 meters and that the SAR is 6°C/1000 meters.

2.   A parcel of air with an initial temperature of 15°C begins to rise in Location A. The LCL of the parcel is 1000 meters. With a red (or labeled) line, carefully draw the temperature decrease of this parcel of air as it rises to 3500 meters. Be sure to consider the LCL, and the DAR and SAR.

   (a)   Describe the stability pattern of this parcel of air:

   (b)   What is the general name for the change observed in the vertical temperature profile between 1000 and 1500 meters?

   (c)   Does the parcel of rising air become highly stable or highly unstable between 1000 and 1500 meters? Why?

3.   A parcel of air with an initial temperature of 35°C begins to rise in Location B. The LCL of the parcel is 2000 meters. With a red (or labeled) line, carefully draw the temperature decrease of this parcel of air as it rises to 5000 meters. Be sure to consider the LCL, and the DAR and SAR.

   (a)   Will this parcel of air begin to rise from the surface on its own? Why?

   (b)   Does the stability of this parcel change with increased elevation? If so, at what elevation does this change occur?

   (c)   How would the pattern of stability below 5000 meters be different if the lifting condensation level was not reached until 4500 meters?

Name _____   Section _____

EXERCISE 15 PROBLEMS—PART II *(English Units)*

1. On the chart below, use the following sets of hypothetical data to plot the vertical temperature profile (the environmental lapse rate) of the atmosphere in two locations. Using a straightedge, connect the temperature points for Location A with blue line, and for Location B with a green line (if you do not use colored lines, label each line clearly). After completing the temperature profiles, answer the questions on the following page.

Elevation	Temperature	
	Location A	Location B
10,000 feet	30°F	33°F
7000 feet	34°F	47°F
5000 feet	41°F	59°F
3000 feet	51°F	67°F
2000 feet	46°F	72°F
0 feet	55°F	80°F

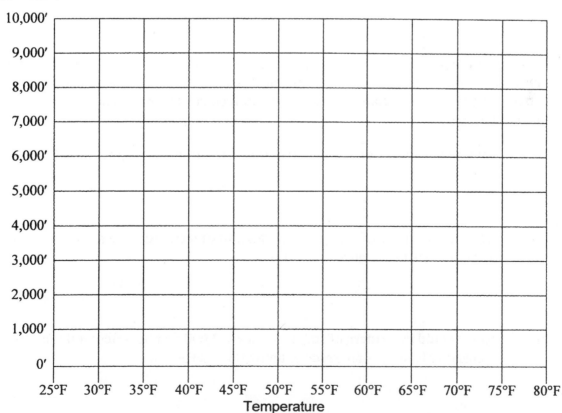

Remember, the vertical temperature profiles show the temperature of the surrounding air through which parcels of air can move. For the following questions, assume that the DAR is 5.5°F/1000 feet and that the SAR is 3.0°F/1000 feet.

2.   A parcel of air with an initial temperature of 55°F begins to rise in Location A. The LCL of the parcel is 2000 feet. With a red (or labeled) line, carefully draw the temperature decrease of this parcel of air as it rises to 8000 feet. Be sure to consider the LCL, and the DAR and SAR.

     (a)   Describe the stability pattern of this parcel of air:

     (b)   What is the general name for the change observed in the vertical temperature profile between 2000 and 3000 feet?

     (c)   Does the parcel of rising air become highly stable or highly unstable between 2000 and 3000 feet? Why?

3.   A parcel of air with an initial temperature of 80°F begins to rise in Location B. The LCL of the parcel is 4000 feet. With a red (or labeled) line, carefully draw the temperature decrease of this parcel of air as it rises to 10,000 feet. Be sure to consider the LCL, and the DAR and SAR.

     (a)   Will this parcel of air begin to rise from the surface on its own? Why?

     (b)   Does the stability of this parcel change with increased elevation? If so, at what elevation does this change occur?

     (c)   How would the pattern of stability below 10,000 feet be different if the lifting condensation level was not reached until 9000 feet?

EXERCISE 16
MIDLATITUDE CYCLONES

Objective:	To study the pressure, wind, and temperature patterns of midlatitude cyclones.
Resources:	Internet access (optional).
Reference:	McKnight and Hess, *Physical Geography*, 9th ed., pp. 182–191.

THE MIDLATITUDE CYCLONE

The **midlatitude cyclone** is the most important storm of the midlatitudes. At the heart of a midlatitude cyclone is an area of low pressure, as much as 1600 kilometers (1000 miles) across.

The low pressure cell produces a converging counterclockwise wind flow that pulls together two unlike **air masses** (the wind flow is converging clockwise in the Southern Hemisphere). Relatively cool air from the high latitudes is brought together with relatively warm air from the subtropics. These unlike air masses do not mix readily. Instead, abrupt transition zones known as **fronts** develop between the air masses. At the surface, a mature midlatitude cyclone has a "cool sector" and a "warm sector," separated by a **cold front** (cold air advancing under the warm) and a **warm front** (warm air advancing over the cold).

Figure 16-1 shows a typical well-developed midlatitude cyclone in the Northern Hemisphere, mapped with **isobars**. The lowest pressure is at the heart of the storm, but a **trough** of low pressure extends down the length of the cold front as well. As the whole storm migrates eastward in the flow of the **westerlies** (left to right in this diagram), air converges counterclockwise into the low. The cold front typically advances faster than the storm itself, and eventually catches up with the warm front. A cross section through the storm is shown in Figure 16-1b.

Figure 16-2 shows the life cycle of a midlatitude cyclone, beginning with the early development of the storm along the **polar front**, through maturity, and finally the process of **occlusion**, in which the cold front catches up with the warm front, lifting all of the warm air off the ground. After occlusion, the storm generally begins to lose strength and die.

The cross sections shown in Figure 16-2 help illustrate the reasons for the weather typically brought by these storms. Generally, the heaviest precipitation is associated with the cold front. The abrupt uplift of the warm air along the advancing, steeply sloping cold front causes the **adiabatic cooling** needed to produce clouds and precipitation. Because of the more gentle slope of the warm front, this region of the storm is usually associated with more widespread but less intense precipitation than the cold front.

FRONTS ON WEATHER MAPS

There are four common kinds of fronts. Cold fronts develop where the cold air is actively advancing under warm air. Warm fronts occur when the warm air is actively advancing over cold air. **Occluded fronts** develop when the cold front catches up with a warm front. **Stationary fronts** represent boundaries between unlike air masses, but neither air mass is actively advancing. Figure 16-3 shows the commonly used weather map symbols for these four kinds of fronts.

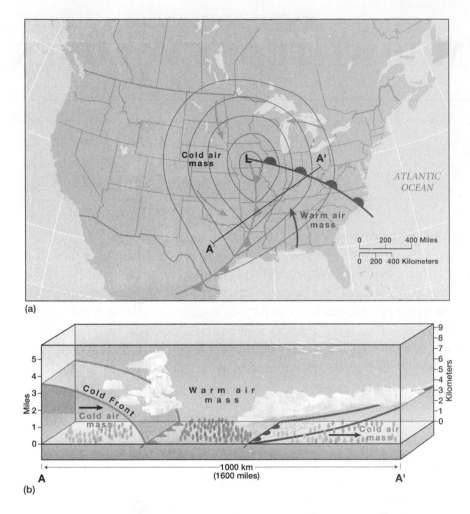

Figure 16-1: A map (a) and a cross section (b) of a typical mature midlatitude cyclone. Arrows in (b) indicate the direction of frontal movement. (From McKnight and Hess, *Physical Geography*, 9th ed.)

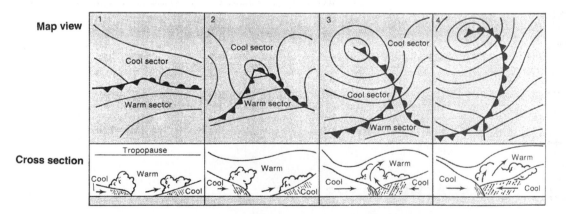

Figure 16-2: Stages in the life of a midlatitude cyclone: (1) early development, (2) maturity, (3) partial occlusion, (4) full occlusion. (Adapted from McKnight, *Physical Geography*, 4th ed.)

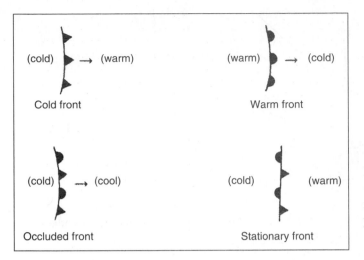

Figure 16-3: Fronts as shown on weather maps. Arrows indicate the direction of movement of the front. The relative temperature of air masses at the surface is shown in parentheses.

While it might seem that the most obvious way to recognize a front would be an abrupt change in temperature from one meteorological data station to the next, such changes are not always obvious on weather maps. Fronts often represent transition zones that may be 15 kilometers (about ten miles) or more wide. It is quite possible that the spacing of meteorological stations is such that a sharp difference in temperature is not clearly visible on a weather map.

Figure 16-4 shows a section of a hypothetical weather map in the Northern Hemisphere (top of map is north) showing isobars, a cold front, and 10 meteorological stations. The weather map **station model** was introduced in Exercise 11. In the simplified form used here, the model shows the temperature, **dew point**, and wind direction. For example:

$$40 \qquad 27$$

In this case, the temperature is 40°F, the dew point is 27°F, and the wind is coming from the northeast at 15 knots (the "feathers" on the wind shaft point *into* the wind). We will take a more complete look at the station model in Exercise 17.

The pattern of dew points may be helpful in locating the position of a front. Dew points are usually lower in relatively dry cold air than in warm air, and so generally there is a drop in dew points across a front.

Wind direction is another useful indication of the location of a front. Notice in Figure 16-4 that a wind direction shift is observed from one side of the front to the other. In this example, the wind direction in the cold sector suggests that the cold air is advancing, and therefore, pushing the position of the cold front toward the southeast.

Also notice the "kink" in the isobars at the position of the front. A cold front is associated with a trough of low pressure. As a cold front passes, the pressure trend changes from falling to rising.

METEOGRAMS

Meteograms are charts that plot changes in a wide range of weather conditions for a location over a 25-hour period. Meteograms may appear in several different formats, but all contain the same general information. Figure 16-5 is a typical meteogram. The top chart shows temperature ("TMPF"), dew point ("DWPF"), and relative humidity ("RELH"). Below the temperature charts, information such as current weather conditions ("WSYM" or "WX"; see Figure I-3 in Appendix I

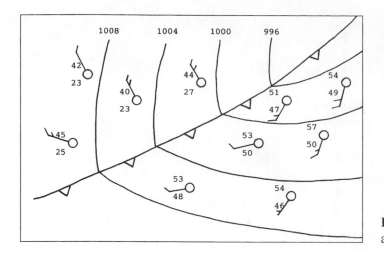

Figure 16-4: Hypothetical weather map showing a cold front.

for an explanation of the symbols used) and wind direction and speed are shown. A middle chart shows the elevation of the cloud base and visibility ("VSBY"), while precipitation amounts ("P06I" or "PREC") are shown below. In the bottom chart, atmospheric pressure ("PMSL") is plotted. The date and time of the meteogram is in **Zulu time** or UTC (Universal Time Coordinated; GMT) (see Exercise 3 for a discussion of time zones and Zulu time).

Meteograms clearly show changing trends in weather, such as that associated with the passing of a midlatitude cyclone. For example, in Figure 16-5 notice the change in wind direction, the drop in temperature, the decreasing visibility and lower cloud cover, and the onset of precipitation associated with the passing of a front. The trough of the front passed through Boothville, Louisiana, at about 1200Z on January 9, 2004.

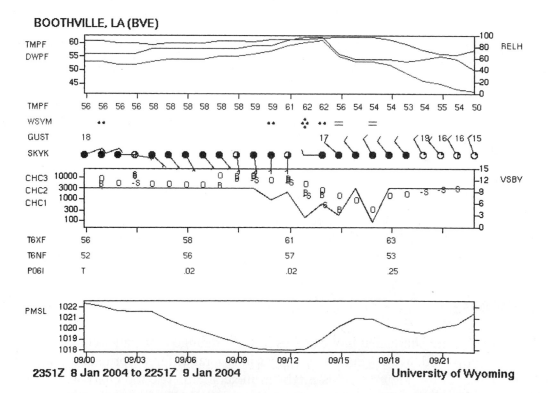

Figure 16-5: Meteogram for Boothville, Louisiana, on 1/8/04–1/9/04. (Meteogram courtesy of the University of Wyoming)

90

EXERCISE 16 PROBLEMS—PART I

The following questions are based on this hypothetical weather map in the Northern Hemisphere showing isobars and the positions of a cold front and a warm front (top of map is north). Six locations are marked on the map (points A, B, C, D, E, and F). A cross-section diagram along points A, B, C, D, E, and F is shown below the map.

Map:

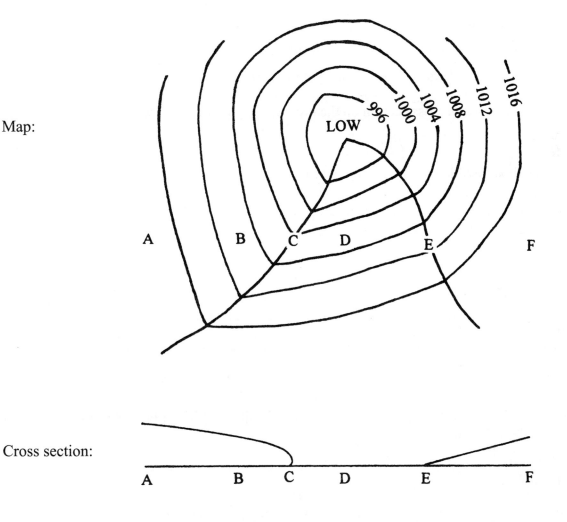

Cross section:

1.   On the map above, label the following:

   (a)   Cold front (use standard weather map symbols)

   (b)   Warm front (use standard weather map symbols)

   (c)   Cool sector of storm

   (d)   Warm sector of storm

2.   On the map on the previous page, use arrows to show the wind direction in the western, southern, eastern, and northern parts of the storm.

3.   In which direction is the storm as a whole moving?   From _____ to _____

4.   On the cross-section diagram, label the following:

   (a)   Cold front

   (b)   Warm front

   (c)   Cold air mass(es)

   (d)   Warm air mass

   (e)   Direction of cold front movement (use arrow)

   (f)   Direction of warm front movement (use arrow)

Using your labeled map and cross section on the previous page for reference, answer the following questions:

5.   What is the most likely wind direction at Point D?   From the _____

6.   (a)   At point D, is the pressure rising or falling?   _____

   (b)   Why?

7.   (a)   Is precipitation more likely at Point D or at Point C?   _____

   (b)   Why?

8.   (a)   At Point C, what general temperature change will take place with the passing of the cold front?

   (b)   Why?

9.   What is the most likely wind direction at Point B?   From the _____

10.   (a)   At point B, is the pressure rising or falling?   _____

   (b)   Why?

EXERCISE 16 PROBLEMS—PART II

1. Two hypothetical weather maps in the Northern Hemisphere are shown below. Using the appropriate symbols (see Figure 16-3), draw in the position of the front on each map (one map shows a cold front, and the other a warm front). Top of each map is north. (Hint: the fronts can be drawn with a nearly straight line.)

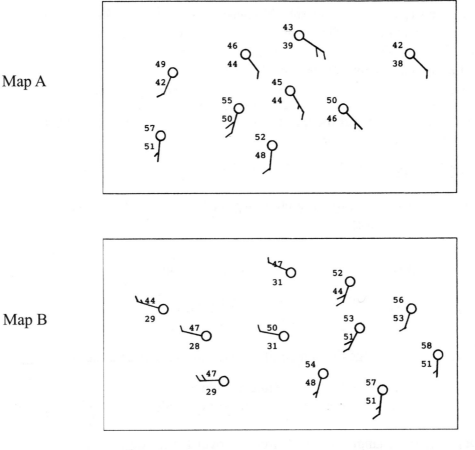

Map A

Map B

2. Is a cold front or warm front shown in Map A?   _____

3. (a) In which direction is the front in Map A advancing?   To the _____

    (b) How can you tell?

4. Is a cold front or warm front shown in Map B?   _____

5. In which direction is the front in Map B advancing?   To the _____

EXERCISE 16 PROBLEMS—PART III—INTERNET

In this exercise, you will use a meteogram to study the weather changes brought by the passing of a midlatitude cyclone. This exercise will work best about 12 hours after a midlatitude cyclone or front passes through your area. If no storms are currently in your area, your instructor may have you choose another city that has experienced a passing storm within the last day.

- Go to the McKnight and Hess textbook Web site, *<http://www.prenhall.com/mcknight>*. Select "Lab Manual," then "Exercise 16." Then select "Go to *University of Wyoming, Information for United States Cities*" for the Department of Atmospheric Science Web page, *<http://weather.uwyo.edu/cities>*. (Your instructor may recommend a different Internet site that provides meteograms.)
- Select your region of the United States to see a map showing cities in the area.
- Under "Observations" select "Meteogram."
- Click on the closest city to your location for the current meteogram in that city.

After viewing the meteogram, answer the questions below. Your instructor may ask that you attach a copy of the meteogram to your answers.

1.   Which city did you study?   _____

2.   What was the date and time of the meteogram studied? (Be sure to also indicate the *local* day and time of the meteogram.)

3.   (a)   Describe the changes in pressure over the 25-hour period.   _____

      (b)   What might explain these pressure changes?

4.   (a)   Describe the changes in temperature over the 25-hour period.   _____

      (b)   What might explain these temperature changes?

5.   (a)   Describe the changes in wind direction over the 25-hour period.   _____

      (b)   What might explain these wind direction changes?

6.   Did any precipitation take place during the 25-hour period? If so, how much and when?

7.   (a)   Based on the information in the meteogram, what time did
             the front(s) and/or storm pass through your city?   _____

      (b)   How can you tell?

EXERCISE 17
WEATHER MAPS

Objective:	To study weather patterns shown on standard weather maps produced by the National Weather Service.
Resources:	Internet access (optional).
Reference:	McKnight and Hess, *Physical Geography*, 9th ed., pp. A13–A17.

THE STATION MODEL

In Exercises 11, 12, and 16 we used a simplified version of the weather map **station model**. We will now introduce the complete station model used on standard National Weather Service maps. Figure 17-1 is a sample station model, with labeled information. A complete description of all standard U.S. Weather Service station model codes is found in Appendix I in the back of the Lab Manual.

In earlier exercises, we introduced the format and position of data to indicate current temperature (upper left of station circle), dew point (lower left of station circle), wind direction, wind speed, and atmospheric pressure.

Wind direction is indicated with a shaft that points *into* the wind, and wind speed is determined by adding up the "feathers" on the wind shaft: $\frac{1}{2}$ feather = 5 knots; full feather = 10 knots; triangular flag = 50 knots (one knot equals one nautical mile per hour, 1.15 statute mph, and 1.85 km/hr). For example, the station model in Figure 17-1 shows a 20-knot wind from the northwest.

Barometric pressure is shown in an abbreviated form on the station model. The first 9 or 10 is left off, and the decimal point removed, so a pressure of 1021.3 is written simply "213." In the example station model in Figure 17-1, "147" indicates a pressure of 1014.7 mb. Immediately below the pressure, the change in pressure in tenths of a millibar (+ or −) over the last three hours is given.

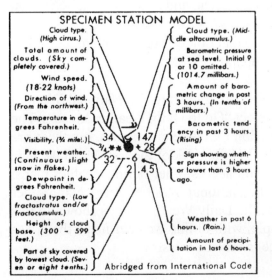

Figure 17-1: Sample weather station model. (From National Weather Service)

95

Every station model on a weather map may not contain all of the information shown in the sample. The position of data around a station model, however, does not vary. For example, in the abbreviated station model below, the temperature is 73°F, the dew point is 47°F, the pressure is 995.3 mb and has decreased 3.1 mb over the last three hours, and the wind is 25 knots from the southeast:

U.S. WEATHER SERVICE MAPS

Figure 17-2 shows a standard set of weather maps produced by the National Weather Service. (The maps are shown here reduced in size; you may also view these maps online by going to *<www.prenhall.com/mcknight>* and then to "Lab Manual" and "Exercise 17.") These maps were published as part of its *Daily Weather Maps: Weekly Series*. These sets contain weather maps for a seven-day period (Monday through Sunday).

Included for each day is a "Surface Weather Map" showing conditions at 7:00 A.M. Eastern Standard Time (Figure 17-3 is a full-size copy of the surface map in Figure 17-2). The surface map provides weather data with station models, gives the position of fronts, and uses shading to indicate areas of precipitation. Isobars are used to map surface pressure (in millibars). Dashed isotherms are provided for 32°F and 0°F.

The tracks of well-defined low pressure areas (midlatitude cyclones and tropical cyclones) are shown by a chain of arrows, with black boxes indicating the position of these lows at 6-hour intervals, usually 6, 12, 18, and 24 hours before the time of the map.

The "500 mb Height Contours Map" illustrates the conditions in the upper atmosphere. (Figure 17-4 in Exercise 17 Problems, Part III, is a full-size copy of this map.) It shows the elevation of 500 mb of pressure, given in dekameters above sea level (1 dekameter = 10 meters). High 500 mb elevations indicate relatively high pressure below, while low 500 mb elevations indicate relative low pressure below (notice also that 500 mb elevations generally decrease with increasing latitude due to cooler surface conditions). For reference, a pressure of 500 mb is found at an average elevation of about 5600 meters (18,400 feet). This map also shows the general trend and speed of upper-elevation winds, locations of upper elevation pressure centers, and isotherms (dashed lines) in degrees Celsius. Note that the area covered by the "500 mb" map is greater than that of the "Surface" map.

Two other maps show the "Highest and Lowest Temperatures" over the last 24 hours, and "Precipitation Amounts" over the last 24 hours.

An online version of recent Daily Weather Maps is available from the National Weather Service in a PDF format (from the Lab Manual Web site, select "Go to Daily Weather Maps"). The station models on some of the online versions of the maps don't include city names, but these are shown on a separate index map (see Figure I-8 in Appendix I at the back of the Lab Manual). This station model index map will also be useful to you when you access other online weather maps. Although online versions of weather maps produced by the National Weather Service and other organizations use the same station model nomenclature as the Daily Weather Maps shown in this exercise, the level of map detail varies greatly. For example, with online weather maps the boxes and arrows used to show the movement of low pressure cells may be missing.

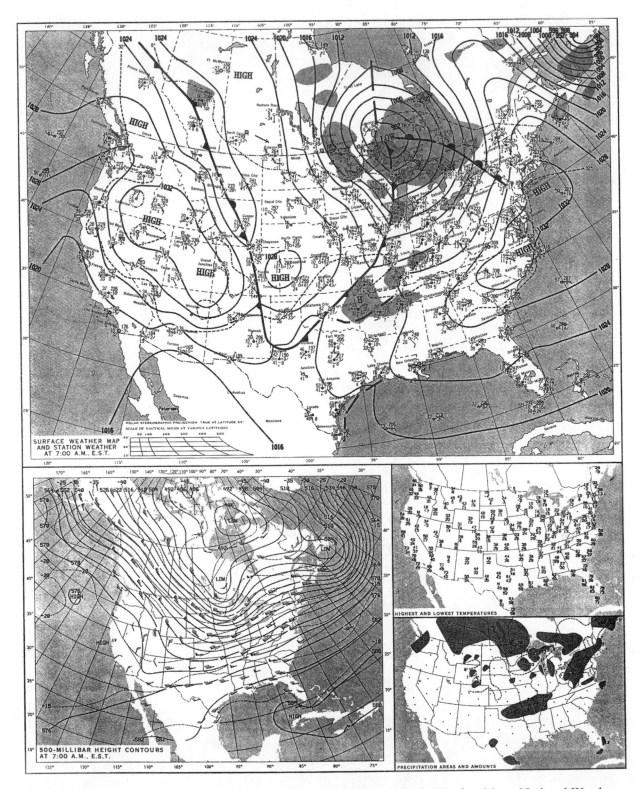

Figure 17-2: Weather maps for December 25, 1992. (From *Daily Weather Maps*, National Weather Service)

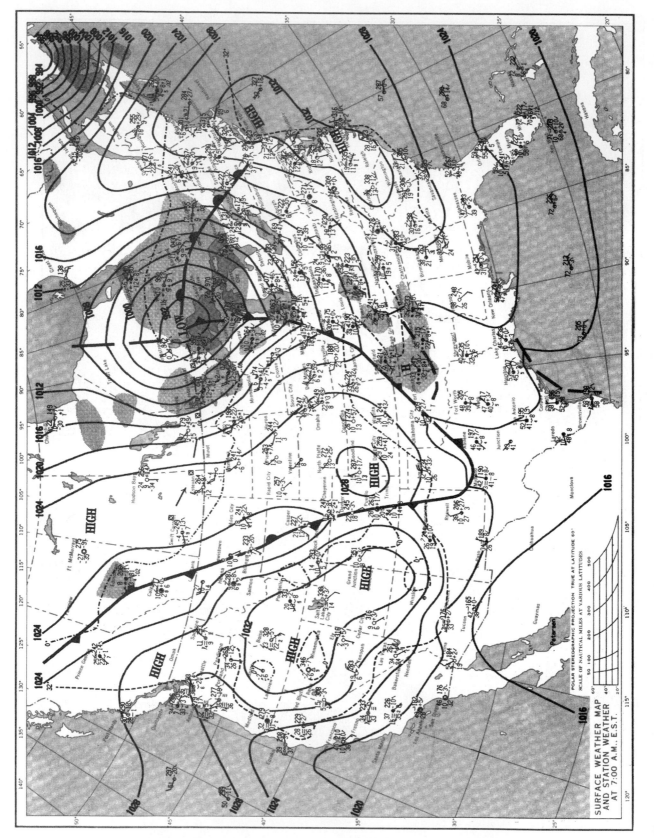

Figure 17-3: Surface Weather Map for December 25, 1992. (From *Daily Weather Maps*, National Weather Service)

Name _____   Section _____

EXERCISE 17 PROBLEMS—PART I

The following questions are based on the surface weather map for December 25, 1992, (Figure 17-3). This day was chosen because of the weather conditions present. There is a well-developed midlatitude cyclone centered over Lake Superior, with a cold front extending to the southwest and a warm front extending to the east. The cold front curves back to the northwest, becoming a stationary front. A trough (shown by a heavy dashed line) extends north of the midlatitude cyclone. Several areas of high pressure are found along the east coast and in the west.

1. Describe the following weather conditions at 7:00 A.M. EST on December 25, 1992, in Indianapolis, Indiana, (40° N, 86° W; an enlarged copy of the station model is shown below).

    (a)   Temperature: _____ °F

    (b)   Dew point: _____ °F

    (c)   Wind speed: _____ knots

    (d)   Wind direction: _____

    (e)   Pressure: _____ mb

    (f)   Pressure change over last 3 hours: _____ mb

    (g)   What explains this change in pressure?

    (h)   What explains the wind direction?

2. (a)   Which city is more likely to receive precipitation during the next 12 hours, Detroit, Michigan (42° N, 83° W) or Des Moines, Iowa, (42° N, 94° W)?   _____

    (b)   Why?

Name _____   Section _____

EXERCISE 17 PROBLEMS—PART II

The following questions are based on the surface weather map shown in Figure 17-3.

1.   Describe the following weather conditions at 7:00 A.M. EST on December 25, 1992, in Minneapolis, Minnesota, (45° N, 93° W; an enlarged copy of the station model is shown below).

   (a)   Temperature: _____ °F

   (b)   Wind direction: _____   Minneapolis

   (c)   Pressure: _____ mb

   (d)   Pressure change over last 3 hours: _____ mb

   (e)   What explains this change in pressure?

   (f)   Approximately how many hours ago did the cold front
         pass through Minneapolis?   _____

   (g)   What explains the difference in temperature between Indianapolis and Minneapolis?

2.   (a)   What general kind of weather should Salt Lake City,
           Utah, (41° N, 112° W), expect over the next 24 hours?   _____

     (b)   Why?

3.   Approximately how far has the midlatitude cyclone traveled over
     the last 24 hours? Give your answer in nautical miles, using the
     "Scale of Nautical Miles at Various Latitudes" shown in the
     lower left corner of the map (use the scale for 50° N latitude).   _____ nautical miles

4.   How fast is the midlatitude cyclone traveling in knots (nautical
     miles per hour)?   _____ knots

100

Name _____   Section _____

EXERCISE 17 PROBLEMS—PART III

The following questions are based on Figure 17-4, the 500 mb map below:

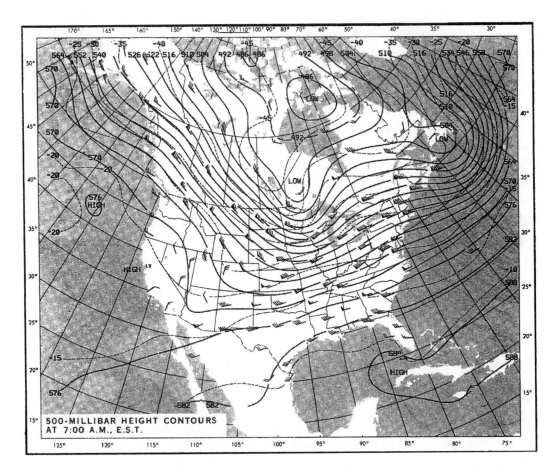

Figure 17-4: 500-Millibar Height Contours map for December 25, 1992. (From *Daily Weather Maps*, National Weather Service)

1. What is the highest recorded velocity of upper elevation
    winds shown on the 500 mb map?   _____ knots

2. With a blue pencil, draw a series of arrows to indicate the approximate position and wind
    direction of the jet stream.

3. Locate the midlatitude cyclone centered over Lake Superior (shown in Figure 17-3).
    Based on the upper elevation wind patterns, in which direction would you expect this
    storm to travel over the next 24 hours? Be as specific as possible.

                                                          To the _____

Name _____   Section _____

EXERCISE 17 PROBLEMS—PART IV—INTERNET

In this exercise, you will use weather maps from the Internet to explain current local weather conditions.

- Before using the weather maps on the Internet, go outside to note the local sky and wind conditions so that you can answer questions 1 and 2.
- Go to the McKnight and Hess textbook Web site, *<http://www.prenhall.com/mcknight>*. Select "Lab Manual," then "Exercise 17." Then select "Go to Unisys Weather," *<http://weather.unisys.com/>*. (Your instructor may recommend a different Internet site that provides weather maps.)
- There are many weather maps available at this site, but a good starting point is to select "Analyses—Surface Data" on the site index. This will take you to the "Surface Data" page.
- From the "Surface Data" page, look at the "Current Surface Map" as well as the simpler "Fronts" map you can access from the "Composite Plots" link in the index. These maps use bold red lines to indicate warm fronts, blue lines for cold fronts, and pink lines for occluded fronts.
- You also might take a look at the "Composite Views" found by selecting "Satellite Images" on the main site index. (Exercise 18 covers weather satellite images.)
- Answer the questions below. Your instructor may ask that you attach a copy of the weather maps you used to your answers.

1.   What sky conditions do you currently observe in your city (cloudy, rainy, clear, etc.)?

2.   What wind direction do you currently observe in your city?

3.   What are the dates and times of the Internet weather maps you used? Indicate both the date and time shown on the maps (usually in Zulu time or UTC), as well as the equivalent local time in your location:

_____ Zulu/UTC = _____ local time.

4.   Based on the weather maps, what might explain the current local weather conditions you observed? (Consider the position of pressure cells, fronts, etc.)

5.   Are nearby cities experiencing the same general weather? If not, suggest a reason why.

6.   How has the weather in your city changed over the last 12 hours, and what might explain these changes?

EXERCISE 18
WEATHER SATELLITE IMAGES

Objective:	To interpret visible light images, infrared images, water vapor images, and movie loops from weather satellites.
Resources:	Internet access (optional).
Reference:	McKnight and Hess, *Physical Geography*, 9th ed., pp. 148 and 152.

GOES WEATHER SATELLITES

The satellite images we commonly see on television weather reports come from a pair of satellites operated by the National Oceanographic and Atmospheric Administration (NOAA). They are known as **GOES**, or **Geostationary Operational Environmental Satellites**. The two GOES satellites orbit at a distance of about 35,800 kilometers (22,300 miles) in fixed locations relative to the surface of Earth below. GOES-East (GOES-12) orbits above the equator in South America (75° W), where it can see the conterminous United States, as well as much of the north and south Atlantic Ocean. GOES-West (GOES-11) orbits above the equator in the Pacific (135° W), where it can see most of the Pacific Ocean from Alaska to New Zealand. (As of this writing, GOES-13 is being stored in orbit as a replacement for either GOES-11 or GOES-12; GOES-10 is being repositioned to 60° W to provide better coverage of South America.) Both GOES satellites (as well as satellites operated by other countries) send back several images each hour, and are important weather forecasting tools. Figures 18-1, 18-2, 18-5, 18-6, and 18-7, showing the west coast of North America, were taken by GOES-West. Figures 18-3 and 18-4, showing North and South America, were taken by GOES-East. You may also view all of these images online by going to *<www.prenhall.com/mcknight>* and then to "Lab Manual" and "Exercise 18."

The GOES satellites have sensors that can detect radiation in several different bands of wavelengths in the electromagnetic spectrum. The intensity of radiation in each wavelength band is recorded and used to produce the images we see. This exercise will focus on satellite images from three wavelength bands—visible light, thermal infrared, and a portion of the infrared spectrum that allows the creation of "water vapor" images.

VISIBLE LIGHT IMAGES

Visible light satellite images show light that has been reflected off the surface of the Earth, or by clouds in the atmosphere. In gray-scale ("black-and-white") images, the intensity of reflected visible light is shown with shades of gray, with white (bright) areas representing surfaces reflecting a great deal of visible light, and black (dark) areas reflecting very little light.

The brightness of a surface depends both upon its **albedo** (reflectance) and the angle of the light striking it. The brightest (high albedo) surfaces in visible light are typically the tops of clouds and snow or ice-covered surfaces. The darkest (low albedo) surfaces are typically land areas (especially unvegetated land surfaces) and the oceans—which are usually the darkest surfaces seen on visible light satellite images. When a region of the Earth is experiencing early morning or late

Figure 18-1: GOES-West visible light image of northern Pacific Ocean on February 26, 2003, 2230Z. (Image courtesy of Naval Research Laboratory, Marine Meteorology Division)

104

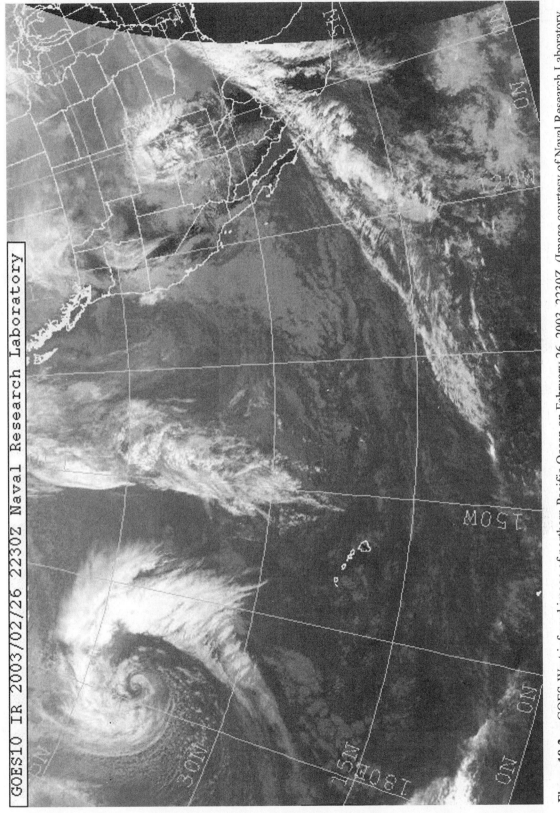

Figure 18-2: GOES-West infrared image of northern Pacific Ocean on February 26, 2003, 2230Z. (Image courtesy of Naval Research Laboratory, Marine Meteorology Division)

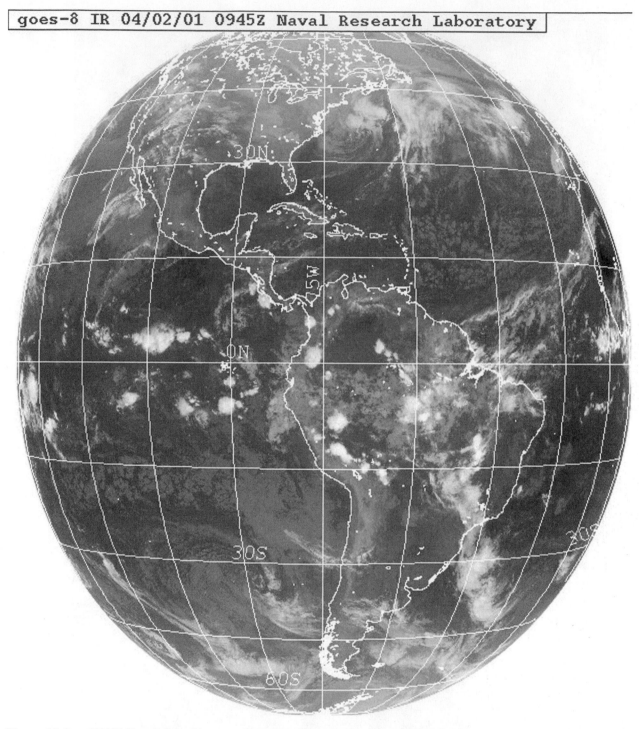

Figure 18-3: GOES-East infrared image of North and South America on April 2, 2001, 0945Z. (Image courtesy of Naval Research Laboratory, Marine Meteorology Division)

Figure 18-4: GOES-East infrared image of North and South America on April 2, 2001, 2045Z. (Image courtesy of Naval Research Laboratory, Marine Meteorology Division)

afternoon, the amount of visible light reflected generally will be reduced, producing a much darker image than at midday. Figure 18-1 is a visible light image of the northern Pacific Ocean and the west coast of North America.

INFRARED IMAGES

Infrared satellite images show the **longwave radiation** (or "thermal infrared") that has been emitted by the surface of the Earth or by clouds in the atmosphere. Warm objects emit more longwave radiation than cold objects, and so infrared images show us differences in temperature. Although infrared radiation is invisible to the human eye, differences in its intensity are shown on gray-scale satellite images so that cooler surfaces (those emitting relatively little longwave radiation) are shown in white, while warmer surfaces (those emitting a great deal of longwave radiation) are shown in black. Since clouds and the surface emit longwave radiation continuously, infrared images are produced by satellites both day and night.

Figure 18-2 is an infrared image of the northern Pacific Ocean and the west coast of North America taken at the same time as the visible light image shown in Figure 18-1. Figures 18-3 and 18-4 are infrared images of North and South America taken 11 hours apart.

In order to distinguish very small differences in temperature, infrared satellite images are frequently computer enhanced with colors to highlight the lowest temperatures. In computer-enhanced infrared images, the lowest temperatures—such as would be found at the tops of the highest clouds—are usually shown in color as shades of green, blue, and purple. These colors help meteorologists recognize the location of the very cold, high tops of the massive **cumulonimbus** clouds associated with thunderstorms and hurricanes. Such detail may be lost on ordinary gray-scale infrared images.

INTERPRETING VISIBLE AND INFRARED IMAGES

Both visible and infrared satellite images are useful in weather forecasting since they provide different kinds of information about the surface of the Earth and the atmosphere—visible light images show differences in the reflectance of light, while infrared images show differences in temperature.

In infrared images, the tops of high clouds are easy to distinguish from low clouds and fog. The tops of high clouds, such as massive cumulonimbus clouds, are much colder than low clouds and fog, and so will appear brighter (white) on gray-scale infrared images. Low clouds and fog tend to have similar temperatures to that of the surface, and so will appear as nearly the same shade of gray as the surface below.

On the other hand, in visible light both high clouds and low clouds may appear equally bright (since they tend to reflect similar amounts of light). It also may be difficult to tell the difference between snow-covered surfaces and clouds in visible light images. By comparing visible and infrared images of the same area, it is possible to distinguish between high clouds and low clouds, as well as to recognize snow- or ice-covered surfaces.

WATER VAPOR IMAGES

In ordinary infrared satellite images, the wavelengths of infrared radiation emitted by the surface and atmosphere are in the portion of the electromagnetic spectrum called the **atmospheric window**. These are the wavelengths of infrared radiation that can transmit through the atmosphere without being absorbed (wavelengths between approximately 8 and 12 micrometers). While such infrared satellite images tell us about the temperature of the surface and cloud tops, they may not tell us much about the characteristics of the air itself.

However, some gases in the atmosphere, such as water vapor and carbon dioxide, absorb and emit wavelengths of infrared radiation that are outside the atmospheric window. By detecting wavelengths of infrared radiation outside the atmospheric window that are emitted by water vapor (specifically, wavelengths of 6.7 micrometers and 7.3 micrometers), we have a way to determine the relative amount of water vapor in the atmosphere—water vapor that may be invisible in visible light and ordinary infrared satellite images. Regions with high emission of infrared wavelengths emitted by water vapor contain relatively large amounts of water vapor, while regions with low emission of these wavelengths contain relatively small amounts of water vapor. Such satellite images are called **water vapor images**.

Water vapor images let us recognize regions of dry air and moist air. In gray-scale water vapor images, darker shades of gray show areas of relatively dry air, while lighter shades of gray show areas of relatively moist air (in color water vapor images, relatively dry air is often shown as dark blue, while relatively moist air is shown in shades of orange and red). Figures 18-3, 18-4, and 18-5 are satellite images of western North America taken on the same day showing visible light, infrared, and water vapor, respectively.

Because water vapor images can only detect infrared emission from water vapor in the middle and upper **troposphere** (above about 4500 meters or 15,000 feet), in addition to telling us about the moisture content of the atmosphere, these images also give us information about wind movement in the upper atmosphere, especially when time-sequence "movie loops" are used.

SATELLITE MOVIE LOOPS

Time-sequence movie loops (or "animations" as they are called on some Web sites) are very useful tools in meteorology. By viewing a sequence of satellite images taken over several hours (or several days in some cases), we can track the development, movement, and changes in air masses, storms, and wind patterns. Because clouds are associated with cyclonic storms, the wind patterns and movement of midlatitude cyclones and hurricanes are usually quite obvious on satellite movie loops. However, by viewing movie loops, the wind patterns and movement in cloudless areas (such as in an anticyclone) may also be determined by viewing the movement of clouds around the margins of these areas, or by viewing the movement of water vapor.

TIME MARKS ON SATELLITE IMAGES

The time and date of a satellite image are usually indicated along the top or bottom of the frame. Since satellite images cover such large areas (and therefore, many time zones), it is impractical to label them using local time. Instead, the images are labeled with the date and time at Greenwich, England. This is known as **Universal Time Coordinated (UTC)** or **Zulu time**. The times are usually given using a 24-hour clock, with a "Z" to indicate Zulu time. For example, "1800Z" would be 6:00 P.M. Greenwich time.

To convert Zulu time to local standard times in North America subtract 5 hours for Eastern Standard Time, subtract 6 hours for Central Standard Time, subtract 7 hours for Mountain Standard Time, and subtract 8 hours for Pacific Standard Time. To convert Zulu time to daylight-saving times, subtract one less hour than indicated above.

Figure 18-5: GOES-West visible light image of northern Pacific Ocean on September 26, 2003, 2000Z. (Image courtesy NOAA)

Figure 18-6: GOES-West infrared image of northern Pacific Ocean on September 26, 2003, 2000Z. (Image courtesy NOAA)

Figure 18-7: GOES-West water vapor image of northern Pacific Ocean on September 26, 2003, 2000Z. (Image courtesy NOAA)

Name _____   Section _____

EXERCISE 18 PROBLEMS—PART I

The following questions are based on Figure 18-1, a visible light image of the northern Pacific Ocean and the west coast of North America, and Figure 18-2, an infrared image of the same region taken at the same time. A well-developed midlatitude cyclone can be seen in the Pacific on the left side of the image.

1.   Determine the center of the low pressure cell associated with the midlatitude cyclone:

   Latitude: _____   Longitude: _____

2.   (a)   Find the band of clouds that cuts diagonally across the southern
             tip of Baja, Mexico from southwest to northeast (at about
             20° N, 115° W). Are these high clouds or low clouds?   _____

      (b)   How can you tell?

The following questions are based on Figures 18-5, 18-6, and 18-7 showing visible light, infrared, and water vapor images of western North America and the northern Pacific Ocean basin taken on the same day and time:

3.   (a)   In the visible light image, notice the clouds along the
             coast of California and Baja, Mexico. Are these high
             clouds or low clouds?   _____

      (b)   How can you tell?

4.   (a)   In the visible light image, find the cloudless area off the
             coast of Oregon and Washington. Does this region contain
             relatively large amounts of water vapor, or relatively little
             water vapor?   _____

      (b)   What might explain the lack of clouds here?

EXERCISE 18 PROBLEMS—PART II—INTERNET

To answer the following questions, go to the Lab Manual Web site, <*www.prenhall.com/mcknight*>, then go to "Lab Manual," and then "Exercise 18."

Problems 1 and 2 are based on "Figure 18-8: West Coast Satellite Movie Loop," a satellite movie loop showing California and the eastern Pacific Ocean basin. You may also want to look at the high-quality single image of the same location: "Figure 18-9: West Coast Image."

1. (a)   Is high or low pressure found just off the coast of
          Oregon and Washington (47° N, 130° W)?   _____

    (b)   Based on the movement of clouds, how can you tell?

2. (a)   Is high or low pressure found just off the coast of southern
          California and Baja (25° N, 125° W)?   _____

    (b)   Based on the movement of clouds, how can you tell?

Problems 3 to 5 are based on Figure 18-10: "Africa Satellite Movie Loop," an infrared satellite movie loop showing Africa over a 16-hour period.

3. What explains the general direction of movement of clouds in the region of the Mediterranean Sea?

4. Why does the location of the land area shown in the darkest shade of gray move from east to west across Africa and then finally to the east coast of South America?

5. What explains the growth of clouds near the equator as the movie loop proceeds?

EXERCISE 18 PROBLEMS—PART III—INTERNET

In this exercise, you will interpret satellite images found on the Internet.

- Before viewing the satellite images, go outside and note the general weather conditions so that you can answer question #1. If your school has a weather station, you will be able to report more information about your local weather conditions than if you are simply relying on your own observations.

- Go to the McKnight and Hess textbook Web site, *<http://www.prenhall.com/mcknight>*. Select "Lab Manual," then "Exercise 18." Then select "Go to Naval Research Laboratory Satellite Images," *<http://www.nrlmry.navy.mil/sat_products.html>*. (Your instructor may recommend a different Internet site that provides satellite images.)

- There are many satellite images to see at this site. Begin with "West Coast & EPAC" if you live on the West Coast and "CONUS" if you live in the Midwest or East Coast. View the infrared, visible light, and water vapor images; you may make movie loops by clicking on the "animate" button in the menu above most images. Also try "Global Imagery" to see images that show both the Northern and Southern Hemisphere in one image.

- Another good Web site for satellite images is NOAA's Geostationary Satellite Server, *<http://www.goes.noaa.gov/>*.

- Your instructor may ask that you attach a copy of the satellite images to your answers.

1. Describe the current weather conditions in your location:

    (a) What is the date and local time of your observations? _____

    (b) What are the general sky conditions you observe outside (cloudy, rainy, clear, etc.)?

    (c) What is the current wind direction?

    (d) Has there been any precipitation over the last 24 hours? If so, how much? (Optional if a rain gauge measurement is not available.)

    (e) What is the current temperature? (Optional if instrument measurement is not available.)

(f)   What is the barometric trend (rising/falling/steady)? (Optional if instrument measurement is not available.)

View the latest weather satellite images showing your city and region of the country, and then answer the following questions.

2.   (a)   What is the date and time stamp on the satellite images?

            Date: _____   Time: _____ Z

       (b)   What is the day and local time (in your city) of these images?

            Date: _____   Time: _____

3.   What kind of sky conditions (high clouds, low clouds, scattered clouds, clear, etc.) do the satellite images suggest are in your immediate location? (You will need to look at both the visible light and infrared images to determine this.)

4.   Do your own observations of the sky (question #1 above) and the satellite images match closely? If not, suggest a reason why.

5.   Based on the satellite images and movie loops (that can help you identify wind direction and major pressure cells), what explains your observations of the following local weather conditions from question #1 above:

       (a)   Wind direction:

       (b)   Precipitation over the last 24 hours:

       (c)   Temperature (optional if instrument measurement is not available):

       (d)   Barometric trend (optional if instrument measurement is not available):

Name _____   Section _____

EXERCISE 18 PROBLEMS—PART IV—INTERNET

The following questions are based on your observations of the current visible light, infrared, and water vapor images and movies loops of North America available on the Internet, such as from the Naval Research Laboratory: *<http://www.nrlmry.navy.mil/sat_products.html>*.

1.   What is the most recent date and time stamp on the satellite images you viewed when answering the problems below?

   Date: _____   Time: _____ Z

2.   Describe the location of any midlatitude cyclones or tropical cyclones you see over (or near) North America in the satellite images (describe the locations with latitude and longitude, or by their position over states/provinces).

3.   (a)   On the satellite images, describe the location of any cloud-free regions near or over North America (describe with latitude and longitude or by their position over states/provinces):

   (b)   Do you think that any of these cloud-free regions are in areas of high pressure? If so, describe which one(s) and explain why you think this is the case:

4.   Using the satellite images, look at the sky conditions in a city far away from your location (for example, if you are in Denver, look at Miami):

   (a)   City: _____

   (b)   What kind of local weather do you expect that city is experiencing at the time the satellite image was taken?

After completing questions #2–4, view a current weather map (such as the weather maps you can access from the Lab Manual Web page for "Exercise 17"):

5.   Are any of the cloud-free areas associated with high pressure cells?

6.   Describe the actual weather in the city you studied in question #4:

115

EXERCISE 18 PROBLEMS—PART V

The following questions are based on Figure 18-3 and Figure 18-4, infrared images of North and South America taken 11 hours apart.

1. Determine the local time of these satellite images at 75° W (the eastern time zone of the United States):

    Figure 18-3: _____   Figure 18-4: _____

2. In Figure 18-4 why does Mexico appear much darker than in Figure 18-3?

3. (a) Has the ocean within the Gulf of Mexico changed temperature during the time between the first image and the second?

    (b) Why?

4. (a) In terms of the general circulation of the atmosphere, what explains the band of clouds near the equator over the Pacific Ocean and South America?

    (b) Why is this area of cloudiness more prominent over the landmass of South America than over the ocean?

    (c) The clouds over the Amazon Basin are much more obvious in Figure 18-4 than in Figure 18-3. What explains this?

5. In terms of the general circulation of the atmosphere, what helps explain the mostly clear skies off the west of South America between about 15° S and 30° S?

EXERCISE 19
DOPPLER RADAR

Objective:	To use Doppler radar images to study storm movement and precipitation patterns.
Resources:	Internet access (optional).
Reference:	McKnight and Hess, *Physical Geography*, 9th ed., p. 202.

DOPPLER RADAR

Radar was developed and used primarily for military purposes during World War II. Since the late 1940s, however, radar has been used by meteorologists to detect precipitation and severe weather such as thunderstorms and tornadoes.

Radar is an acronym for *ra*dio *d*etection *a*nd *r*anging. The principle of radar is simple. A rotating antenna emits short bursts of radio waves that transmit through the atmosphere until they reflect off an object and return to the antenna where they are detected. The time lag between the emission of a radio wave pulse and the return of its "echo" is used to calculate the distance to the reflecting object—the greater the time lag, the greater the distance. In meteorological applications, radar "targets" in the atmosphere are mostly raindrops and hailstones—generally the larger the droplets, the stronger the return echo.

Modern meteorological radar units emit pulses of radio waves lasting only about 0.0000016 seconds, followed by a 0.00019-second listening period for the echo. This process is repeated as many as 1300 times each second (because of the extremely short pulse of radio waves emitted relative to the listening period, a radar antenna is actually transmitting for only a total of about 7 seconds each hour). Meteorological radar typically emits pulses of "microwaves" with wavelengths of about 10 centimeters.

Because of the curvature of Earth and the reduction of signal strength over distance, most weather radar is limited to a distance of about 260 kilometers (about 160 miles) from the antenna; light rain can be detected perhaps only 150 kilometers (90 miles) away from the antenna. Generally speaking, the closer a storm is to the radar station, the higher the resolution of the radar image. In most cases, meteorologists like to view radar images of storms from two or more radar locations in order to overcome deficiencies of coverage and resolution.

Not only can radar detect distances to reflecting objects, but by taking advantage of the **Doppler effect** meteorological radar can help determine the relative speed and direction of water droplets within a storm. You've experienced the Doppler effect if you have ever listened to an approaching emergency vehicle siren: When the siren is approaching, the sound waves are compressed—this leads to a higher frequency and, therefore, a higher pitch of the sound waves. As the siren passes and moves away, the sound waves are stretched—this leads to a lower frequency and lower pitch of the sound waves. Doppler radar detects changes in the "pitch" of radio wave echoes. When an object is moving away from the radar antenna, the radio waves of the returning echo are stretched, leading to a lower frequency; when an object is moving toward the radar antenna, the radio waves of the echo are compressed, leading to a higher frequency.

117

TYPES OF RADAR IMAGES

There are three main types of radar images used in meteorology: reflectivity, velocity, and precipitation totals. Current weather radar images for the United States may be viewed at Internet sites such as *<http://radar.weather.gov/>*. (All of the images shown in this exercise of the Lab Manual, along with supplementary images, may be viewed online on the Lab Manual Web site, *<www.prenhall.com/mcknight>*. Then go to "Lab Manual" and "Exercise 19.")

Reflectivity: Reflectivity images display the intensity of the return echoes, usually measured in decibels of "Z"—the reflected energy (dBZ). In most reflectivity images, low reflectivity is indicated by the colors blue and green, with increasing reflectivity shown as yellow, red, and fuchsia. **Base reflectivity** images show the intensity of echoes when the radar is scanning the atmosphere very close to the horizon—usually about 0.5° above the horizon. Base reflectivity images are helpful in showing precipitation reaching the surface, but do not show activity high in storms or in storms that are distant from the radar station.

By making a series of sweeps at increasingly higher angles (up to about 19.5° above the horizon), a radar unit can detect precipitation high above the ground. A **composite reflectivity** radar image displays the strongest echo detected in each direction from the radar unit—showing precipitation and storm structure well above the horizon (Figure 19-1). Since it takes about five or six minutes for a radar unit to complete a full set of sweeps to complete a composite image, the time of the base reflectivity image and the composite reflectivity image may be different. As with weather satellite images, radar images are given a date and time stamp using **UTC** or **Zulu time**; for example, 1800Z indicates an image taken at 6:00 P.M. UTC or Greenwich Mean Time (for a review of time zones, see Exercise 3).

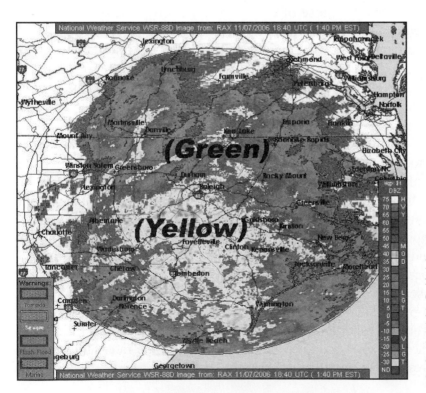

Figure 19-1: Composite reflectivity radar image for Raleigh, North Carolina (in center of image), on November 7, 2006, at 18:40 UTC (1840Z). Areas labeled "green" display low radar reflectivity while areas labeled "yellow" display higher reflectivity. (Image courtesy of National Weather Service)

Both base reflectivity and composite reflectivity images are useful to meteorologists. For example, strong echoes in the composite reflectivity image that are lacking in the base reflectivity image may indicate areas within a storm where falling precipitation evaporates before reaching the surface, or where strong updrafts of hail or rain may be present.

Velocity: Radar velocity images indicate the strength of wind moving directly toward or directly away from the radar unit. The color red indicates wind moving away from the radar antenna, the color green indicates movement toward the antenna, while the gray areas are transition zones between incoming and outgoing wind. The color purple indicates areas where the radar is unable to determine velocity (what are called "folded" areas). **Base velocity** images show the overall pattern of movement within a storm (Figure 19-2), while **storm relative motion** images show the winds as if the storm were stationary (Figure 19-3)—such images can reveal circulation within a storm. Strong local circulation, such as is associated with the formation of tornadoes, is indicated by strong inbound wind (shown as green) adjacent to an area of strong outbound wind (shown as red). Such areas would be carefully watched by meteorologists for the development of tornadoes.

Precipitation: Within a storm, raindrops and hail are good reflectors of radar waves, so the relative strength of a radar echo can be an indication of the amount of precipitation that is falling within a storm. Generally, an echo value of 20 dBZ indicates that light rain is falling, while values of 60 dBZ or greater indicate that large hail (hail with a diameter of more than about 2 centimeters [3/4"]) can occur—conditions associated with severe weather. Not only can the echo intensity indicate the size of precipitation that is falling, but it can also indicate the rate of precipitation. For example, a 20 dBZ value suggests that only a trace of rain may fall over the period of an hour, while a 47 dBZ value indicates a rain rate of about 3.2 centimeters per hour (1.25"/hour) and 60 dBZ indicates a rain rate of over 20 centimeters per hour (8.0"/hour).

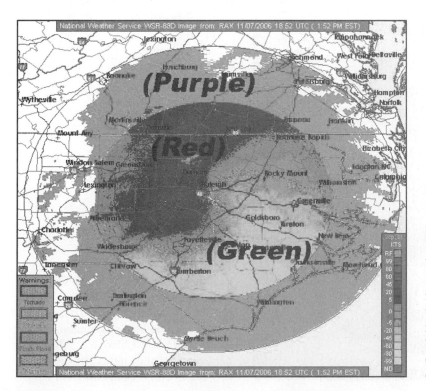

Figure 19-2: Base velocity radar image for Raleigh, North Carolina, on November 7, 2006, at 18:52 UTC (1852Z). Areas labeled "green" indicate movement toward the radar antenna, while areas labeled "red" indicate movement away from the antenna; in "purple" areas the direction of motion cannot be determined. (Image courtesy of National Weather Service)

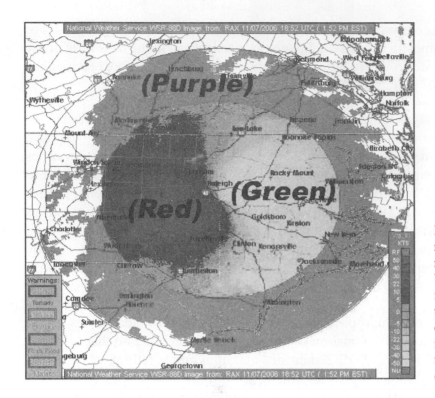

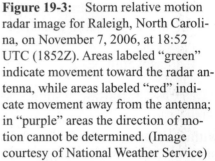

Figure 19-3: Storm relative motion radar image for Raleigh, North Carolina, on November 7, 2006, at 18:52 UTC (1852Z). Areas labeled "green" indicate movement toward the radar antenna, while areas labeled "red" indicate movement away from the antenna; in "purple" areas the direction of motion cannot be determined. (Image courtesy of National Weather Service)

One-hour precipitation radar images provide estimates of precipitation that has fallen over the last hour (Figure 19-4). Such images are used to assess the potential for flash floods in a region. Trace amounts of precipitation are shown in light blue, with increasing amounts of one-hour precipitation indicated with dark blue, green, orange, and red. **Storm total precipitation** radar images estimate the total amount of precipitation that has fallen since the last one-hour pause in rainfall.

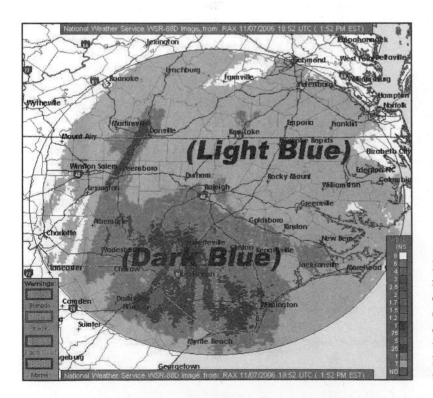

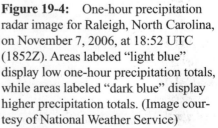

Figure 19-4: One-hour precipitation radar image for Raleigh, North Carolina, on November 7, 2006, at 18:52 UTC (1852Z). Areas labeled "light blue" display low one-hour precipitation totals, while areas labeled "dark blue" display higher precipitation totals. (Image courtesy of National Weather Service)

EXERCISE 19 PROBLEMS—PART I

The following questions are based on Figures 19-1, 19-2, 19-3, and 19-4, radar images of Raleigh, North Carolina, on November 7, 2006. The Doppler radar site in Raleigh is in the center of the image; north is to the top of each radar image. Full-color versions of these figures may be viewed on the Lab Manual Web site: *<www.prenhall.com/mcknight>*, then select "Lab Manual," and then "Exercise 19."

1. (a) Where is the area of greatest precipitation around Raleigh: to the north or to the south of the city?

   (b) How do you know? (You should note the radar image or images you refer to and what evidence supports your answer.)

2. (a) In what direction is the rain generally moving: toward Raleigh or away from Raleigh?

   (b) How do you know? (You should note the radar image or images you refer to and what evidence supports your answer.)

3. (a) Is the direction of wind within the storm the same as the overall direction of movement of the storm itself? If not, describe how they are different.

   (b) How do you know? (You should note the radar image or images you refer to and what evidence supports your answer.)

EXERCISE 19 PROBLEMS—PART II—INTERNET

The following questions are based on radar images and satellite movie loops available on the Lab Manual Web site: *<www.prenhall.com/mcknight>*, then select "Lab Manual," and then "Exercise 19."

View Figures 19-5 and 19-6, radar movie loops showing base reflectivity and composite reflectivity for Raleigh, North Carolina, on November 7, 2006 between 18:06 and 18:46 UTC (1806Z to 1846Z). Green indicates low radar reflectivity while yellow indicates higher reflectivity. In one radar movie loop, precipitation (shown as areas of yellow and orange) is shown passing over Raleigh, while in the other radar movie loop of the same time period the precipitation doesn't quite reach Raleigh.

1. Which radar movie loop—base reflectivity or composite reflectivity—shows precipitation over Raleigh?

2. What explains why the radar base reflectivity and composite reflectivity loops don't show precipitation taking place in the same location?

View Figure 19-7, an infrared satellite movie loop recorded at about the same time as the radar images of Raleigh.

3. Does the pattern of cloud movement over Raleigh shown in the satellite movie loop match the general direction of movement indicated in Figure 19-2, the base velocity radar image?

4. What can you see in the pattern of cloud movement around Raleigh shown in the satellite movie loop that explains the difference in motion shown in Figure 19-2 (base velocity) and Figure 19-3 (storm relative motion)?

EXERCISE 20
HURRICANES

Objective:	To use weather maps and satellite images to study the weather patterns of hurricanes.
Resources:	Internet access (optional).
Reference:	McKnight and Hess, *Physical Geography*, 9th ed., pp. 193–200.

HURRICANES

Tropical cyclones are intense, low pressure disturbances that develop in the tropics and occasionally move up into the midlatitudes. When wind speed reaches 64 knots (64 nautical miles per hour; 119 kilometers per hour or 74 statute miles per hour) tropical cyclones are officially classified as **hurricanes** in North America and the Caribbean and typhoons in eastern Eurasia (in this exercise we use "hurricane" as a generic term for all such storms).

At the center of a hurricane is an intense low pressure cell with a steep pressure gradient, which produces a converging counterclockwise wind flow pattern in the Northern Hemisphere (the wind flow is converging clockwise in the Southern Hemisphere). The converging wind pattern pulls in warm, moist air—the "fuel" for a hurricane. After air spirals into the storm at the surface, it rises in intense updrafts within towering **cumulonimbus clouds**, often reaching altitudes of 15 kilometers (10 miles) before flowing out into the upper atmosphere—typically in a clockwise direction in the Northern Hemisphere (Figure 20-1).

As the air rises, **adiabatic cooling** causes water vapor to condense out of the air. Condensation provides the moisture for the massive cloud development and heavy rain associated with hurricanes. Condensation also releases **latent heat**. This heat powers the storm by increasing the

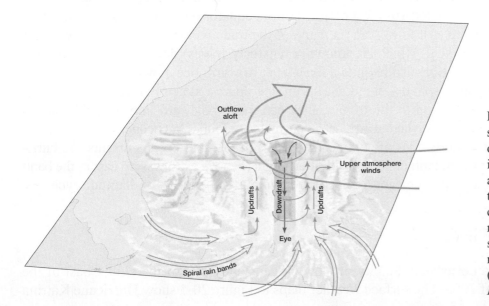

Figure 20-1: Idealized cross section through a well-developed hurricane. Air spirals into the storm horizontally and rises rapidly to produce towering cumulonimbus clouds that produce torrential rainfall. In the center of the storm is the eye, where air movement is downward. (From: McKnight and Hess, *Physical Geography*, 9th ed.)

Figure 20-2: GOES-West visible light satellite image of Hurricane Isabel off the east coast of North America on September 11, 2003. (Image courtesy of Naval Research Laboratory, Marine Meteorology Division)

instability of the air. As latent heat is released into the storm, air rises faster, intensifying the low pressure cell—which in turn pulls in more warm, moist air.

The **eye** in the center of a hurricane is a bit of a paradox. The eye is an area of relative calm and often clear skies, while just beyond the eye wall is the most intense part of the storm. The eye is associated with a downdraft of air (the opposite direction of air flow in a typical low-pressure cell). Hurricane diameters range from 160 to 1000 kilometers (100–600 miles)—much smaller than midlatitude cyclones—with eye diameters ranging from about 16 to 40 kilometers (10–25 miles). A well-defined eye is usually an indication of a well-developed hurricane. Figure 20-2 is a satellite image of Hurricane Isabel off the west coast of North America in September 2003. (All of the images for this exercise may be viewed online by going to *<www.prenhall.com/mcknight>* and then to "Lab Manual" and "Exercise 20.")

Hurricanes develop over warm, tropical oceans—typically with water temperatures of at least 26.5°C (80°F). The period of greatest hurricane activity each year is toward the end of summer, when the ocean water reaches its warmest point. Hurricanes need warm water to survive—they will quickly lose strength and die when they move over land or over cooler water (although powerful hurricanes may remain very destructive even after they make landfall and begin to weaken).

Hurricanes generally develop 10–15° poleward of the equator out of preexisting low pressure disturbances moving from east to west in the band of the trade winds. Not all of these minor low pressure disturbances (some of which are known as **easterly waves**) develop into hurricanes. Conditions for hurricane formation also include a deep layer of warm ocean water and the lack of vertical **wind shear** in the atmosphere—wind shear can tear apart a storm before it strengthens.

Although hurricanes develop in the tropics, they can move poleward into the midlatitudes along the eastern sides of continents where warm ocean currents are found; hurricanes are very rare in the midlatitudes along the western sides of continents because of the cool ocean currents. As hurricanes move poleward into the midlatitudes, they will often begin to move from west to east in the band of the westerlies; in some cases, the remnants of hurricanes will turn into milder midlatitude cyclones.

HURRICANE KATRINA

Hurricane Katrina devastated the city of New Orleans and parts of the Gulf Coast of the United States in August of 2005. The surface weather maps in Figure 20-3 show Hurricane Katrina

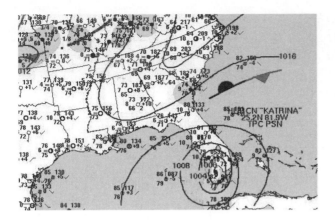

(a)   August 26th

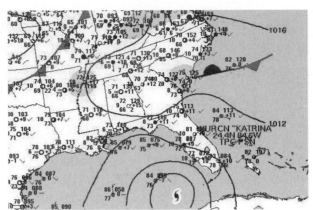

(b)   August 27th

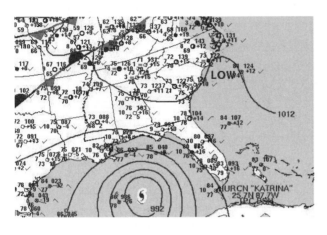

(c)   August 28th

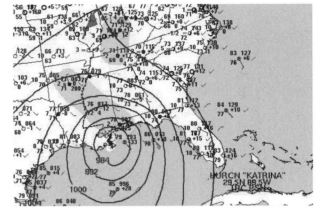

(d)   August 29th

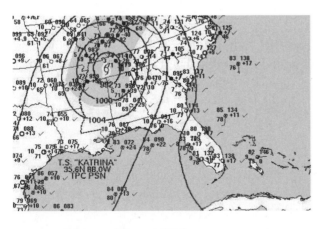

(e)   August 30th

Figure 20-3: Weather maps showing Hurricane Katrina at 7:00 A.M. EST, on August 26–30, 2005. (From *Daily Weather Maps*, National Weather Service)

Hurricane Katrina August 24 to August 30, 2005			
Date	Time	Central Pressure (millibars)	Sustained Wind Speed (knots)
August 24	0300Z	1007	30
	1500Z	1006	35
August 25	0300Z	1001	45
	1500Z	997	50
August 26	0300Z	984	65
	1500Z	981	70
August 27	0300Z	965	90
	1500Z	940	100
August 28	0300Z	939	100
	1500Z	907	150
August 29	0300Z	904	140
	1500Z	927	110
August 30	0300Z	973	50
	1500Z	985	30

Figure 20-4: Central pressure and sustained wind speed of Hurricane Katrina between August 24 and August 30, 2005. (Data compiled from National Weather Service/National Hurricane Center Forecast Advisories)

at 7:00 A.M. Eastern Standard Time on August 26th, 27th, 28th, 29th, and 30th. Figure 20-4 is a table listing the central pressure and sustained wind speed of Hurricane Katrina between August 24 and August 30, 2005.

EXERCISE 20 PROBLEMS—PART I

The following questions are based on Figure 20-3, weather maps showing Hurricane Katrina between August 26 and August 30, 2005 (the full maps may be viewed in color online by going to *<www.prenhall.com/mcknight>* and then to "Lab Manual" and "Exercise 20"), and Figure 20-4, a table showing the central pressure and sustained wind speed of the storm between August 24th and August 30th.

1. What is the general relationship between the central pressure of Hurricane Katrina and its sustained wind speed?

2. What explains the increase in the intensity of Hurricane Katrina (as reflected in the central pressure) between August 26th and 28th?

3. What explains the decrease in the intensity of Hurricane Katrina (as reflected in the central pressure) between August 29th and 30th?

4. The following question is based on the enlarged portion of the weather map for August 29th shown at right. Three weather stations, marked Land 1 (Lake Charles, LA), Gulf 1 and Gulf 2 (weather buoys in the Gulf of Mexico) are labeled. What explains the difference in wind direction between the three weather stations?

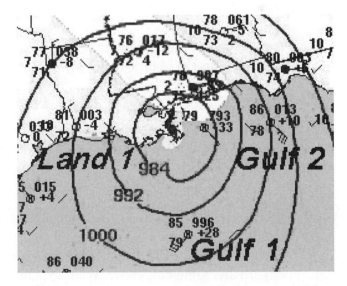

EXERCISE 20 PROBLEMS—PART II—INTERNET

The following questions are based on satellite movie loops available on the Lab Manual Web site. Go to the McKnight and Hess textbook Web site *<http://www.prenhall.com/mcknight>*, then select "Lab Manual," and then "Exercise 20." First, select Figure 20-5, "Hurricane Katrina Movie Loop," to see an infrared satellite movie loop of Hurricane Katrina from August 24th to August 30, 2005, as it moves across Florida into the Gulf of Mexico and finally comes onshore near New Orleans. You may also want to view Figure 20-6, a close-up movie loop of Hurricane Katrina on August 29th. After viewing the satellite movie loops several times, answer the following questions:

1. (a) Assuming that a well-defined eye and a tightly circular shape are indications of a strong hurricane, what generally happens to the strength of Hurricane Katrina between August 24th and August 28th?

    (b) What can explain this change in strength?

2. (a) What is the general direction of movement of Hurricane Katrina on August 24th (at the beginning of the movie loop)?

    To the _____

    (b) What is the general direction of movement of Hurricane Katrina on August 30th (at the end of the movie loop)?

    To the _____

    (c) What may explain this change in direction?

3. Look at Hurricane Katrina on August 29th (the Figure 20-6 movie loop will be especially helpful here). Although the overall pattern of cloud movement is converging counterclockwise, notice that some of the clouds (such as those you see just to the west of Florida) are diverging clockwise. What explains these diverging clouds?

EXERCISE 20 PROBLEMS—PART III—INTERNET

In this exercise, you will log the changes in a hurricane over several days by gathering data on the Internet. This exercise works best during the peak of hurricane season (from August through November in the Northern Hemisphere and from February through May in the Southern Hemisphere), when you are most likely to encounter well-developed tropical cyclones.

You will choose an active tropical cyclone (preferably of hurricane strength), and follow its progress over a period of three to seven days. During the period of your study, you will log changes in position, as well as changes in the weather associated with the storm. Because of the many variables in this exercise, your instructor may offer further guidance in gathering information and in reporting the progress of your storm.

- Go to the McKnight and Hess textbook Web site, *<http://www.prenhall.com/mcknight>*. Select "Lab Manual," then "Exercise 20." Click on "Go to *Tropical Cyclones Web Page, Naval Research Laboratory.*" This will take you to the Naval Research Laboratory, Marine Meteorology Division, in Monterey, California: *<http://www.nrlmry.navy.mil/tc_pages/tc_home.html>*. This site lists all currently active tropical cyclones in the world. Generally the most powerful—or most noteworthy—storm will be shown when the page first comes up, but you may choose any storm from the lists on the left side of the page. Before choosing a storm for your study, spend a few minutes reviewing the kind of information that is available. Note that in addition to visible light and infrared satellite images, this Web site provides tracking maps, information about official watches and warnings, satellite movie loops, and satellite image overlays that show wind speed and precipitation rates.

- Another good starting point is the *National Hurricane Center, Tropical Prediction Center*, Web page: *<http://www.nhc.noaa.gov/>*.

- To gather additional information about your storm, such as current eye pressure or speed of movement, you may want to go to general weather Internet sites, such as *Unisys Weather*: *<http://weather.unisys.com>* (also see Exercise 17).

- After choosing a storm, use the charts on the following page to log your information (attach additional sheets if necessary). Depending on the storm you choose, the information available may vary. Your instructor may specify additional information to log. Your instructor may also ask that you download images and/or tracking maps of your storm.

Storm Name: _____

Days of Study: From _____ to _____

Day 1 Date: _____ Time(s) of Observation: _____

Latitude: _____ Longitude: _____ Wind speed: _____ knots

Heading: _____ at _____ knots (speed) Eye Pressure: _____ mb

Additional information:

_____

Day 2 Date: _____ Time(s) of Observation: _____

Latitude: _____ Longitude: _____ Wind speed: _____ knots

Heading: _____ at _____ knots (speed) Eye Pressure: _____ mb

Additional information or significant changes since previous day:

_____

Day 3 Date: _____ Time(s) of Observation: _____

Latitude: _____ Longitude: _____ Wind speed: _____ knots

Heading: _____ at _____ knots (speed) Eye Pressure: _____ mb

Additional information or significant changes since previous day:

_____

Day 4 Date: _____ Time(s) of Observation: _____

Latitude: _____ Longitude: _____ Wind speed: _____ knots

Heading: _____ at _____ knots (speed) Eye Pressure: _____ mb

Additional information or significant changes since previous day:

_____

Day 5 Date: _____ Time(s) of Observation: _____

Latitude: _____ Longitude: _____ Wind speed: _____ knots

Heading: _____ at _____ knots (speed) Eye Pressure: _____ mb

Additional information or significant changes since previous day:

EXERCISE 21
CLIMATE CLASSIFICATION

Objective:	To use average monthly temperature and precipitation data to classify climates with the Köppen climate classification system.
Resource:	Internet access (optional).
Reference:	McKnight and Hess, *Physical Geography*, 9th ed., pp. 212–246.

KÖPPEN CLIMATE CLASSIFICATION SYSTEM

The modified **Köppen system** is the most widely used climate classification system. With the Köppen system, all climates of the world can be grouped into just 15 types, based simply on **average monthly temperature** and **average monthly precipitation**.

In the Köppen system, each climate type is given a descriptive name, as well as a code based on two or three letters. The first letter refers to the major climate group, the second letter generally refers to the precipitation pattern, and the third letter generally refers to the temperature pattern.

There are actually several different versions of the modified Köppen system in use—the definitions of some climate types vary slightly from version to version. Also, while there are specific boundaries for each climate type, in reality the borders between climates should be thought of as transition zones, rather than sharp boundaries.

CLIMOGRAPHS

One of the key tools used in climate study is the **climograph** or **climatic diagram** (Figure 21-1). In a single chart, the climatic regime of a location can be summarized. The months of the year are indicated along the bottom. The average monthly temperature is shown with a solid line (the temperature scale is along the left side of chart), and the average monthly precipitation is indicated with bars (the precipitation scale is along the right side of chart).

In the sample diagram, notice that in St. Louis the average temperature in January is about −1°C (30°F), while in July the average temperature is 27°C (80°F). Precipitation is evenly distributed throughout the year, each month receiving approximately 8 to 13 centimeters (3–5 inches).

USING THE MODIFIED KÖPPEN SYSTEM CHARTS

Each of the climate types in the Köppen system has a specific definition. The "Modified Köppen System Charts" on the following pages of the Lab Manual provide concise definitions for 14 climate types (plus the special category of "Highland" climate). *In order to use these charts you must follow the procedure for classifying climates listed below.*

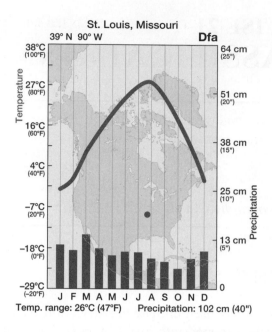

Figure 21-1: Climograph for St. Louis, Missouri. (From McKnight and Hess, *Physical Geography*, 9th ed.)

At the top of each chart, the basic definition for the major climate group is given. Next, the different climate types found within the major group are listed (in some cases a climate type is represented by several different letter combinations). Finally, the specific definitions of the second and third letters for each climate type are provided. Note that the "C" and "D" climates have been grouped together, and that not all second and third letters can be combined with both C and D.

PROCEDURE FOR CLASSIFYING CLIMATES

Construct a climograph for the location by plotting the average monthly temperature and average monthly precipitation (this step is actually optional, but it usually makes classification easier). Then, calculate the average annual temperature and average annual precipitation for the location. (This has been done for you in the problems for this exercise.)

Next, determine the major climate group. If you go through the following steps *in sequence*, you will find the correct major climate group. With experience, you will learn shortcuts to narrow your choices more quickly:

1. If the average temperature of *every* month is below 10°C (50°F), go to the "E" climate chart. (Note: some "H" climates may also exhibit this temperature pattern.)

2. If the total annual precipitation is *more* than 89 centimeters (35 inches), continue to #4.

3. If the total annual precipitation is *less* than 89 centimeters (35 inches), determine if it is a dry climate by using the "Dry Climate Boundary Charts" under "B—Dry Climates." If it is a dry climate, continue with the "B" climate chart; if not a dry climate, continue to #4. (A detailed description of dry climates and using these charts is given below.)

4. If the average temperature of *every* month is above 18°C (64.4°F), go to the "A" climate chart.

5. If at least one winter month is colder than −3°C (26.6°F), go to the "D" climate chart.

6. If the coldest winter month is between −3°C (26.6°F) and 18°C (64.4°F), go to the "C" climate chart.

After establishing the major climate group, determine which climate type is correct by checking the definitions of the second, and if necessary, third letters. When assessing seasonal patterns of temperature or precipitation, be sure to consider if the station is in the Northern or Southern Hemisphere. If you are unsure of the hemisphere of the station in question, look at the temperature pattern. If the coolest months are in December, January, and February, it is in the Northern Hemisphere. If the coolest months are in June, July, and August, it is in the Southern Hemisphere.

CLASSIFYING DRY CLIMATES IN THE KÖPPEN SYSTEM

The basic definition of a dry ("B") climate in the Köppen system is one in which the **potential evaporation** exceeds **precipitation**. There is a complex relationship between temperature, precipitation, and the dryness of a region. For example, because of the lower potential for evaporation, a very cold region with an average annual precipitation of 25 centimeters (10 inches) would not be classified as a dry climate, while a hot region receiving 25 centimeters (10 inches) of precipitation would be. These relationships are shown on the "Dry Climate Boundary Charts."

In order to use the "Dry Climate Boundary Charts," you need to know the average annual precipitation, the average annual temperature, and if there is a "seasonal concentration" of precipitation. A seasonal concentration means that more than 70% of the precipitation comes in either the six summer months or six winter months. For purposes of classification, April to September are considered the six summer months in the Northern Hemisphere. (These would be the six winter months in the Southern Hemisphere.)

To determine if a seasonal concentration is present, add up the precipitation amounts for the months April to September, and divide this by the total annual precipitation. For example, if a Northern Hemisphere location with annual precipitation of 38 centimeters (15 inches) receives 30 centimeters (12 inches) of rain between April and September, make the following calculation: 30 cm/38 cm = 0.8 or 80% (12"/15" = 0.8 or 80%). Since more than 70% of the precipitation comes between April and September, this location has a summer concentration of rainfall.

Modified Köppen System Charts

To use these charts, go through the following steps *in sequence*:

1. If average temperature of every month is below 10°C (50°F), go to "E" climate chart.
2. If total annual precipitation is more than 89 centimeters (35 inches), continue to #4.
3. If total annual precipitation is less than 89 centimeters (35 inches), determine if it is a dry climate by using "Dry Climate Boundary Charts" under "B—Dry Climates." If a dry climate, continue with "B" climate chart; if not a dry climate, continue to #4.
4. If average temperature of every month is above 18°C (64.4°F), go to "A" climate chart.
5. If at least one winter month is colder than −3°C (26.6°F), go to "D" climate chart.
6. If coldest winter month is between −3°C (26.6°F) and 18°C (64.4°F), go to "C" climate chart.

A—TROPICAL HUMID: Temperature of every month above 18°C (64.4°F).

Group A Climate Types
Af —Tropical Wet
Am—Tropical Monsoon
Aw —Tropical Savanna

Second Letters	Definition
f —Wet All Year	Every month has at least 6 cm (2.4") of rainfall.
m—Monsoon Pattern	Short dry season; pronounced rainy season.*
w —Winter Dry	Winter dry season of 3 to 6 months.*

*To calculate boundaries between "Am" and "Aw," determine the average rainfall and the average rainfall of the driest month; then use the chart below. For example, a location with an average annual rainfall of 200 cm (about 80") and 5 cm (2") of rainfall in the driest month is an "Am" climate.

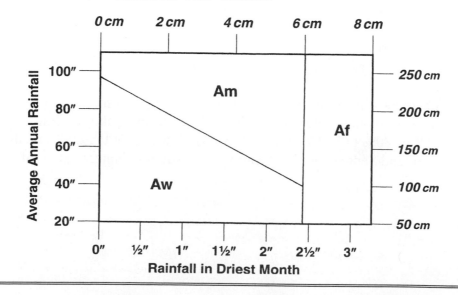

B—DRY CLIMATES: Evaporation exceeds precipitation.

Group B Climate Types

BWh	—Subtropical Desert	(Ave. annual temperature above 18°C [64.4°F]).
BSh	—Subtropical Steppe	" " " " "
BWk	—Midlatitude Desert	(Ave. annual temperature below 18°C [64.4°F]).
BSk	—Midlatitude Steppe	" " " " "

DRY CLIMATE BOUNDARY CHARTS

1. Determine the average annual temperature and average annual precipitation.
2. Determine if the precipitation is distributed evenly during the year:

    (a) If more than 70% of the precipitation comes in the 6 summer months (April to September in Northern Hemisphere), use "Summer Concentration" chart.

    (b) If more than 70% of the precipitation comes in the 6 winter months (October to March in Northern Hemisphere), use "Winter Concentration" chart.

    (c) If precipitation is evenly distributed throughout year (neither a or b), use "Even Distribution" chart.

3. Line up the average annual temperature with the average annual precipitation to find the climate.

Example: If a location has an annual precipitation of 38 cm (15") with a winter concentration, use the "Winter Concentration" chart. If the average annual temperature is 21°C (70°F), the climate is BSh; if the average annual temperature is 10°C (50°F), it is not a dry climate.

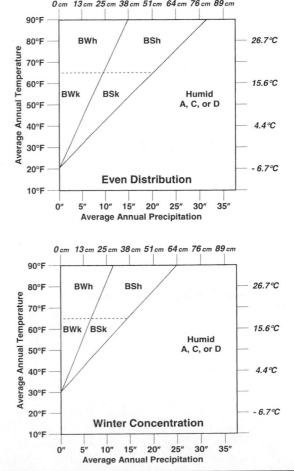

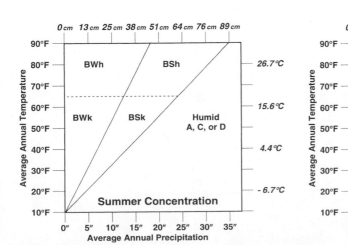

135

C—MILD MIDLATITUDE:

Temperature of warmest month above 10°C (50°F); coldest month between −3°C (26.6°F) and 18°C (64.4°F).

D—SEVERE MIDLATITUDE:

Warmest month above 10°C (50°F); coldest month below −3°C (26.6°F).

Group C & D Climate Types

Cs	— Mediterranean	(includes Csa and Csb)
Cfa	— Humid Subtropical	(also includes Cwa)
Cfb	— Marine West Coast	(also includes Cfc)
Dfa	— Humid Continental	(also includes Dwa, Dfb, and Dwb)
Dfc	— Subarctic	(also includes Dwc, Dfd, and Dwd)

Second Letters

Definition

s—Summer Dry — Wettest winter month has at least 3× precipitation of driest summer month.

w—Winter Dry — Wettest summer month has at least 10× precipitation of driest winter month.

f—Wet All Year — Neither "s" nor "w" above.

Third Letters

Definition

a—Hot Summer — Warmest month above 22°C (71.6°F).

b—Warm Summer — Warmest month below 22°C (71.6°F); at least 4 months above 10°C (50°F).

c—Cool Summer — Warmest month below 22°C (71.6°F); 1 to 3 months above 10°C (50°F); coldest month above −38°C (−36.4°F).

d—Severe Winter — Coldest month below −38°C (−36.4°F).

136

E—POLAR CLIMATES: Temperature of every month below 10°C (50°F).

Group E Climate Types
ET—Tundra
EF—Ice Cap

Second Letters	Definition
T—Tundra	At least one month above 0°C (32°F).
F—Ice Cap	All months below 0°C (32°F).

H—HIGHLAND CLIMATES: Significant variation or modification of a climate type due to high elevation.

Highland climates are not defined in the same way as other climates in the Köppen system. Rather, these are regions in high mountain areas where the climate has been significantly modified from the adjacent lowlands by high elevation.

FINAL SUGGESTIONS ON CLIMATE CLASSIFICATION

You may also want to compare the climograph of the station in question with those in your textbook. This is a quick way to determine if your classification is reasonable. If you know the location of the station in question, look at the generalized map of climate inside the front cover of the Lab Manual. This map may help narrow down the climate type to several possibilities. However, because there are local variations in climate, this map alone is *not* enough to accurately determine all climates. You will need to use the charts defining each climate type to verify your answer.

KÖPPEN CLASSIFICATION AND CLIMATE CONTROLS

Köppen climate classification is based solely on temperature and precipitation patterns. Although the Köppen system does not consider the origin of a climate, the location and dominant controls of each climate type are quite predictable.

This regularity is illustrated with the hypothetical continent shown in Figure 21-2. This idealized distribution pattern predicts quite closely the actual arrangement of climate types on the continents, and reflects the dominant controls that produce each of these climates. These dominant controls include latitude, continent–ocean temperature contrasts, ocean currents, the general circulation of the atmosphere, and the most important kinds of storms.

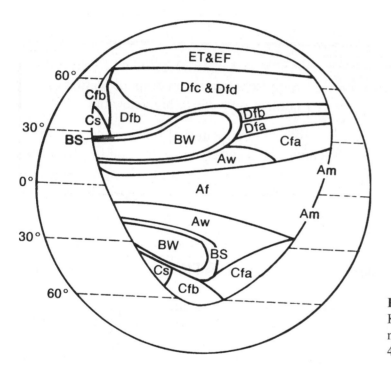

Figure 21-2: The presumed arrangement of Köppen climatic types on a hypothetical continent. (From McKnight, *Physical Geography*, 4th ed.)

EXERCISE 21 PROBLEMS—PART I

For each of the following six locations, complete the climograph using the average monthly temperature ("Temp") given in degrees Celsius and Fahrenheit, and the average monthly precipitation ("Precp") given in centimeters and inches. The average annual temperature and precipitation are provided for you. After completing the climographs, answer the questions at the end of Part I. You may plot data on the climographs using either S.I. or English (note that the English unit and S.I. unit scales on the climographs are not exactly equivalent). It may be helpful to locate each of these stations on a map. No "H" climates are given.

1. Cuiabá, Brazil					Average Annual: 26°C (78°F); 138.8 cm (54.6")							
	JAN	**FEB**	**MAR**	**APR**	**MAY**	**JUN**	**JUL**	**AUG**	**SEP**	**OCT**	**NOV**	**DEC**
Temp	81°F 27°C	80°F 27°C	81°F 27°C	80°F 27°C	75°F 24°C	72°F 22°C	73°F 23°C	75°F 24°C	79°F 26°C	82°F 28°C	81°F 27°C	81°F 27°C
Precp	9.6" 24.4 cm	8.9" 22.6 cm	8.1" 20.6 cm	4.1" 10.4 cm	2.0" 5.1 cm	0.3" 0.8 cm	0.2" 0.5 cm	1.1" 2.8 cm	2.0" 5.1 cm	4.4" 11.2 cm	6.0" 15.2 cm	7.9" 20.1 cm

2. Kashi (Kashgar), China					Average Annual: 12°C (54°F); 8.7 cm (3.4")							
	JAN	**FEB**	**MAR**	**APR**	**MAY**	**JUN**	**JUL**	**AUG**	**SEP**	**OCT**	**NOV**	**DEC**
Temp	22°F −6°C	34°F 1°C	47°F 8°C	61°F 16°C	70°F 21°C	77°F 25°C	80°F 27°C	76°F 24°C	59°F 15°C	56°F 13°C	40°F 4°C	26°F −3°C
Precp	0.3" 0.8 cm	0.0" 0.0 cm	0.2" 0.5 cm	0.2" 0.5 cm	0.8" 2.0 cm	0.4" 1.0 cm	0.3" 0.8 cm	0.7" 1.8 cm	0.3" 0.8 cm	0.0" 0.0 cm	0.0" 0.0 cm	0.2" 0.5 cm

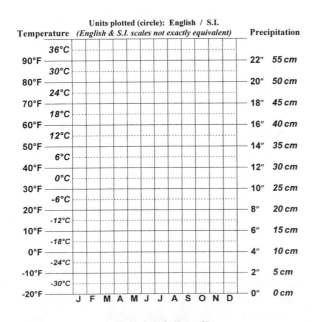

1. Cuiabá, Brazil

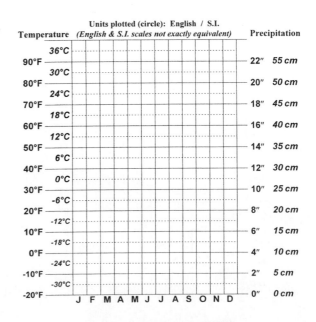

2. Kashi (Kashgar), China

3. New Orleans, Louisiana — Average Annual: 21°C (70°F); 161.8 cm (63.6″)

	JAN	FEB	MAR	APR	MAY	JUN	JUL	AUG	SEP	OCT	NOV	DEC
Temp	56°F 13°C	58°F 14°C	63°F 17°C	70°F 21°C	76°F 24°C	82°F 28°C	83°F 28°C	83°F 28°C	80°F 27°C	73°F 23°C	62°F 17°C	57°F 14°C
Precp	4.8″ 12.2 cm	4.2″ 10.7 cm	6.6″ 16.8 cm	5.4″ 13.7 cm	5.4″ 13.7 cm	5.6″ 14.2 cm	7.1″ 18.0 cm	6.4″ 16.3 cm	5.8″ 14.7 cm	3.7″ 9.4 cm	4.0″ 10.2 cm	4.6″ 11.9 cm

4. Palau, Caroline Islands — Average Annual: 27°C (81°F); 396.2 cm (155.9″)

	JAN	FEB	MAR	APR	MAY	JUN	JUL	AUG	SEP	OCT	NOV	DEC
Temp	81°F 27°C	80°F 27°C	81°F 27°C	82°F 28°C	82°F 28°C	82°F 28°C	81°F 27°C	81°F 27°C	81°F 27°C	81°F 27°C	81°F 27°C	81°F 27°C
Precp	15.3″ 38.9 cm	9.4″ 23.9 cm	6.8″ 17.3 cm	7.6″ 19.3 cm	15.5″ 39.4 cm	12.4″ 31.5 cm	19.9″ 50.5 cm	14.0″ 35.6 cm	15.7″ 39.9 cm	14.8″ 37.6 cm	11.8″ 30.0 cm	12.7″ 32.3 cm

5. Irkutsk, Siberia — Average Annual: 0°C (31°F); 37.0 cm (14.6″)

	JAN	FEB	MAR	APR	MAY	JUN	JUL	AUG	SEP	OCT	NOV	DEC
Temp	−5°F −21°C	1°F −17°C	17°F −8	37°F 3°C	48°F 9°C	59°F 15°C	65°F 18°C	60°F 16°C	48°F 9°C	33°F 1°C	13°F −11°C	1°F −17°C
Precp	0.6″ 1.5 cm	0.5″ 1.3 cm	0.4″ 1.0 cm	0.6″ 1.5 cm	1.2″ 3.0 cm	2.3″ 5.8 cm	2.9″ 7.4 cm	2.4″ 6.1 cm	1.6″ 4.1 cm	0.7″ 1.8 cm	0.6″ 1.5 cm	0.8″ 2.0 cm

6. Dublin, Ireland — Average Annual: 9°C (48°F); 70.4 cm (27.7″)

	JAN	FEB	MAR	APR	MAY	JUN	JUL	AUG	SEP	OCT	NOV	DEC
Temp	40°F 4°C	41°F 5°C	42°F 6°C	45°F 7°C	49°F 9°C	55°F 13°C	58°F 14°C	57°F 14°C	54°F 12°C	48°F 9°C	44°F 7°C	41°F 5°C
Precp	2.2″ 5.6 cm	1.9″ 4.8 cm	1.9″ 4.8 cm	1.9″ 4.8 cm	2.1″ 5.3 cm	2.0″ 5.1 cm	2.6″ 6.6 cm	3.1″ 7.9 cm	2.0″ 5.1 cm	2.6″ 6.6 cm	2.9″ 7.4 cm	2.5″ 6.4 cm

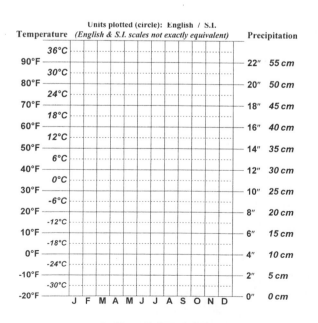

3. New Orleans, LA

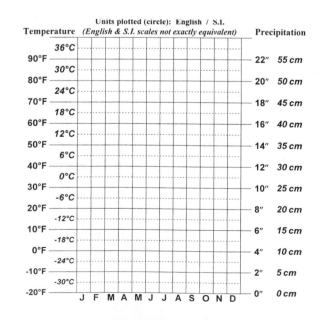

4. Palau, Caroline Islands

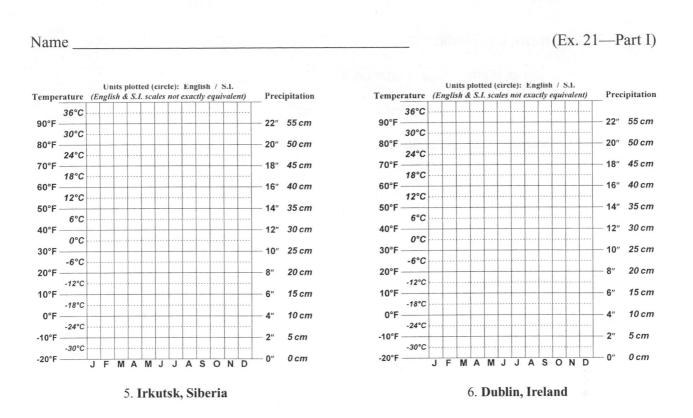

5. Irkutsk, Siberia   6. Dublin, Ireland

After completing the climographs, answer the following questions about each location:

1.   **Cuiabá, Brazil:**

     (a)   Köppen climate type: Letter code: _____

                           Descriptive name: _____

     (b)   Dominant climate controls for this location:

2.   **Kashi (Kashgar), China:**

     (a)   Köppen climate type: Letter code: _____

                           Descriptive name: _____

     (b)   Dominant climate controls for this location:

3.　**New Orleans, Louisiana:**

(a)　Köppen climate type: Letter code: _____

Descriptive name: _____

(b)　Dominant climate controls for this location:

4.　**Palau, Caroline Islands:**

(a)　Köppen climate type: Letter code: _____

Descriptive name: _____

(b)　Dominant climate controls for this location:

5.　**Irkutsk, Siberia:**

(a)　Köppen climate type: Letter code: _____

Descriptive name: _____

(b)　Dominant climate controls for this location:

6.　**Dublin, Ireland:**

(a)　Köppen climate type: Letter code: _____

Descriptive name: _____

(b)　Dominant climate controls for this location:

EXERCISE 21 PROBLEMS—PART II

For each of the following six locations, complete the climograph using the average monthly temperature ("Temp") given in degrees Celsius and Fahrenheit, and the average monthly precipitation ("Precp") given in centimeters and inches. The average annual temperature and precipitation are provided for you. After completing the climographs, answer the questions at the end of Part II. You may plot data on the climographs using either S.I. or English units (note that the English unit and S.I. unit scales on the climographs are not exactly equivalent). No "H" climates are given.

1.									Average Annual: 10°C (50°F); 31.4 cm (12.3″)			
	JAN	**FEB**	**MAR**	**APR**	**MAY**	**JUN**	**JUL**	**AUG**	**SEP**	**OCT**	**NOV**	**DEC**
Temp	21°F -6°C	30°F -1°C	42°F 6°C	54°F 12°C	63°F 17°C	70°F 21°C	73°F 23°C	71°F 22°C	61°F 16°C	51°F 11°C	35°F 2°C	23°F -5°C
Precp	0.1″ 0.3 cm	0.1″ 0.3 cm	0.3″ 0.8 cm	0.5″ 1.3 cm	0.7″ 1.8 cm	1.5″ 3.8 cm	2.6″ 6.6 cm	3.6″ 9.1 cm	2.2″ 5.6 cm	0.6″ 1.5 cm	0.1″ 0.3 cm	0.0″ 0.0 cm

2.									Average Annual: −12°C (10°F); 13.4 cm (5.2″)			
	JAN	**FEB**	**MAR**	**APR**	**MAY**	**JUN**	**JUL**	**AUG**	**SEP**	**OCT**	**NOV**	**DEC**
Temp	−20°F -29°C	−13°F -25°C	−13°F -25°C	−2°F -19°C	22°F -6°C	35°F 2°C	41°F 5°C	39°F 4°C	32°F 0°C	16°F -9°C	0°F -18°C	−15°F -26°C
Precp	0.1″ 0.3 cm	0.4″ 1.0 cm	0.2″ 0.5 cm	0.3″ 0.8 cm	0.3″ 0.8 cm	0.8″ 2.0 cm	0.3″ 0.8 cm	0.9″ 2.3 cm	0.5″ 1.3 cm	0.7″ 1.8 cm	0.3″ 0.8 cm	0.4″ 1.0 cm

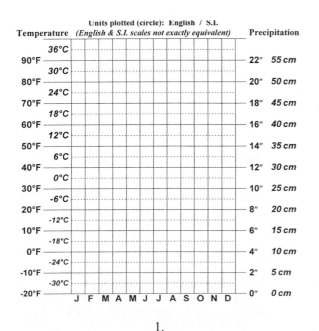

1.

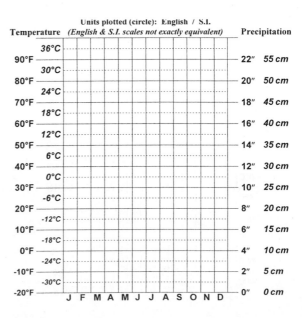

2.

3.   Average Annual: 16°C (61°F); 52.6 cm (20.7″)

	JAN	FEB	MAR	APR	MAY	JUN	JUL	AUG	SEP	OCT	NOV	DEC
Temp	69°F 21°C	68°F 20°C	66°F 19°C	61°F 16°C	57°F 14°C	55°F 13°C	53°F 12°C	54°F 12°C	57°F 14°C	59°F 15°C	64°F 18°C	67°F 19°C
Precp	0.4″ 1.0 cm	0.6″ 1.5 cm	0.5″ 1.3 cm	2.1″ 5.3 cm	3.5″ 8.9 cm	3.3″ 8.4 cm	3.3″ 8.4 cm	2.9″ 7.4 cm	1.8″ 4.6 cm	1.2″ 3.0 cm	0.7″ 1.8 cm	0.4″ 1.0 cm

4.   Average Annual: 27°C (81°F); 291.4 cm (114.7″)

	JAN	FEB	MAR	APR	MAY	JUN	JUL	AUG	SEP	OCT	NOV	DEC
Temp	81°F 27°C	82°F 28°C	84°F 29°C	85°F 29°C	84°F 29°C	80°F 27°C	79°F 26°C	79°F 26°C	80°F 27°C	80°F 27°C	81°F 27°C	81°F 27°C
Precp	0.8″ 2.0 cm	0.8″ 2.0 cm	1.7″ 4.3 cm	3.7″ 9.4 cm	11.4″ 29.0 cm	27.8″ 70.6 cm	25.3″ 64.3 cm	12.5″ 31.8 cm	9.22″ 23.4 cm	12.9″ 32.8 cm	6.7″ 17.0 cm	1.9″ 4.8 cm

5.   Average Annual: 10°C (50°F); 83.6 cm (32.9″)

	JAN	FEB	MAR	APR	MAY	JUN	JUL	AUG	SEP	OCT	NOV	DEC
Temp	25°F −4°C	27°F −3°C	36°F 2°C	48°F 9°C	58°F 14°C	68°F 20°C	74°F 23°C	72°F 22°C	66°F 19°C	54°F 12°C	40°F 4°C	30°F −1°C
Precp	1.9″ 4.8 cm	1.9″ 4.8 cm	2.7″ 6.9 cm	2.9″ 7.4 cm	3.5″ 8.9 cm	3.7″ 9.4 cm	3.3″ 8.4 cm	3.1″ 7.9 cm	3.0″ 7.6 cm	2.6″ 6.6 cm	2.3″ 5.8 cm	2.0″ 5.1 cm

6.   Average Annual: 21°C (70°F); 25.2 cm (9.9″)

	JAN	FEB	MAR	APR	MAY	JUN	JUL	AUG	SEP	OCT	NOV	DEC
Temp	84°F 29°C	82°F 28°C	77°F 25°C	68°F 20°C	60°F 16°C	54°F 12°C	53°F 12°C	58°F 14°C	65°F 18°C	73°F 23°C	79°F 26°C	82°F 28°C
Precp	1.7″ 4.3 cm	1.3″ 3.3 cm	1.1″ 2.8 cm	0.4″ 1.0 cm	0.6″ 1.5 cm	0.5″ 1.3 cm	0.3″ 0.8 cm	0.3″ 0.8 cm	0.3″ 0.8 cm	0.7″ 1.8 cm	1.2″ 3.0 cm	1.5″ 3.8 cm

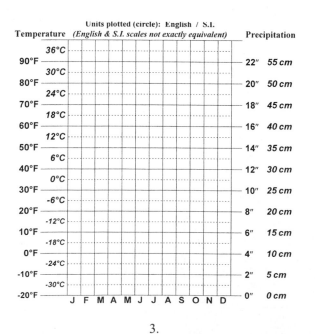

3.

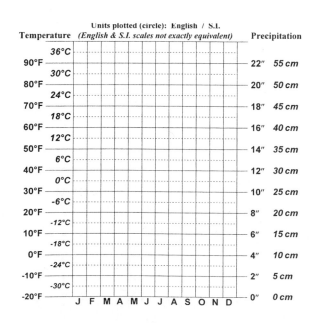

4.

144

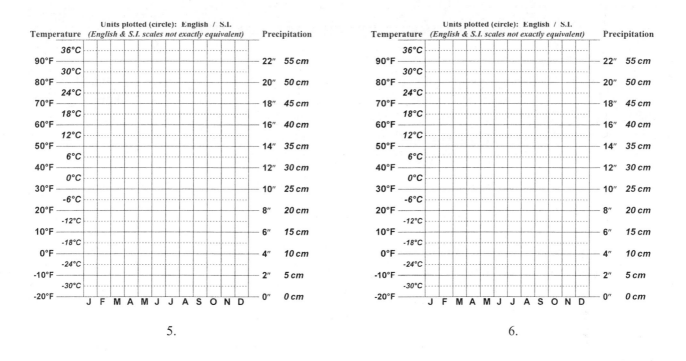

5.   6.

After completing the climographs, assign a Köppen letter code and descriptive climate name to each location:

1.   Köppen climate type: Letter code: _____

          Descriptive name: _____

2.   Köppen climate type: Letter code: _____

          Descriptive name: _____

3.   Köppen climate type: Letter code: _____

          Descriptive name: _____

4.   Köppen climate type: Letter code: _____

          Descriptive name: _____

5.   Köppen climate type: Letter code: _____

          Descriptive name: _____

6.   Köppen climate type: Letter code: _____

          Descriptive name: _____

EXERCISE 21 PROBLEMS—PART III

Before answering the following questions, assign Köppen climate types to each of the six locations in Part II. Match each of the locations in Part II (1 through 6) with its most likely city from the list below:

Alice Springs, Australia	Cochin, India
Capetown, South Africa	Lanzhou, China
Chicago, Illinois	Barrow, Alaska

1. (a)   Most likely city: _____

    (b)   Why is this the most likely city?

2. (a)   Most likely city: _____

    (b)   Why is this the most likely city?

3. (a)   Most likely city: _____

    (b)   Why is this the most likely city?

4. (a)   Most likely city: _____

    (b)   Why is this the most likely city?

5. (a)   Most likely city: _____

    (b)   Why is this the most likely city?

6. (a)   Most likely city: _____

    (b)   Why is this the most likely city?

EXERCISE 21 PROBLEMS—PART IV

The following questions are based on the diagram of the Köppen climate distribution on a hypo-thetical continent (Figure 21-2). It may also be helpful to compare the hypothetical continent with the map of actual climate distribution shown on the inside cover of the Lab Manual. In answering the questions, consider both the characteristics of a climate and the dominant controls producing that climate.

1. Why are Aw (tropical savanna) climates found in bands north and south of the Af (tropical wet) climates?

2. Why do the Af climates extend farther toward the poles along the east coast than along the west coast?

3. What explains the distribution of BW (desert) climates centered at about 25° to 30° north and south latitude along the west coast?

4. On the hypothetical continent, why does the BW climate extend farther inland in the Northern Hemisphere than in the Southern Hemisphere?

5. What explains the distribution of BS (steppe) climates?

6. What explains the narrow coastal band of Cs (mediterranean) climates at about 35° north and south latitude along the west coast?

7. Why do the Cfb (marine west coast) climates, just poleward of the dry summer Cs climates, receive rain all year?

8. Why do Cfa (humid subtropical) climates along the east coast receive rain all year, but at the same latitude along the west coast, the Cs climates have dry summers?

9. Why is the Dfb (humid continental) climate in a band just north of the band of Dfa climate?

10. Why is the high latitude interior of the continent dominated by Dfc and Dfd (subarctic) climates?

11. Why are no D or E climates shown in the Southern Hemisphere?

Name _____   Section _____

EXERCISE 21 PROBLEMS—PART V—INTERNET

In this exercise, you will use the Internet to find the climate record of the city where you live, and then classify its climate with the Köppen system.

- Go to the McKnight and Hess textbook Web site, <*http://www.prenhall.com/mcknight*>. Select "Lab Manual," then "Exercise 21." Then select "Go to *Regional Climate Centers*" under NOAA: <*http://www.ncdc.noaa.gov/oa/climate/regionalclimatecenters.html*>. (Your instructor may recommend a different Internet site that provides climate data.)

- From the map of the United States, select the Regional Climate Center for your state, and then look for the historical climate summary for your city.

- To properly classify the climate of your city, you will need the average monthly temperature and average monthly precipitation. (If "Average" or "Mean" Monthly Temperature is not given, it may be calculated by taking the average of a month's "Mean Maximum Temperature" and its "Mean Minimum Temperature.") The averages should be based on weather data over at least a 25-year period. If you choose not to print out the data, write down the information in the chart on the following page. Also note the years on which the averages are based.

- Indicate if your data are in S.I. or English units.

- Note (or calculate) the average annual temperature and precipitation.

- Using the graph on the following page, complete a climograph for your city.

- Use the "Modified Köppen System Charts" to classify the climate of your city.

As an alternative assignment, your instructor may ask that you classify the climate of a city other than where you live.

City: _____

Years of climate record: From _____ to _____

Units used: S.I. or English (circle)

	JAN	FEB	MAR	APR	MAY	JUN	JUL	AUG	SEP	OCT	NOV	DEC
Temp												
Precp												

Average Annual Temperature: _____

Average Annual Precipitation: _____

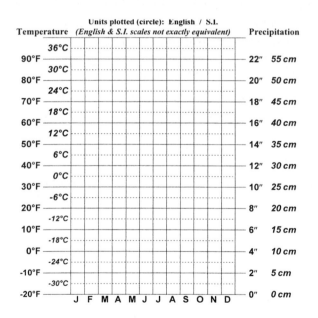

Köppen climate type: Letter code: _____

Descriptive name: _____

EXERCISE 22
BIOME DISTRIBUTION AND CLIMATE

Objective: To analyze the relationships between the distribution of biomes and global patterns of climate.

Reference: McKnight and Hess, *Physical Geography*, 9th ed., pp. 331–343.

ECOSYSTEMS AND BIOMES

Of the many interrelationships in the natural world, among the most striking is the relationship between the local physical environment—especially climate—and the local biological community.

Biogeographers describe biological communities using two important concepts: the **ecosystem** and the **biome**. An ecosystem is a fundamental biological community of plants and animals that is tied together through **biogeochemical cycles** by the flow of energy and nutrients with the surrounding nonliving environment.

The difficulty of studying the distribution of ecosystems is that this concept can be used to describe biological communities at many different scales, from the microscopic world in a drop of water to the planetary scale. In order to study biological communities in a meaningful way at the global scale, we usually describe patterns of ecosystems in terms of biomes. A biome is a large, recognizable assemblage of plants and animals in functional interaction with its environment.

THE MAJOR BIOMES

The 10 major biomes of the world are shown in Figure 22-1. These biomes are primarily distinguished by the dominant types of vegetation they contain, although each biome generally includes characteristic animals and soil types, and is usually associated with characteristic climatic regions as well.

This map shown in Figure 22-1 is highly generalized. In reality, the natural patterns of vegetation and animal life have been significantly altered in many locations. Further, the boundaries between these biomes should be viewed as transition zones rather than abrupt borders.

The following brief descriptions highlight just one or two important or distinguishing characteristics of each biome—see your textbook for additional information about each.

Tropical Rainforest: Tropical rainforests are characterized by very high species diversity (many different species present, but with just a few individuals of each species in a given area), and by relatively infertile soils. Tropical rainforests typically include a thick, continuous canopy of leaves produced by **broadleaf evergreen trees**, along with **epiphytes** (plants living above ground level without direct contact with the soil), vines, and a dense understory of vegetation on the surface.

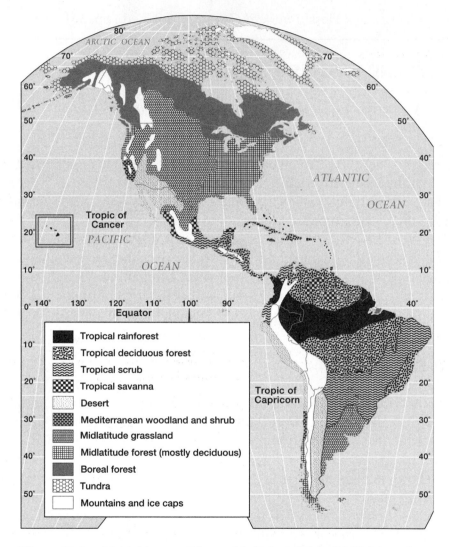

Figure 22-1: Major biomes of the world. (Adapted from McKnight and Hess, *Physical Geography*, 9th ed.)

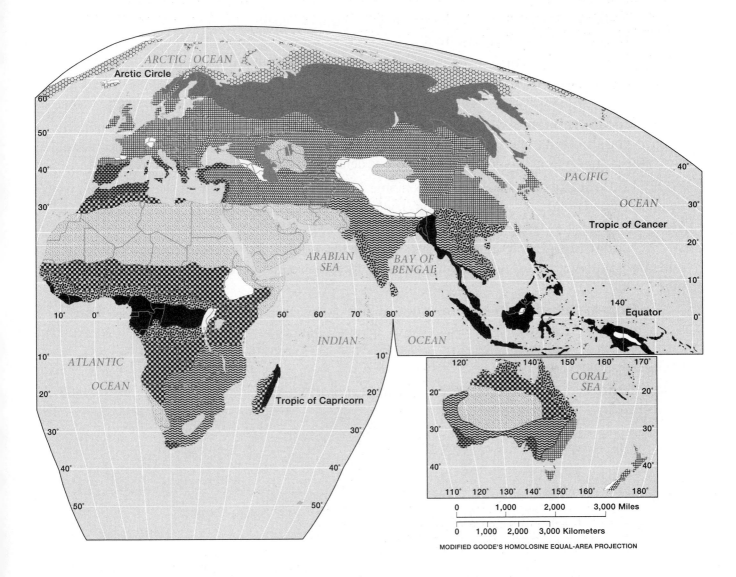

ARCTIC OCEAN
Arctic Circle

60°
50°
40°
30°

PACIFIC

OCEAN

Tropic of Cancer

40°
30°
20°
10°

ARABIAN
SEA

BAY OF
BENGAL

10°
0°
10°

ATLANTIC

OCEAN

20°

INDIAN   OCEAN

140°

Equator

0°

10°
20°
Tropic of Capricorn

30°
40°
50°

10°

30°
40°
50°

CORAL
SEA

120°   140° 150°   160° 170°

20°   20°

30°   30°

40°   40°

110° 120° 130° 140° 150° 160° 180°

0   1,000   2,000   3,000 Miles

0   1,000   2,000   3,000 Kilometers

MODIFIED GOODE'S HOMOLOSINE EQUAL-AREA PROJECTION

Tropical Deciduous Forest: Unlike the tropical rainforest biome, in the tropical deciduous forests many broadleaf trees shed their leaves during part of the year.

The usual transition between the tropical deciduous forest biome and the desert biome is either the tropical scrub or tropical savanna biome.

Tropical Scrub: Tropical scrub biome typically contains thorny or spiny **shrubs**. The density of vegetation cover varies from areas of thick undergrowth to open growth of trees such as acacias.

Tropical Savanna: These tropical **grasslands** typically contain a wide variety of tall grasses, interspersed with scattered trees.

Desert: This biome includes both hot and relatively cool arid areas of the world, so the appearance of the vegetation cover varies greatly. Hot deserts often include dry shrubs and varieties of cactus and **succulents**, while cold deserts typically include short dry grasses and shrubs.

Mediterranean Woodland and Shrub: The mediterranean woodland is comprised of open grassland with interspersed trees (such as the oak in California), while the mediterranean shrub (also known as **chaparral**) consists of low, dense stands of shrubs and small trees.

Midlatitude Grassland: This biome includes grasslands such as the *pampa* of Argentina and the prairies of North America. The natural vegetation varies from the short grasses of the Asiatic steppes to the tall grasses of the North American prairie.

Midlatitude Deciduous Forest: These forests consist primarily of **broadleaf deciduous trees**, although many midlatitude deciduous forests also include **evergreen conifers** such as pines.

Boreal Forest: The boreal forest biome forms an almost unbroken belt across the whole of North America and Eurasia between about 50° and 60° north latitude. This biome typically consists of forests composed of just a few species of evergreen conifers such as pine, fir, larch, and spruce.

Tundra: The tundra biome consists of treeless plains with low-lying shrubs, mosses, and sedges.

EXERCISE 22 PROBLEMS

Using the global map of biome distribution (Figure 22-1), the map of climate distribution on the inside front cover of the Lab Manual, as well as information about Köppen climate types from Exercise 21, answer the following questions.

1. (a) Which Köppen climate type (or types) is most closely associated with the tropical rainforest biome?

    (b) Describe the general temperature and precipitation characteristics of the climate in regions of the tropical rainforest biome:

2. (a) Describe the general locations of the tropical deciduous forest biome relative to the tropical rainforest biome (especially note the pattern in South America and Africa):

    (b) Based on the differences in location noted in question 2a above, in what way(s) will the climate in regions of tropical deciduous forest differ from the climate in regions of tropical rainforest?

    (c) How do the climate differences noted in question 2b above help explain the presence of large numbers of deciduous trees in the tropical deciduous forest biome?

3. (a) Which Köppen climate type (or types) is most closely associated with regions of the tropical scrub and the tropical savanna biomes?

    (b) What characteristics of the climate in these regions would tend to limit the growth of extensive forest (such as those found in the tropical rainforest and tropical deciduous forest biomes)?

4.   Which Köppen climate type (or types) is most closely associated with the desert biome?

5.   (a)   Which Köppen climate type (or types) is most closely associated with the mediter-
             ranean woodland and shrub biome?

      (b)   Describe the general seasonal patterns of temperature and precipitation in these
             locations:

6.   (a)   Which Köppen climate type (or types) is most closely associated with the midlati-
             tude grassland biome?

      (b)   What characteristics of the climate in these regions would tend to limit the growth
             of forest?

7.   Describe the general climate characteristics of regions of the midlatitude deciduous forest
      biome (you may specifically note the Köppen climate type or types, but this isn't necessary):

8.   (a)   Which Köppen climate type (or types) is most closely associated with the distribu-
             tion of the boreal forest biome?

      (b)   Describe the general characteristics of temperature and precipitation in these
             regions:

9.   (a)   Which Köppen climate type (or types) is most closely associated with the distribu-
             tion of the tundra biome?

      (b)   Describe the temperature and precipitation characteristics of the climate in these
             regions:

EXERCISE 23
CONTOUR LINES

Objective: To learn to interpret elevation contour lines.

Reference: McKnight and Hess, *Physical Geography*, 9th ed., pp. 39–41 and A3–A4.

CONTOUR LINES

In previous exercises, we used **isolines** to illustrate the distribution of various phenomena. We used isotherms to show patterns of temperature, and isobars to show patterns of pressure. In the study of landforms, we often use maps showing elevation with isolines known as **contour lines**.

Contour lines are lines that connect points of equal elevation. Contour lines enable us to study the topography of a region from a two-dimensional map. Figure 23-1 shows a simple contour line map and a profile cross section through the landscape.

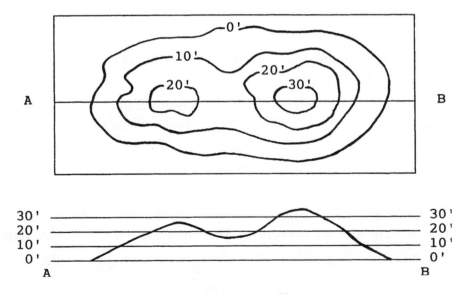

Figure 23-1: Simple contour line map and profile.

157

SAMPLE CONTOUR LINE MAP

Figure 23-2 shows a fictitious landscape and a contour line map of the same landscape with various elevations and features labeled.

CONTOUR LINE RULES

The following rules will help you interpret contour lines:

1. A contour line connects points of equal elevation.

2. The difference in elevation between two contour lines is known as the **contour interval**.

3. Usually every fifth contour line is a darker **index contour**. (On some maps, every fourth line is an index contour.)

4. Elevations on one side of a contour line are higher than on the other side.

5. Contour lines never cross one another, although they may touch at a vertical cliff.

6. Contour lines have no beginning or end. Every line closes on itself, either on or off the map.

7. Uniformly spaced contours indicate a uniform slope.

8. If spaced far apart, contour lines indicate a gentle slope. If spaced close together, they represent a steep slope.

9. When crossing a valley, gully, or "draw," a contour line makes a "V" pointing up-hill.

10. When crossing a spur or a ridge running down the side of a hill, a contour line makes a "V" pointing downhill.

11. A contour line that closes within the limits of the map represents a hill or rise. The land within the closed contour is higher than the land outside the closed contour.

12. The top of a hill shown with closed contour lines is higher than the uppermost closed contour, but lower than the next highest contour that hasn't been shown on the map.

13. A small depression is represented by a closed contour line that is hachured on the side leading into the depression. Hachured contours are called **depression contours**.

(a)

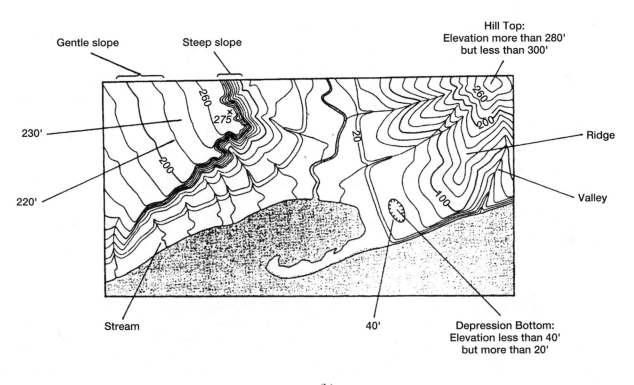

(b)

Figure 23-2: (a) Fictitious landscape; (b) Sample contour line map (contour interval 20'; adapted from U.S. Geological Survey).

159

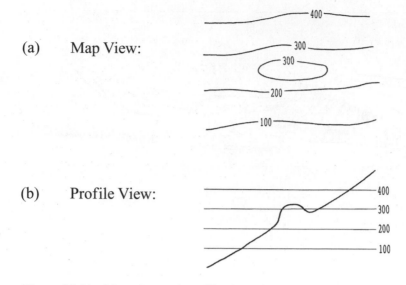

(a)   Map View:

(b)   Profile View:

Figure 23-3:   Map view and profile view of a closed contour line on a slope.

14.   A closed contour line between two other contours (such as would show a bump on the side of a hill) is the same elevation as the adjacent upslope contour line (Figure 23-3).

15.   Unless otherwise marked, the elevation of a depression contour is the same as that of the adjacent lower regular contour (Figure 23-4).

Unless otherwise noted in a Lab Manual exercise or by your instructor, estimate elevations between contour lines to the nearest half-contour interval, and estimate the elevation of the top of a hill to be one-half-contour interval higher than the highest contour line shown.

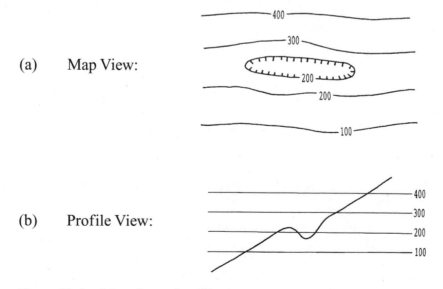

(a)   Map View:

(b)   Profile View:

Figure 22-4:   Map view and profile view of depression contour line on a slope.

160

EXERCISE 23 PROBLEMS

The questions in this exercise are based on this contour line map with elevations shown in feet.

- North is to the top of the map.

- Streams are shown with dashed lines.

- A graphic scale for measuring horizontal distances is shown below the map.

- Estimate elevations between contour lines to the nearest half-contour interval; assume that the top of a hill is one-half-contour interval higher than the highest contour line shown.

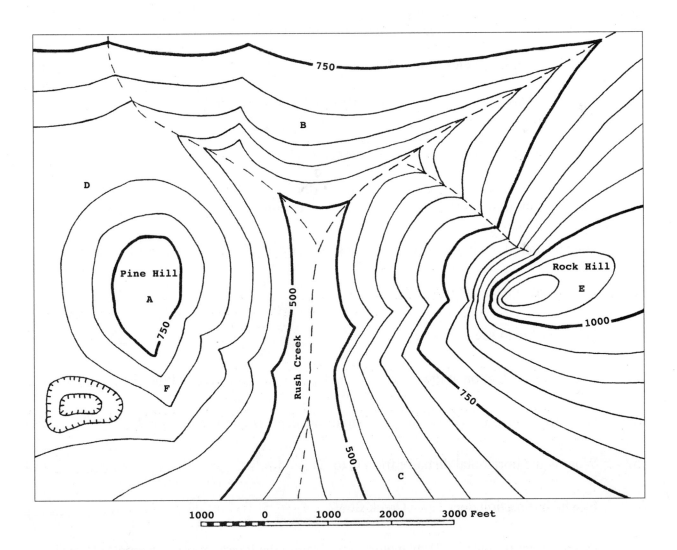

1.   What is the contour interval?   _____ feet

2.   What is the elevation of Point A?   _____ feet

3.   What is the elevation of Point B?   _____ feet

4.   What is the elevation of Point C?   _____ feet

5.   Which lettered point has the highest elevation?   _____

6.   Which lettered point has the lowest elevation?   _____

7.   (a)   Where is the highest elevation shown in this landscape?
               (It may not be a location marked with a letter.)   _____

        (b)   What is the elevation of this highest location?   _____ feet

8.   (a)   Where is the lowest elevation shown in this landscape?
               (It may not be a location marked with a letter.)   _____

        (b)   What is the elevation of this lowest location?   _____ feet

9.   What is the "local relief" of this landscape (the difference
        in elevation between the highest and lowest locations)?   _____ feet

10.   Which lettered point is most clearly on a spur or ridge running down the side of a hill? ____

11.   Is it possible to see D from F?   _____

12.   Is it possible to see D from B?   _____

13.   What is the elevation at the bottom of the depression southwest of Pine Hill? _____ feet

14.   How deep is the depression (from the lip of the depression to its bottom)?   _____ feet

15.   What is the horizontal distance from C to B?   _____ feet

16.   In which direction does Rush Creek flow?   From _____ to _____

17.   Draw a 1 centimeter ($^{1}/_{2}$") diameter circle around the location of the steepest slope shown
        on the map.

18.   Draw in three more streams as indicated by the contour pattern (but not shown on the map
        with dashed lines).

EXERCISE 24
U.S. GEOLOGICAL SURVEY
TOPOGRAPHIC MAPS

Objective:	To learn the features of standard U.S. Geological Survey topographic maps.
Materials:	A complete USGS topographic quadrangle is helpful, but not required.
Resources:	Internet access (optional).
Reference:	McKnight and Hess, *Physical Geography*, 9th ed., pp. A3–A7.

TOPOGRAPHIC MAPS

Topographic maps are large-scale maps that use contour lines to portray the elevation and shape of the topography. Topographic maps show and name both natural and human-made features. The U.S. Geological Survey (USGS) is the principal government agency that provides topographic maps of the United States. USGS topographic maps cover the entire United States at several different scales.

The largest scale maps are those at a scale of 1:24,000 (1" represents 2000'; 1 cm represents 0.24 km). The long-established 1:62,500 scale maps (1" represents about 1 mile; 1 cm represents about 0.6 km) have been replaced by 1:100,000 scale maps (1" represents about 1.6 miles; 1 cm represents 1 km). The entire country is also mapped at a scale of 1:250,000 (1" represents about 4 miles; 1 cm represents 2.5 km). The primary scale for mapping Alaska remains 1:63,360 (1" represents 1 mile; 1 cm represents 0.63 km), although larger scale maps will eventually cover this entire state as well. Printed versions of topographic maps are available for purchase through the USGS, however, the *National Map* is an interactive online map that lets you quickly access both detailed topographic maps, aerial photographs, and satellite images of most locations within the United States.

MARGINAL DATA ON USGS MAPS

In this exercise we will focus primarily on the information found in the margins of these maps (this information has been omitted from most of the maps reproduced for future exercises). Figure 24-1 shows the lower right corner of a standard USGS topographic map with a scale of 1:24,000 (sometimes referred to as a "7$\frac{1}{2}$ minute" map). (The map has been reproduced here at 90% of its original size in order to fit on a two-page spread in the Lab Manual.)

The name of this map, or **quadrangle**, is "Greasewood Spring, Arizona." Below the name is the date of publication, in this case, 1972. The date of any revisions would also be listed here. To the left of the name, is a small map showing the quadrangle location in Arizona.

The latitude and longitude are printed at each corner of the quadrangle. The coordinates of the lower right (southeast) corner of this map are 35°22'30" N latitude, 109°52'30" W longitude (on these maps, "north" latitude and "west" longitude are understood). Below the name, notice that quadrangles are also identified by the latitude and longitude of the lower right corner of the map, in this case, "N3522.5—W10952.5/7.5" (35°22.5' N latitude; 109°52.5' W longitude; 7.5 minute series map).

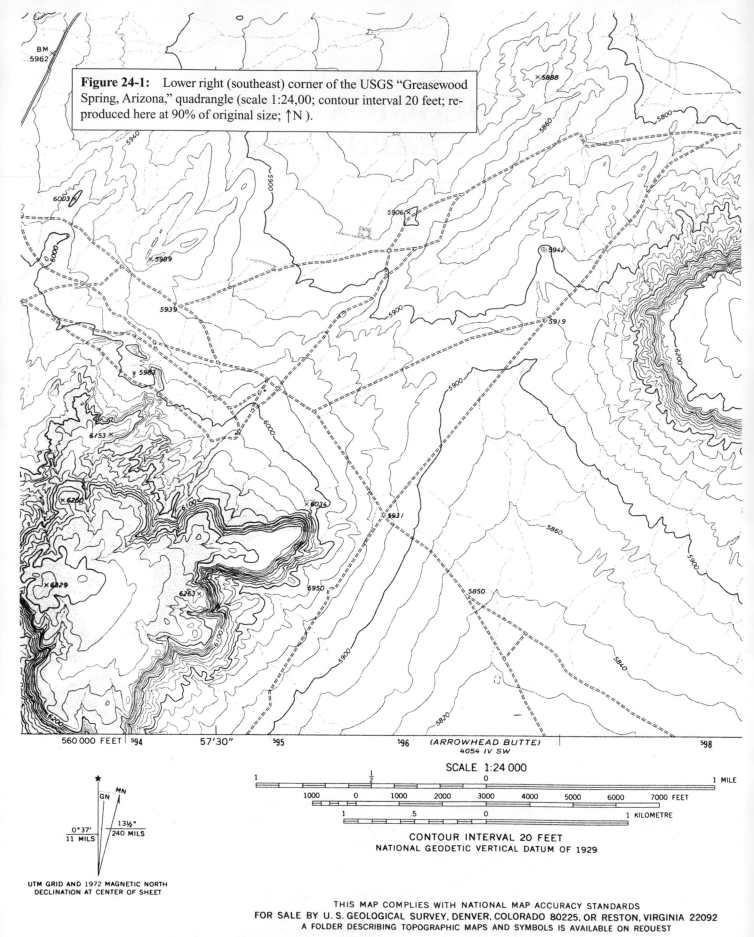

Figure 24-1: Lower right (southeast) corner of the USGS "Greasewood Spring, Arizona," quadrangle (scale 1:24,00; contour interval 20 feet; reproduced here at 90% of original size; ↑N).

(ARROWHEAD BUTTE)
4054 IV SW

SCALE 1:24 000

CONTOUR INTERVAL 20 FEET
NATIONAL GEODETIC VERTICAL DATUM OF 1929

GN MN

0°37'
11 MILS

13½°
240 MILS

UTM GRID AND 1972 MAGNETIC NORTH
DECLINATION AT CENTER OF SHEET

THIS MAP COMPLIES WITH NATIONAL MAP ACCURACY STANDARDS
FOR SALE BY U. S. GEOLOGICAL SURVEY, DENVER, COLORADO 80225, OR RESTON, VIRGINIA 22092
A FOLDER DESCRIBING TOPOGRAPHIC MAPS AND SYMBOLS IS AVAILABLE ON REQUEST

164

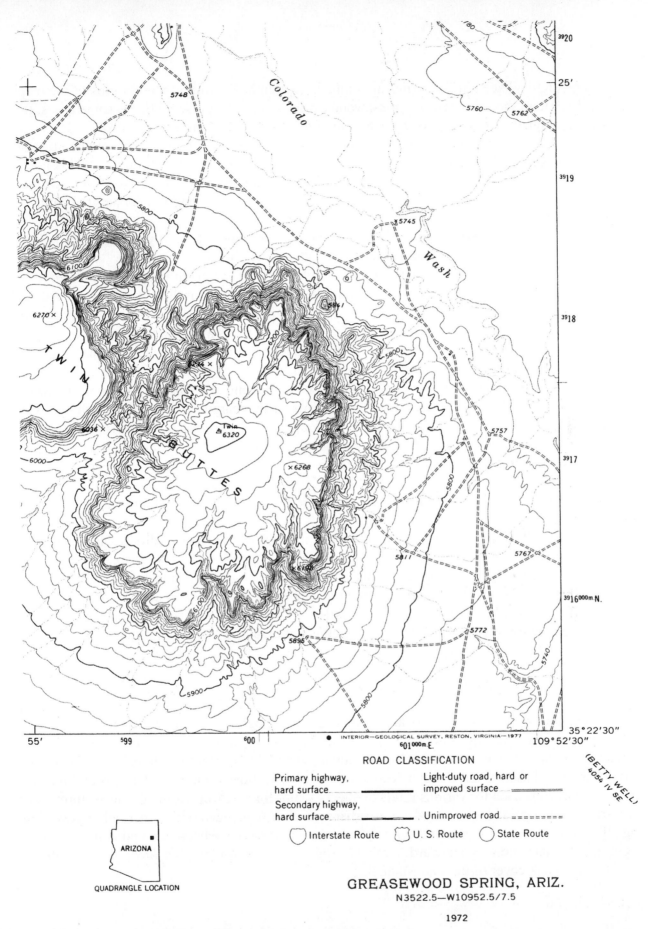

ROAD CLASSIFICATION

Primary highway,
hard surface...........

Light-duty road, hard or
improved surface............

Secondary highway,
hard surface.............

Unimproved road....======

◯ Interstate Route   ▢ U. S. Route   ◯ State Route

ARIZONA

QUADRANGLE LOCATION

GREASEWOOD SPRING, ARIZ.

N3522.5—W10952.5/7.5

1972

INTERIOR—GEOLOGICAL SURVEY, RESTON, VIRGINIA—1977

(BETTY WELL)
4054 IV SE

The eight adjacent quadrangles are named in parentheses around the margins of the map. The quadrangle to the southeast of Greasewood Spring is called "Betty Well." In some cases, the eight adjacent quadrangles are shown with a small diagram at the bottom of the map.

The scales are shown at the bottom center of the map. Below the fractional scale (1:24,000), three graphic scales are shown, in miles, feet, and kilometers. Note that "0" is not at the far left edge of the graphic scales. Below the scales the contour interval is given. The **datum** is the reference point from which elevations are measured. On USGS topographic maps the datum is normally mean sea level.

The **declination arrow** (or *declination diagram*) is found at the lower left corner of the map. True north is shown with the tallest arrow, labeled with either a star or a large "N." The "MN" arrow shows the direction of **magnetic north**. The location of the north magnetic pole is not the same as the true geographical North Pole, so it is necessary to adjust for this difference when using a magnetic compass. The position of the north magnetic pole changes with time, and so the compass correction indicated on the map may not be exact some years after the original survey.

The "GN" arrow shows **grid north**. In addition to the grid system of latitude and longitude, other kinds of grids are also marked on many topographic maps. Grid north refers to the orientation of the **Universal Transverse Mercator grid** (UTM) used by the military. Abbreviated numbers for the UTM grid are marked every 1000 or 10,000 meters around the margins of the map. North–south locations are indicated in meters north or south of the equator, while east–west locations are indicated in meters from a standard meridian. Similar state grids are often marked every 1000 or 10,000 feet.

UTM grid numbers are shown along the right and bottom margins of the map. Along the right margin of the map, the number $^{39}16^{000m.}$N indicates a location 3,916,000 meters north of the equator, while along the bottom margin of the map, the number $^{6}01^{000m.}$E indicates a location 601,000 meters east of a standard meridian.

In addition to the UTM numbers along the margins of the map, additional indications of latitude and longitude are also provided. Notice along the right margin of the map, near the top of Figure 24-1, the number 25' appears—this marks the location where the latitude is 35°25' N. Along the bottom margin of the map, near the left side of Figure 24-1, you see the number 57'30" —this marks the location where the longitude is 109°57'30" W. Most topographic maps will have these supplementary marks for latitude and longitude at regular intervals along the margins.

TOPOGRAPHIC MAP SYMBOLS

Standard symbols and colors are used on USGS topographic maps. Brown lines are elevation contours. Spot elevations are shown by black numbers next to an "X," while more precisely surveyed points known as **benchmarks** are shown as numbers next to the letters "BM." Blue lines and numbers are used to show water features (blue contour lines on a white background indicate glaciers). Green is used for various kinds of vegetation or forest cover. Human-built features, such as roads, are shown in black and red, while urbanized areas are shown with either red or gray shading. "Photorevised" features are shown in purple on maps that have been updated with aerial photographs. A chart showing standard symbols used on USGS topographic maps is found on the inside of the back cover of the Lab Manual.

Name _____   Section _____

EXERCISE 24 PROBLEMS—PART I

The following questions are based on the lower right (southeast) corner of the "Greasewood Spring, Arizona," quadrangle (Figure 24-1):

1.   What is the contour interval of the map?   _____ feet

2.   What is the difference in elevation between index contours?   _____ feet

3.   What is the elevation of the bench mark at the top of the
      eastern Twin Butte?   _____ feet

4.   Estimate (to the nearest half-minute [30"] the latitude of the
      bench mark at the top of the eastern Twin Butte: _____

5.   What do the dashed double lines represent?   _____

6.   What is the name of the adjacent quadrangle to the south?_____

7.   The latitude of the upper right (northeast) corner of the map is 35°30' N, while the longitude of the lower left (southwest) corner of the map is 110°00' W. Why is this called a "7.5 minute" topographic map?

8.   At the time this quadrangle was printed, what was the difference
      (in degrees) between true north and magnetic north for this map?   _____ degrees

9.   On all three graphic scales for the map, "0" is not at the far left. Explain the reason for this.

10.   Using the graphic map scales, determine the maximum
      width of the eastern Twin Butte (use the 6100' contour
      to be the outer edge of the butte):   _____ feet

                                                                                                             _____ kilometers

Name _____   Section _____

EXERCISE 24 PROBLEMS—PART II—INTERNET

In this exercise, you will use the online *National Map* to answer questions about your school campus.

- Go to the McKnight and Hess textbook Web site <***http://www.prenhall.com/mcknight***>. Select "Lab Manual" and then "Exercise 24." Select "Go to *National Map*" <***http://nationalmap.gov/***>.
- From the National Map main page, select "Go to Viewer."
- Click on the map of the United States. By repeatedly clicking on the map, you can zoom in to the location of your campus.

Notice that to the right of the map there is a list of map "Layers" you can view—most have drop-down menus with multiple options in each category, although not all layers are available for all locations and at all map scales. Each time you select a new layer to view, you may need to click "Refresh Map." As you move the cursor across the map, notice that the latitude and longitude appear along the bottom (west longitude reads as a negative value; north latitude reads as a positive value).

From the Layers menus, select "Topographic Maps" and then "USGS Raster Graphics (Topo Maps)." Zoom in until you can locate your campus on the topographic map (if you zoom in too far, the topographic map base may not be available).

1.   Using the contour lines, estimate the elevation of the building in which you are taking your laboratory class. (You may need to view other sections of the map in order to determine the contour interval; indicate if in feet or meters.) _____

2.   Location of your building: Latitude _____ Longitude _____

Select "Imagery" and then either "DOQ—TerraServer DOQ," or "USGS DOQ" (DOQ stands for "digital orthophoto quadrangle"), or "Other Imagery—TerraServer USA Urban Area," to see an aerial photograph of this area. Zoom in on your school to the point that the maximum detail is available. (You may want to turn off all "Transportation" layers to make viewing easier.)

3.   Using the menu to the left of the map, click "Elevation". Center your cursor and click on your campus building (to end this function, scroll down the left menu and click "clear").   Elevation _____

4.   (a)   What time of day was this image taken? (circle) Morning / Midday / Afternoon

     (b)   How can you tell?

5.   (a)   Were these images taken from directly overhead? _____

     (b)   How can you tell?

EXERCISE 25
TOPOGRAPHIC PROFILES

Objective: To learn to draw and interpret topographic profiles.

TOPOGRAPHIC PROFILES

Features on topographic maps are shown in "plan view," looking down on the surface. A **topographic profile** is a diagram showing the changes in elevation of the landscape along a line. It creates a "side view" of the landscape, much like the silhouette of a skyline. Topographic profiles are used in the study of landforms to help emphasize patterns in the topography.

In this example, we will draw a topographic profile of a simple contour line map showing a hill (Figure 25-1). We will draw the profile along line AB, using a profile graph to show vertical and horizontal distance.

We begin by laying the edge of a piece of paper along line AB (Figure 25-2). At each place where a contour line meets the edge of the paper, make a short mark and write down the elevation. Continue across the map, also marking the positions of mountain peaks, passes, streams, and any important cultural features along the line of the profile. Next, line up the edge of paper along the bottom of the graph (Figure 25-3). Carefully mark the elevations of each point along the profile on the graph. Finally, connect these points with a smooth line (Figure 25-4).

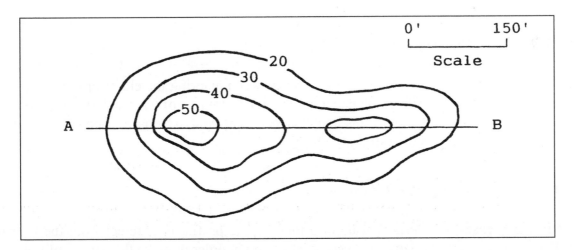

Figure 25-1: Sample contour line map.

169

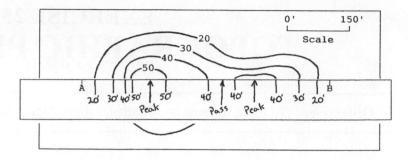

Figure 25-2: Marking elevations along profile line.

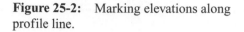

Figure 25-3: Transferring elevations to profile graph.

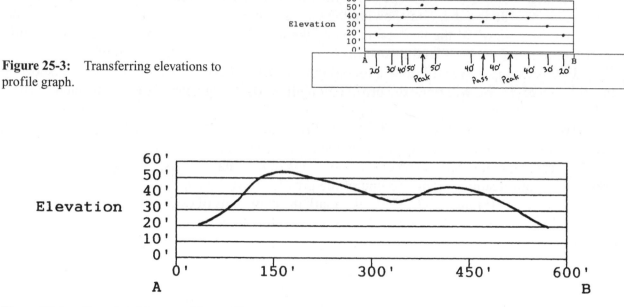

Figure 25-4: Completed topographic profile.

(As an alternative to using a separate piece of paper when marking the elevations along a profile, you can simply fold the profile graph paper along the bottom line of the graph, then mark the elevations of the profile directly below this line; this technique cannot be used when the map and profile chart are reproduced on the same page.)

VERTICAL EXAGGERATION

In many cases, the vertical scale of a topographic profile is different from the horizontal scale. This is done to emphasize differences in elevation in order to make the pattern of relief more obvious. We say that such profiles have been drawn with **vertical exaggeration**. If great vertical exaggeration is being used, small hills can begin to appear as tall peaks. To determine the amount of vertical exaggeration, compare the horizontal and vertical scales. In the example above, the horizontal scale is 1 inch represents 150 feet, while the vertical scale is 1 inch represents 60 feet. Therefore:

$$\text{Vertical Exaggeration} = \frac{\text{Horizontal}}{\text{Vertical}} = \frac{150'}{60'} = 2.5\times$$

170

EXERCISE 25 PROBLEMS

1. Construct a topographic profile of the map below along line AB. Draw your profile in the graph provided.

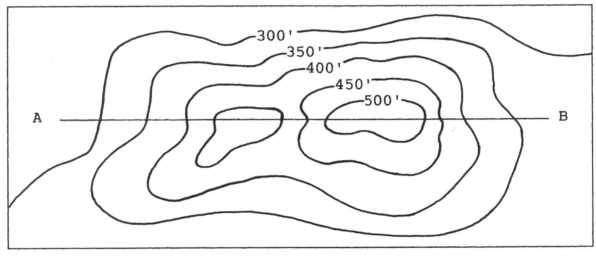

0'   3000'

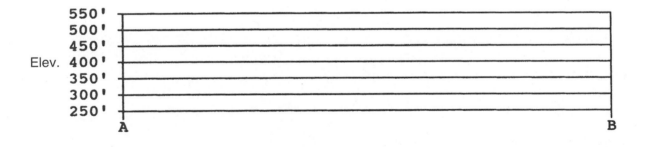

After completing the profile, answer the questions on the following page.

2. Calculate the vertical exaggeration of your profile in Problem #1:

    (a)   Horizontal Scale: 1 inch = _____ feet

    (b)   Vertical Scale: 1 inch = _____ feet

    (c)   Vertical Exaggeration   = _____ ×

EXERCISE 26
U.S. PUBLIC LAND SURVEY SYSTEM

> **Objective:** To learn to use the Public Land Survey System.

PUBLIC LAND SURVEY SYSTEM

The **Public Land Survey**, or **township grid**, was established by the federal government in 1785 in order to keep track of land ownership in the American frontier. This grid covers most of the continental United States west of the Mississippi and Ohio rivers, with the exception of some regions such as those under old Spanish land grants.

The starting point for the grid is a series of parallels known as **base lines**, and a series of **principal meridians** (Figure 26-1). Beginning at the intersection of a base line and a principal meridian, rows of 36 square-mile tracts of land known as **townships** were established (Figure 26-2a).

TOWNSHIP AND RANGE

Each township is a square tract of land, 6 miles to a side, and is identified by its position north or south of a base line, and east or west of a principal meridian. The first position north of a base line is called "Township 1 North" (T1N), the second position north is T2N, and so on. The first position south is T1S.

The first position west of a principal meridian is called "Range 1 West" (R1W), and the first position east is R1E. Each 36 square-mile township is identified by both a **township** and a **range**. For example, one of the townships would be designated "Township 3 North, Range 2 East" (see Figure 26-2a).

(Note: the term "township" has two meanings in the context of the Public Land Survey—a 36-square mile tract of land, as well as the positions of these tracts north and south of a base line. It may help to think of "T1N" and "T2N" as referring to "Tier" 1 North, "Tier" 2 North, and so on.)

A township is divided into 36 **sections**. Each section is 1 square mile (640 acres) in area and is given a number, from 1 to 36. Notice the specific numbering pattern of sections within a township (Figure 26-2b). Each section is subdivided into "quarter sections" (160 acres), and each quarter section is further divided into "quarters of quarter sections" (40 acres), or as shown in Figure 26-2c, into even smaller tracts of land. The shaded 10-acre plot shown in Figure 26-2c would be called the "Southeast Quarter of the Southwest Quarter of the Northeast Quarter, Section 24, Township 2 South, Range 3 West" ($SE^1/_4$, $SW^1/_4$, $NE^1/_4$, Sec. 24, T2S, R3W).

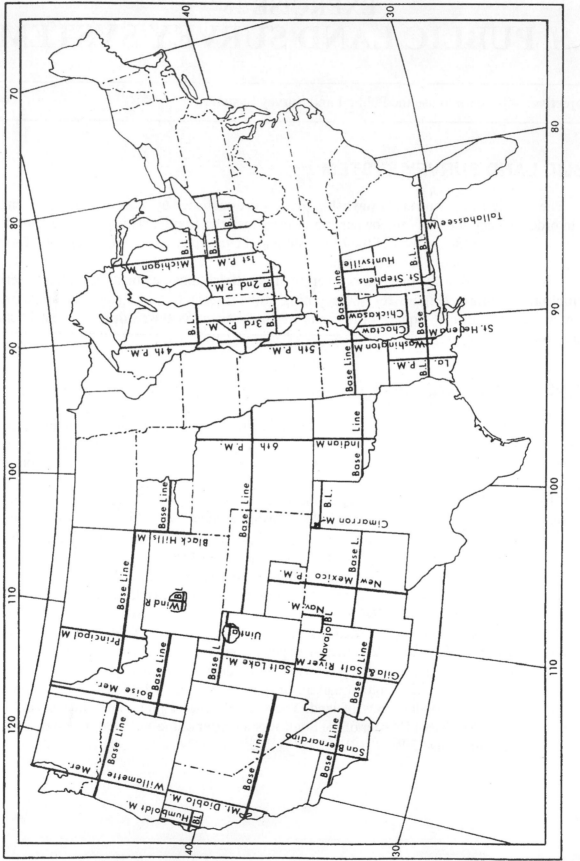

Figure 26-1: Baselines and principal meridians of the Public Land Survey System. (From U.S. Geological Survey)

174

Figure 26-2: Public Land Survey System.

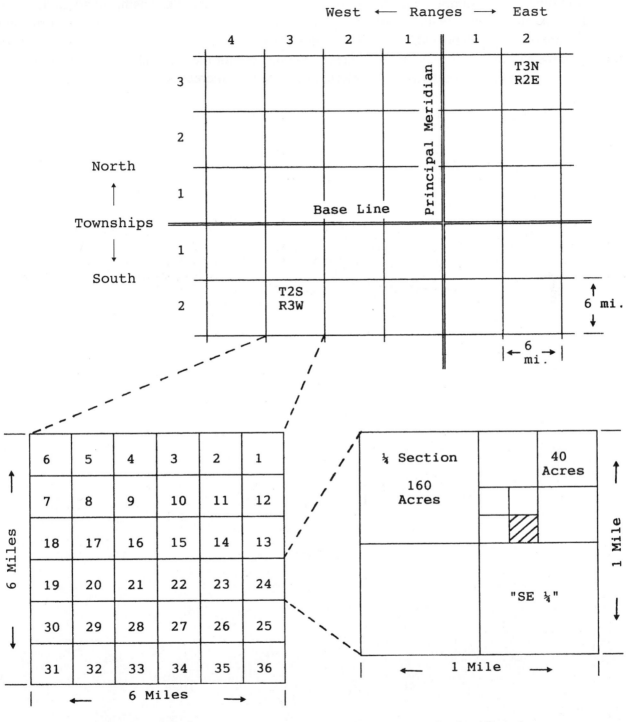

(a) Township & Range Grid

(b) One "Township"

(c) One "Section"

TOWNSHIP GRID ON TOPOGRAPHIC MAPS

On USGS topographic maps, the public land survey grid is usually shown with red lines and section numbers (for example, look at Map T-11, the "Whitewater, Wisconsin," quadrangle). The township and range numbers are shown along the margins of the map. The base line and principal meridian are often not identified. You will also notice that a row of townships is occasionally offset relative to the row to the north or south. This is to compensate for the constriction of a township that would result from the convergence of the meridians as latitude increases.

EXERCISE 26 PROBLEMS

The following questions are based on Figure 26-3 on the following page, showing a portion of the "Antelope Peak, Arizona," quadrangle (scale 1:62,500; contour interval 25 feet). The map's marginal information is visible along the left and top margins ("T.5S," "R.2E," etc.). On the original USGS map, this information was printed in red.

1.   The word "Hidden" appears on the map within which township?

        Township _____, Range _____

2.   The words "Vekol Wash" appear within which township?

        Township _____, Range _____

3.   The "Booth Hills" are found within which section and township?

        Section _____, Township _____, Range _____

4.   Find the hill in Sec. 8, T6S, R2E. This hill covers approximately how many acres?   _____ acres

5.   With a red pencil, carefully mark off and shade in:

     (a)   The Northeast Quarter of Section 25, T5S, R1E.

     (b)   The Northwest Quarter of the Southeast Quarter of Section 5, T6S, R2E.

6.   Describe two kinds of human/cultural features that follow the Public Land Survey grid.

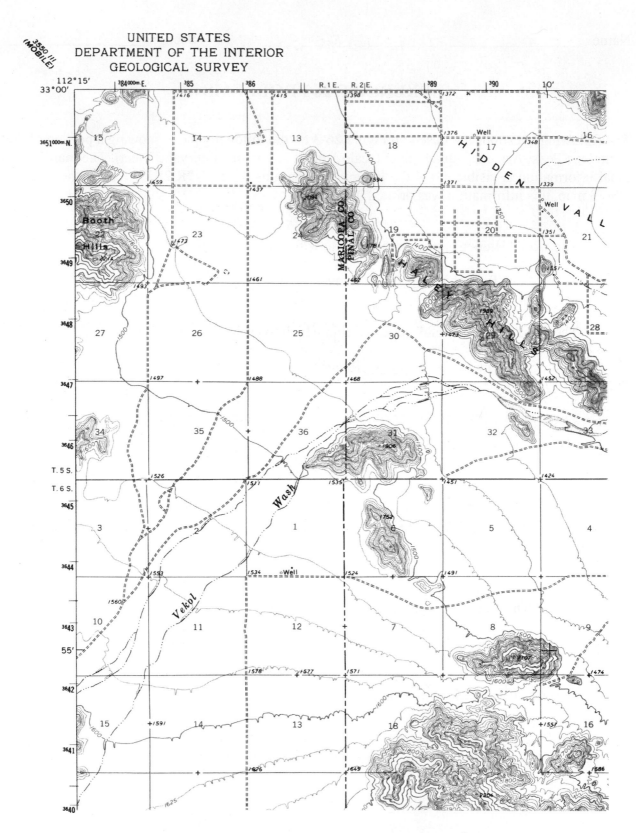

Figure 26-3: USGS "Antelope Peak, Arizona," quadrangle (scale 1:62,500; contour interval 25 feet; ↑N).

EXERCISE 27
STEREO AERIAL PHOTOGRAPHS

Objective:	To learn to interpret stereo aerial photographs.
Materials:	Lens stereoscope.
Reference:	McKnight and Hess, *Physical Geography*, 9th ed., p. 43.

STEREOGRAMS

A **stereogram** or **stereopair** is a set of carefully matched **vertical aerial photographs**. A sample stereogram is shown in Figure 27-3. At first glance, a stereogram may look like two identical photographs, but it actually consists of two slightly different photographs.

Stereograms come from photographs taken from an airplane with a camera pointing directly down toward the surface. As the plane flies over an area, it takes a sequence of photographs so that the area shown in one photograph overlaps the area shown in the next photograph by about 60% (Figure 27-1). Stereograms are produced from two of these photographs. Both photographs in the pair show the same area, but from slightly different angles.

Stereograms are useful in the study of landforms, since by viewing the stereograms with simple equipment we can see the landscape in "three dimensions." We see in stereo with depth perception because our two eyes see an object from slightly different angles. Since the two photographs in a stereogram also show objects from slightly different angles, if we view the right photograph with our right eye and the left photograph with our left eye, we can produce a stereovision view of the landscape.

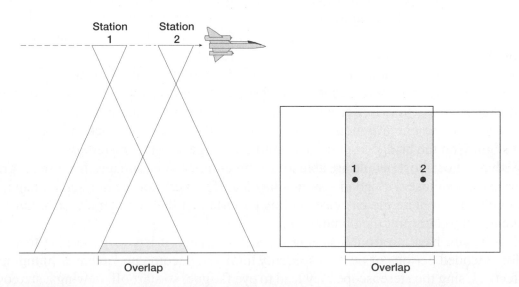

Figure 27-1: Overlapping vertical aerial photographs taken from an airplane. (From McKnight and Hess, *Physical Geography*, 9th ed.)

179

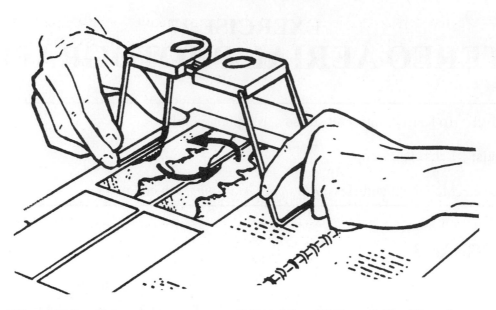

Figure 27-2: Using a lens stereoscope. (Adapted from W. Kenneth Hamblin and James D. Howard, *Exercises in Physical Geology*, 9th ed. Englewood Cliffs, NJ: Prentice Hall, 1995, p. 71.)

THE LENS STEREOSCOPE

The images in stereograms are separated by a distance of 63 mm (about 2.5 inches)—this is the approximate distance between our eyes. They are designed to view with an instrument called a **lens stereoscope** (Figure 27-2). A lens stereoscope consists of a pair of magnifying lenses, usually supported with an adjustable stand. A simple handheld stereoscope is included with the Lab Manual.

To view a stereogram, set the spacing of an adjustable stereoscope to 63 mm (or approximately so). Set the stereoscope on the stereogram so that the right lens is directly over one image of the stereogram and the left lens is directly over the other image. Slowly rotate the stereoscope slightly clockwise and counterclockwise until the stereo image comes into view.

To use the simple handheld stereoscope included with the Lab Manual, holding the handle of the stereoscope, rest the stereoscope on the bridge of your nose (much like holding a pair of glasses in front of your eyes. Lower your head toward the stereogram until the image is sharp (it may be easiest to close one eye momentarily as you do this), and then rock the stereoscope back and forth slightly on the bridge of your nose until the image appears in stereo.

With practice, most people are able to see three-dimensional images from stereograms, but some people—even those with good vision—may not. If you cannot see the stereo image, you still should be able to complete the exercises in this Lab Manual that use stereograms, but it will require more effort to interpret the photographs.

Even if you have no trouble seeing the stereo image, it isn't a good idea to view stereograms for extended periods of time—especially until you become proficient at lining up the images perfectly. Using the stereoscope may lead to eye fatigue, so start off viewing a stereogram for no longer than about five seconds without looking away for a few seconds to relax your eyes.

Although the stereograms in the Lab Manual have a nominal image separation of 63 mm, in some cases it is impossible to optimize the image separation for all parts of the stereogram. This is especially true in scenes with very high relief. This means that you may not see a clear stereo image over an entire stereogram. Also, some stereograms (including several of the stereograms in the Lab Manual) consist of three photographs instead of two. To view these stereograms, simply match the center photograph with one of the side photographs.

VERTICAL EXAGGERATION

Since the photographs in a stereogram were taken perhaps a kilometer or so apart, when viewed with a stereoscope, the vertical dimension in the landscape is exaggerated. When you view a stereogram, you are viewing the landscape below as if your eyes were separated by a kilometer or so. This **vertical exaggeration** means that slopes will look steeper, mountain peaks will look higher, and depressions will look deeper. Often this vertical exaggeration is helpful to us by accentuating the surface features, but you need to keep in mind that the topography isn't really as steep as it appears.

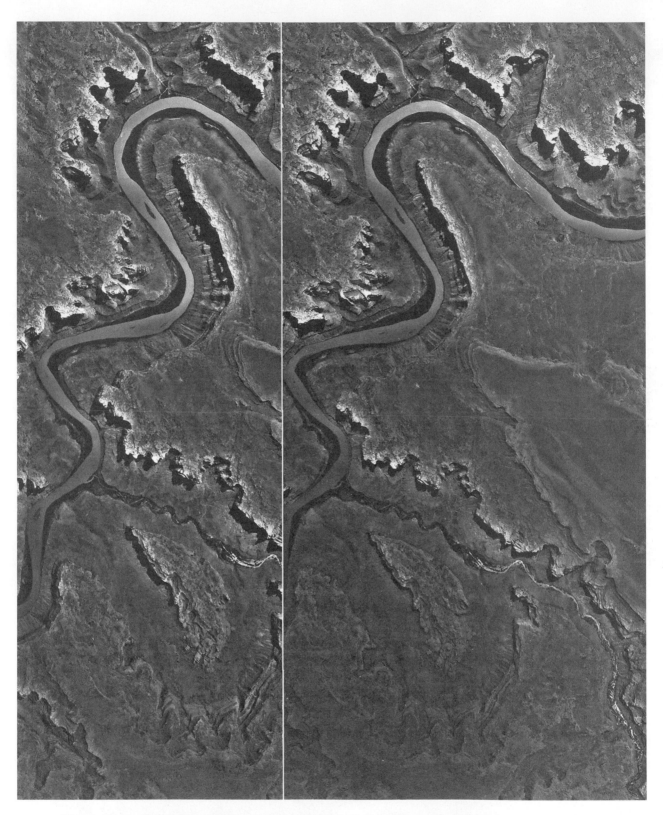

Figure 27-3: Stereogram of the entrenched meanders of the Green River in Utah. North is to the left side of the page (scale 1:40,000; USGS photographs, 1993; ← N).

EXERCISE 27 PROBLEMS

The questions on the following page are based on Figure 27-3, a stereogram showing the entrenched meanders of the Green River in Utah; and Figure 27-4, a topographic map of the same region. A larger portion of this topographic map is reproduced in color as Map T-7 in the back of the Lab Manual.

Figure 27-4: USGS "Canyonlands National Park, Utah," topographic map. North is to the left side of the page (scale 1:62,500; contour interval 80′; ← N).

Begin by looking at the flat-topped, half-circle-shaped hill about 4 centimeters (1.5 inches) from the bottom of the stereogram.

1. When viewed without a stereoscope, the shadow on the left side (the north side) of this hill appears larger in the left image than in the right image. Why?

2. Locate the dry gorge that circles around this half-circle-shaped hill. With the stereoscope, view this dry gorge on the left (north) side of the hill:

    (a) This dry gorge is approximately 2000 feet (about 600 meters) wide. Viewing the stereogram, approximately how deep does the gorge *appear*? (As a starting point for your estimate, consider if the gorge appears deeper than it is wide, wider than it is deep, or equally deep and wide):

    Apparent depth _____ feet

    (b) Use the topographic map on the previous page (Figure 27-4) to determine the *actual* depth of the dry gorge.

    Actual depth _____ feet

    (c) Was your estimate in Problem #2a far off? If so, why?

3. Using the stereogram, describe the location of an apparent overhanging cliff:

4. Locate "Cottonwood Bottom" at the top (east side) of both the topographic map and the stereogram. Describe one kind of detail on the surface of the cliffs that is visible in the stereogram, but not on the topographic map.

EXERCISE 28
PLATE TECTONICS

Objective:	To study the tectonic processes and topographic features associated with plate boundaries and mantle plumes.
Reference:	McKnight and Hess, *Physical Geography*, 9th ed., pp. 415–428.

PLATE TECTONICS

The model of **plate tectonics** is the starting point for understanding the distribution and formation of many collections of landforms around the world. Figure 28-1 is a map showing the principal plates and plate boundaries. These **lithospheric plates** are 65 to 100 kilometers (40 to 60 miles) thick and consist of the crust and upper mantle. The plates move over the layer of the mantle known as the **asthenosphere** at speeds averaging from 2.5 to 10 centimeters (1 to 4 inches) per year.

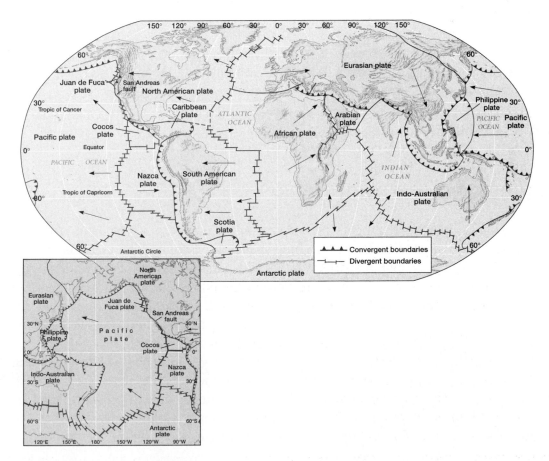

Figure 28-1: Major lithosphere plates. Barbed lines show collision; lines with offsets show spreading; single lines show transform boundaries; arrows indicate generalized direction of plate movement. (From McKnight and Hess, *Physical Geography*, 9th ed.)

PLATE BOUNDARIES

The three different kinds of plate boundaries are associated with different kinds of topographic features and tectonic activity.

Divergent Boundaries: At divergent boundaries (also called "spreading centers"), plates are moving apart. The most common kind of spreading center is the **midocean ridge** where new basaltic ocean floor is created (Figure 28-2). Spreading may also take place within a continent. In this case, blocks of crust may drop down as the land is pulled apart, producing a **continental rift valley**.

Convergent Boundaries: At convergent boundaries, where plates collide, three circumstances are possible:

1. If the edge of an oceanic plate collides with the edge of a continental plate a **subduction** zone is formed. The denser oceanic plate is subducted below the continent, producing a deep **oceanic trench**. As the oceanic lithosphere descends, water and other volatile materials are driven out of the ocean rocks, leading to the partial melting of the mantle. The **magma** that is generated rises, producing intrusions of **plutonic rock** such as granite and a chain of andesitic **volcanoes**, such as the Andes in South America or the Cascades in North America (Figure 28-2).

2. If the edge of an oceanic plate collides with the edge of another oceanic plate, subduction also takes place. A deep oceanic trench forms, along with a chain of andesitic volcanic islands known as an **island arc**, such as the Aleutian Islands in Alaska and the Mariana Islands of the western Pacific Ocean.

3. If the edge of a continent collides with the edge of another continent, the relatively buoyant continental material is not subducted. Instead, a mountain range is uplifted. The Himalayas are a dramatic example of this kind of plate boundary interaction.

Transform Boundaries: Plates slide past each other at transform boundaries, such as along the San Andreas fault system in California (Figure 28-3).

EVIDENCE OF PLATE TECTONICS

Evidence supporting the theory of plate tectonics comes from global patterns of landforms and tectonic activity. In addition to the matching shape of the continental margins on both sides of the Atlantic Ocean (which spread apart from the Mid-Atlantic Ridge), the age of the ocean floor provides evidence of movement. The ocean floors are youngest at midocean ridges, where new lithosphere is being formed, and become progressively older away from a ridge in both directions. This was verified through ocean core samples, as well as **paleomagnetic** evidence (changes in the Earth's magnetic field that have been recorded in the volcanic rocks of the ocean floor).

Plate boundaries are often the sites of significant volcanic activity. At spreading centers, magma is moving up to the surface, creating new lithosphere as the plates spread apart. Magma generated in subduction zones can produce a chain of continental volcanoes or a volcanic island arc.

The distribution of **earthquakes** also provides clues to plate activity. Most earthquakes around the world occur in association with plate boundaries. Shallow-focus earthquakes, within

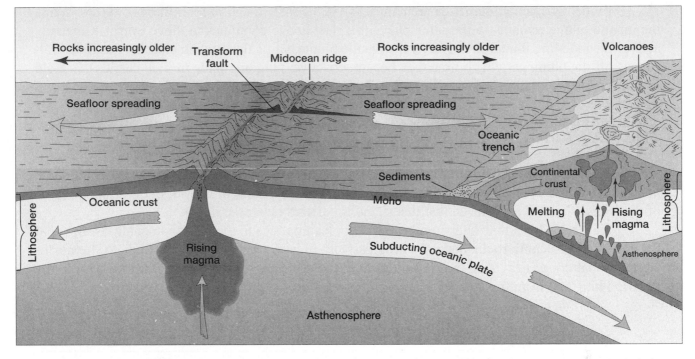

Figure 28-2: Plates move apart at spreading centers such as midocean ridges, collide at convergent boundaries such as subduction zones, and slide past each other along transform faults. (From McKnight and Hess, *Physical Geography*, 9th ed.)

about 70 kilometers (45 miles) of the surface, occur at all plate boundaries. However, in subduction zones, bands of progressively deeper earthquakes are observed, produced when an oceanic plate is thrust down into the asthenosphere.

MANTLE PLUMES

One of the important modifications of basic plate tectonic theory is the concept of the **mantle plume** or **hot spot**. These are locations where a fairly narrow plume of magma is rising from the asthenosphere to the surface, producing volcanoes.

Mantle plumes may occur well away from plate boundaries, often in the middle of a plate. It is not yet completely understood why these hot spots occur where they do, but the existence of mantle plumes has been helpful in verifying plate motion.

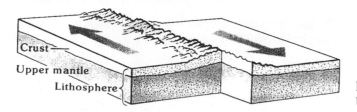

Figure 28-3: Transform plate boundary. (From U.S. Geological Survey Bulletin 1595)

187

Evidently, mantle plumes can remain active in the same location for millions of years. While the mantle plume remains in the same place, the plate above continues to move over it. Currently active volcanoes are found directly over the mantle plume, while the moving plate carries older volcanoes off the plume, at which time they become inactive. Ongoing plate motion carries these old volcanoes farther and farther away from the plume, resulting in a chain of extinct volcanoes.[1]

THE HAWAIIAN HOT SPOT

The Hawaiian Islands are the best-known example of an island chain produced by a mantle plume. The only currently active volcanoes are found on the island of Hawaii in the southeast part of the island chain. It is believed that this island is currently over the hot spot.

Figure 28-4 is a map showing the ages of volcanic rocks in the Hawaiian chain. Notice that the age of the volcanic rocks becomes progressively older as we follow the islands to the northwest. The pattern of islands in the Hawaiian chain shows the general direction of movement of the Pacific Plate, and from the ages of the rocks, we can infer the rate of plate movement.

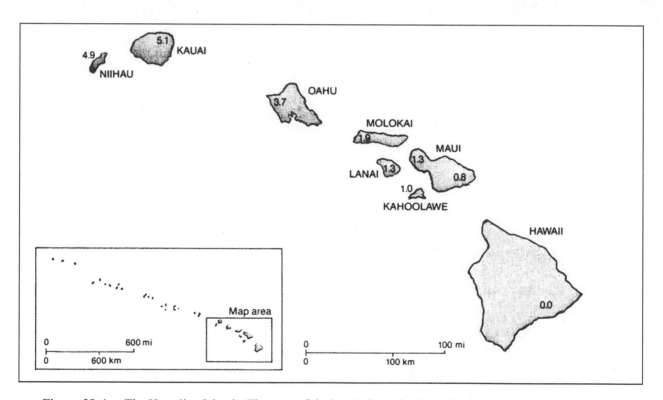

Figure 28-4:   The Hawaiian Islands. The ages of the basalt from the Hawaiian volcanoes are shown in millions of years; map scale 1:4,200,000. (Adapted from McKnight, *Physical Geography*, 4th ed.)

[1]Recent geophysical evidence suggests that the locations of some mantle plumes may slowly change over time, making a complete explanation of some hot spots more complex than geologists once thought.

EXERCISE 28 PROBLEMS – Part I

In the problems for this exercise, you will study the tectonic map of a hypothetical ocean basin (shown on page 191). The map shows the location of volcanoes, earthquakes, and the age of ocean floor rocks. From this map, you will determine the probable location of the plate boundaries and the locations of major topographic features in the region.

On the map, the edges of two continents are shown (in the upper right corner and the lower left corner). Six islands are also shown in the ocean basin.

The symbols used on the tectonic map are described below.

Earthquake Epicenter Location and Depth:

The locations of earthquake **epicenters** are shown with letters. The depth of an earthquake (the distance of the earthquake hypocenter or "focus" below the surface) is indicated with an "S" (shallow focus), "I" (intermediate focus), or "D" (deep focus):

S	=	Shallow Earthquakes	0–70 kilometers (0–45 miles) deep
I	=	Intermediate Earthquakes	70–200 kilometers (45–125 miles) deep
D	=	Deep Earthquakes	200–500 kilometers (125–310 miles) deep

Active Volcano:

Continent or Island:

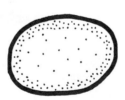

Age of Volcanic Ocean Floor Rocks:

The circled numbers represent the age of volcanic ocean floor rocks in millions of years.

For example, ⃝20 indicates the location of 20 million year old rocks.

EXERCISE PROCEDURE:

The first step of the exercise is to draw in the approximate plate boundaries as indicated by the tectonic activity on the map.

Clues include:

(a)   The pattern of earthquakes. For example, subduction produces a pattern of deeper and deeper earthquakes as one plate plunges below the other.

(b)   The age pattern of volcanic ocean floor rocks suggests the location where new ocean floor is being created at a midocean ridge.

(c)   Volcanic activity may be associated with subduction, spreading centers, or mantle plumes.

Use the following symbols to indicate the extent of all plate boundaries. Both the map symbols, and a side view of the circumstance they represent, are shown below. Arrows indicate direction of plate movement.

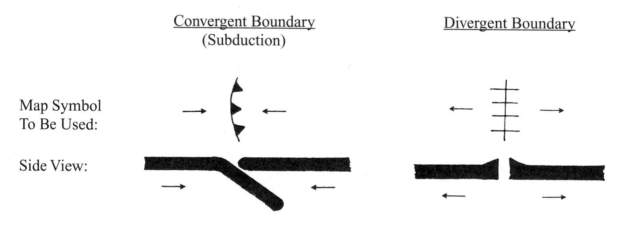

Convergent Boundary
(Subduction)

Divergent Boundary

Map Symbol
To Be Used:

Side View:

Note:

• No transform boundaries are found on the map.

• Assume that only one of the volcanoes on the map has been produced by a mantle plume.

EXERCISE 28 PROBLEMS—PART I

After drawing in the plate boundaries on the tectonic map below, answer the questions on the following page.

TECTONIC MAP OF HYPOTHETICAL OCEAN BASIN

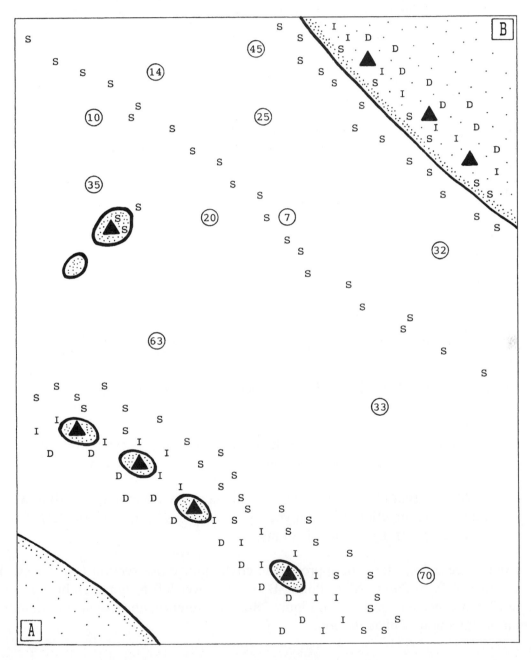

Scale: 1 cm = 300 km (1 inch = 500 miles)

1. (a) How many different *plates* are clearly shown on the map? _____

   (b) How many of the plates on the map consist entirely of ocean floor (or ocean floor with islands)? _____

2. (a) With the number "2" indicate the most likely location on the map of a midocean ridge (such as the Mid-Atlantic Ridge).

   (b) What type of plate boundary is this? _____

   (c) What evidence *shown on the map* suggests that this type of boundary is present?

3. (a) With the number "3" indicate the most likely location on the map of a major volcanic mountain range similar to the Andes in South America.

   (b) What type of plate boundary is this? _____

   (c) What evidence *shown on the map* suggests that this type of boundary is present?

4. (a) With the number "4" indicate the most likely location on the map of a volcanic island arc.

   (b) What type of plate boundary is this? _____

   (c) What evidence *shown on the map* suggests that this type of boundary is present?

5. With the number "5" label all plate boundaries where deep oceanic trenches should be found.

6. (a) Assume that only one of the volcanoes on the map has been produced by a mantle plume (a "hot spot"). With the number "6" label this volcano.

   (b) With a 2-centimeter (about one-inch) long arrow extending from this volcano, indicate the direction in which you would expect to find progressively older *extinct* volcanoes left by the mantle plume.

7. In the space below, draw an approximate continuous cross section ("side view") of the ocean basin from Point "A" to Point "B" (from lower left to upper right). Use the "side view" drawings on page 190 and Figure 28-2 for reference, and use arrows to indicate the relative direction of plate motion.

A
Lower Left

B
Upper Right

EXERCISE 28 PROBLEMS—PART II

Using the map of the Hawaiian Islands and the ages of the basaltic lava (Figure 28-4), compute the approximate rate of movement of the Pacific Plate as it passes over the Hawaiian hot spot.

You will compare the age and distance between several different volcanoes on the islands. The ages of volcanic rocks on the islands are given in millions of years. Assume that the decimal point of an age marks the location of a volcano. For example, on the island of Hawaii, "0.0" marks the location of the currently active volcano, Kilauea.

In this exercise, you will compare Hawaii (0.0 years—currently active volcanoes), Molokai (1.9 million years), Oahu (3.7 million years), and Kauai (5.1 million years). For the purposes of this exercise, we will take the position of the Kilauea volcano to represent the location of the Hawaiian hot spot (keep in mind that this is a simplistic assumption). We also assume that the Hawaiian hot spot is completely stationary over long periods of time.

1.   Complete the chart on the following page:

   (a)   First, determine the distance between each pair of locations listed on the chart. With a ruler, carefully measure the distance between locations on the map to the nearest millimeter if you use S.I. units and to the nearest 1/16 inch if you use English units. (If you use English units, convert fractions of inches to decimals to make other calculations easier.) This figure is the "Measured Distance On Map." Then multiply this measured distance on the map by 4,200,000 (the denominator of the fractional map scale) to determine the "Actual Distance" in millimeters (or inches).

   (b)   Next, determine the "Age Difference" in years between each pair of locations. (Be sure to include the correct number of zeros in your figure.)

   (c)   Finally, divide the "Actual Distance" between locations by the "Age Difference" to estimate the rate of plate movement in millimeters (or inches) per year.

Locations	Measured Distance on Map (in mm or inches)	Actual Distance (in mm or inches)	Age Difference (in years)	Rate of Plate Movement (mm or inches per year)
Kauai to Hawaii				
Oahu to Hawaii				
Molokai to Hawaii				
Kauai to Oahu				
Kauai to Molokai				

2. Based on the average of your five answers in Problem #1 above, what has been the approximate rate of movement of the Pacific Plate in the area of the Hawaiian Islands over the last 5.1 million years?

3. Midway Island, to the northwest of Hawaii, is also part of the Hawaiian chain and is believed to have been produced by the same hot spot. Midway is about 2430 kilometers (1510 miles) from the Kilauea volcano on Hawaii. Use the average rate of plate movement you calculated in Problem #2 above to estimate the age of volcanic rocks you would expect to find on Midway Island.

4. The actual age of the volcanic rock on Midway is about 27.7 million years. Suggest a reason why your answer for Problem #3 above differs noticeably from this.

EXERCISE 29
VOLCANOES

Objective:	To compare different kinds of volcanic mountains.
Materials:	Lens stereoscope.
Resources:	Internet access (optional).
Reference:	McKnight and Hess, *Physical Geography*, 9th ed., pp. 428–437.

TYPES OF LAVA AND STYLES OF ERUPTION

There is a close relationship between the shape of a volcanic mountain, the style of a volcano's eruption, and the mineral composition of the **magma** associated with the volcano. In general, **lava** with relatively little **silica**, such as forms the volcanic rock **basalt**, tends to be quite fluid. (The viscosity of a lava, its mineral composition, and its temperature are all interrelated.) Basaltic lava usually flows from a volcano in quiet, non-explosive eruptions. The Hawaiian volcanoes erupt in this fashion. The term "quiet" is of course relative, and refers to the non-explosive venting of fluid lava.

In contrast, lavas with greater amounts of silica, such as **andesite** (an "intermediate" lava whose plutonic equivalent is diorite), and high silica lavas such as **rhyolite** (whose plutonic equivalent is granite), tend to be more viscous. Unlike the fluid basaltic lavas, gas bubbles can rise only slowly through these viscous lavas. As the magma moves toward the surface during an eruption, the reduction of pressure causes these gas bubbles to expand and escape in an explosive fashion. Explosive eruptions entail the ejection of **pyroclastics**—solid pieces of shattered volcanic rock of various sizes.

TYPES OF VOLCANIC MOUNTAINS

Shield Volcanoes: Quiet, fluid eruptions of basaltic lava tend to produce wide, gently sloping mountains known as **shield volcanoes** (Figure 29-1b). The Hawaiian volcanoes are of this type. Shield volcanoes can be very high, but they are not steep-sided.

Mauna Loa volcano in Hawaii is an exceptionally large shield volcano. Map T-1 is a topographic map showing the southern portion of the island of Hawaii. Mauna Loa has been active many times over the last century, but since the 1950s, Kilauea (seen on the eastern part of the map) has been the most active of the Hawaiian volcanoes.

Composite Volcanoes: Explosive eruptions are common with volcanoes that emit higher silica intermediate lavas, such as andesite. These volcanoes tend to develop into symmetrical, steep-sided mountains known as **composite volcanoes** (also called **stratovolcanoes**). Mount Fuji in Japan and Mount Rainier in Washington are examples of composite volcanoes.

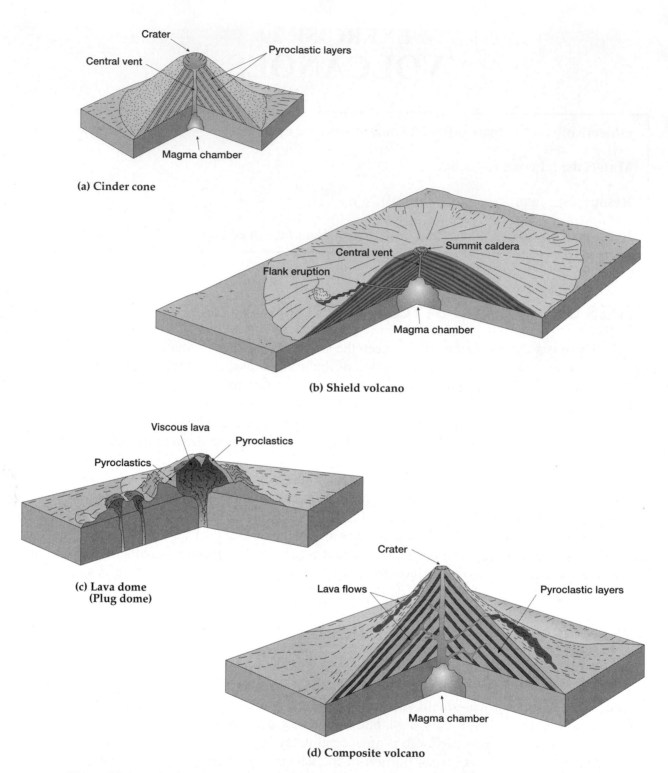

Figure 29-1: The four principal types of volcanic cones. (From McKnight and Hess, *Physical Geography*, 9th ed.)

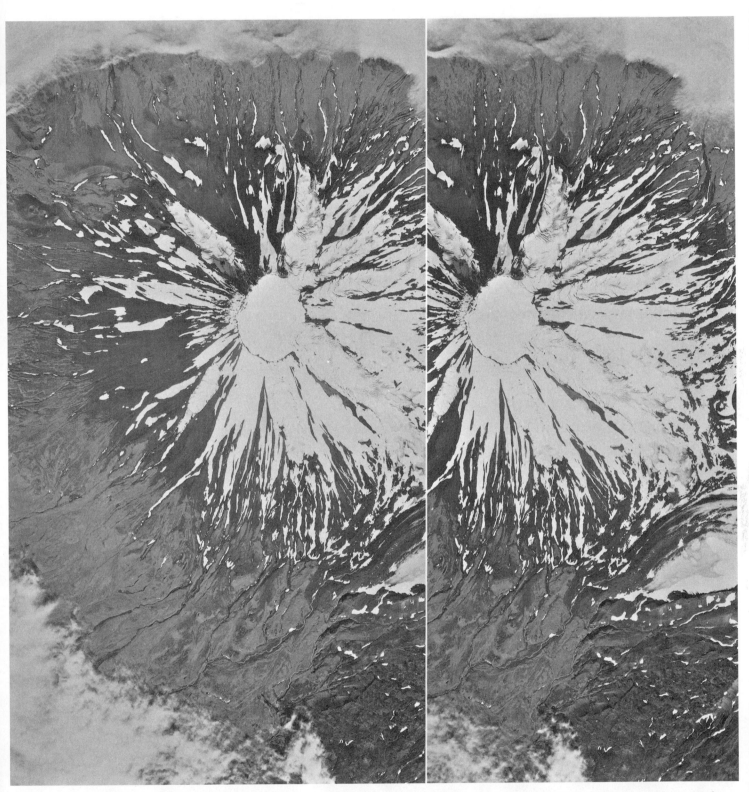

Figure 29-2: Stereogram of Mt. Vsevidof in the Aleutian Islands, Alaska (scale 1:60,000; USGS photographs, 1983; N↗).

Figure 29-3: USGS "Mono Craters, California," quadrangle; north is to left side of page (scale 1:62,500; contour interval 80 feet; ← N).

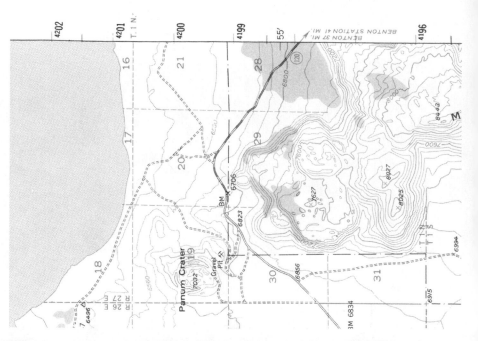

Figure 29-4: Stereogram of Mono Craters, California; north is to left side of page (scale 1:40,000; USGS photographs, 1998; ← N).

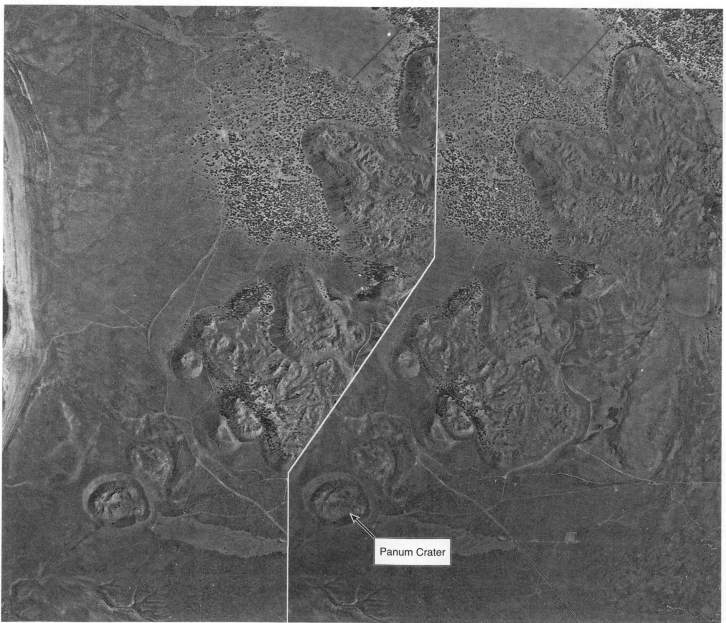

Panum Crater

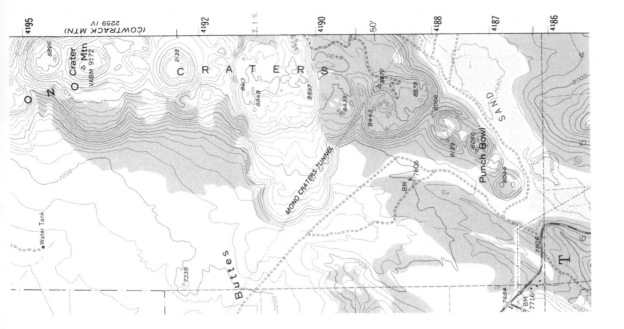

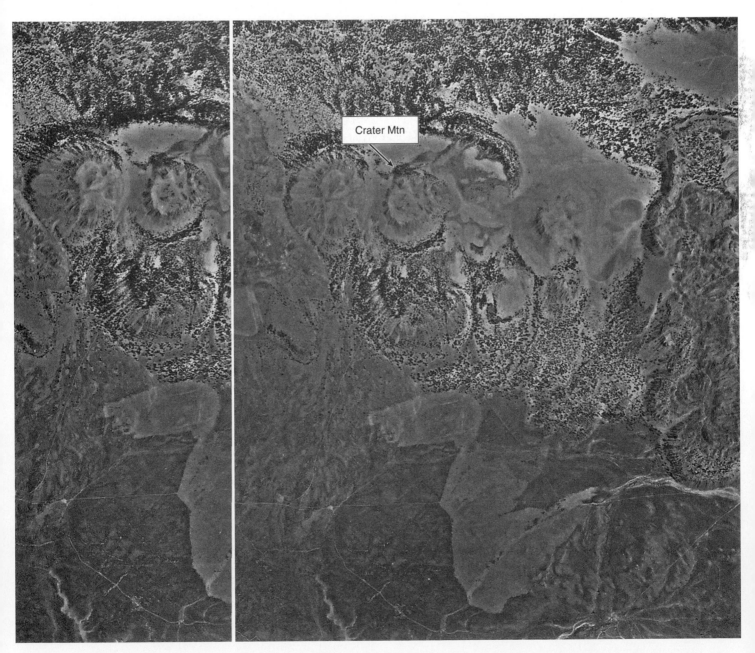

Crater Mtn

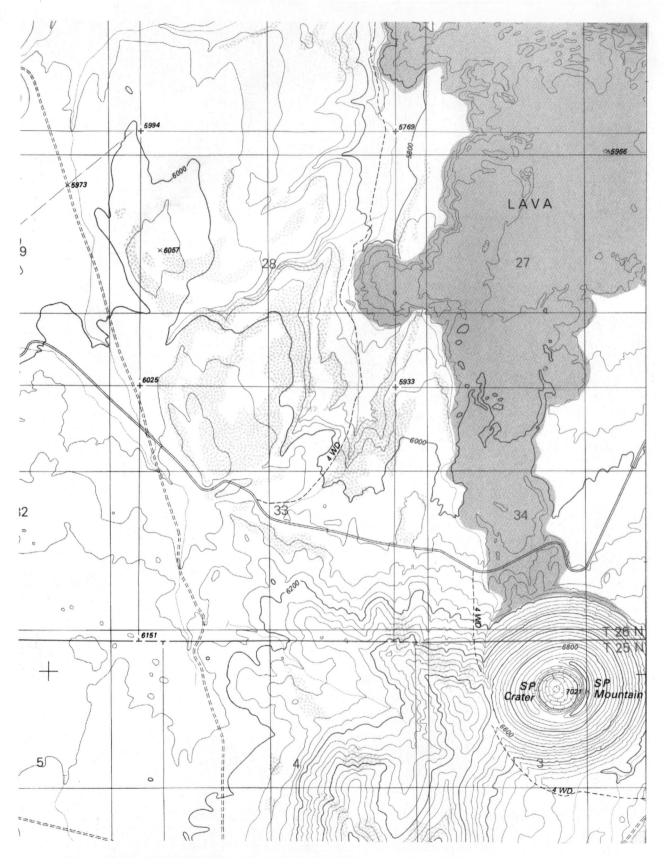

Figure 29-5: USGS "SP Mountain, Arizona," quadrangle (scale 1:24,000; contour interval 40 feet; ↑N).

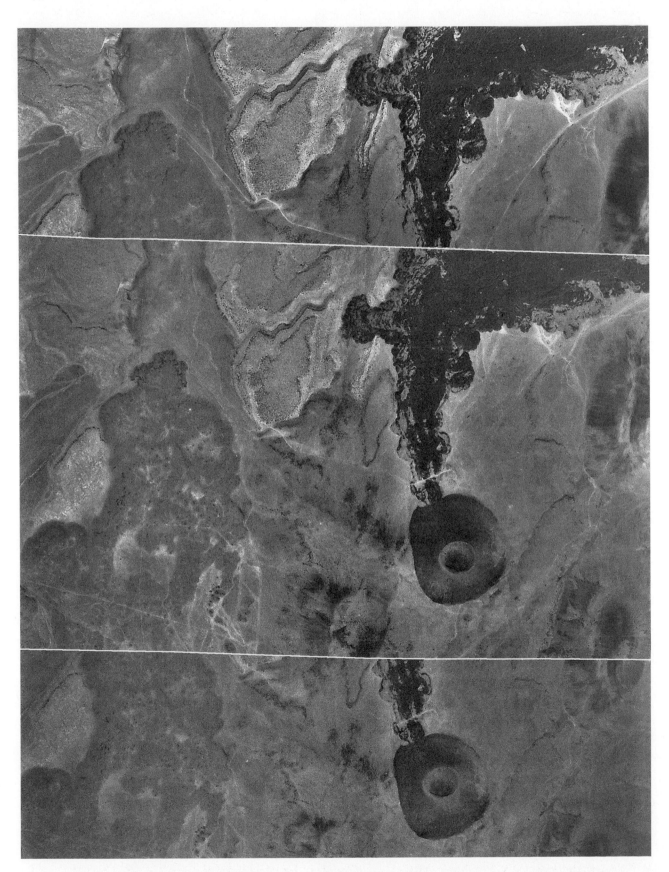

Figure 29-6: Stereogram of SP Mountain, Arizona, (scale 1:40,000; USGS photographs, 1992; ↑N).

These mountains develop steep sides by the buildup of alternating layers of ejected pyroclastic material (ash and cinders) from explosive eruptions, and lava flows from non-explosive eruptions. The explosively erupted ash and cinders tend to produce the steep slopes, while the lava flows tend to hold this loose material together (Figure 29-1d).

Mount Vsevidof in the Aleutian Islands is a typical moderate-sized composite volcano. Map T-2 is a topographic map of Umnak Island, Alaska, showing Mount Vsevidof, along with other volcanic mountains. A stereogram of Mount Vsevidof is shown in Figure 29-2. Mount Vsevidof was most recently active in 1957 with an eruption of ash, and in 1999 with a small steam plume.

Plug Domes: **Lava domes**, or **plug domes**, develop from masses of very viscous lava, such as rhyolite, that are too thick to flow very far. Instead, lava bulges up from the vent, and the dome grows largely by expansion from below and from within (Figure 29-1c). When viscous lava does flow from the vent of a plug dome, it tends to produce a short, steep-sided lava flow called a "coulee."

The Mono Craters are a chain of very young, mostly rhyolitic plug domes south of Mono Lake in California. Figure 29-3 is a topographic map showing the Mono Craters; Figure 29-4 is a matching stereogram of the same area. A flow of rhyolite and rhyolitic obsidian is shown on the map below the words "Mono Craters Tunnel."

Cinder Cones: **Cinder cones** are the smallest kind of volcanic mountain. They are cone-shaped peaks that build up from pyroclastics ejected into the air from a small volcanic vent (Figure 29-1a). The steepness of the slope of a cinder cone is generally related to the size of the particles being ejected. Volcanic ash (particles less than 2 mm in diameter) can produce slopes as steep as 35 degrees, while the larger cinders (particles between 2 mm and 64 mm in diameter) will produce slopes up to about 25 degrees. Cinder cones are generally less than 500 meters (1600 feet) high, and are often found in association with other volcanoes. Occasionally lava flows issue from the same vent that produces a cinder cone.

SP Mountain in Arizona is a young cinder cone in a volcanic field at the southern margin of the Colorado Plateau (Figure 29-5). A lava flow of basaltic andesite (the dark region on the map labeled "lava") flowed north from the cinder cone vent. Note that the scale of this map is 1:24,000. Figure 29-6 is a stereogram of the same region.

GRADIENT

A simple way to compare the steepness of slopes is to use the **gradient**. If working with English units of measure, the gradient is usually stated in feet of elevation change per mile. For example, if a mountain increases elevation by 3200 feet over a distance of 2.5 miles, the gradient is:

$$\text{Gradient} = \frac{\text{Elevation Change}}{\text{Number of Miles}} = \frac{3200 \text{ ft}}{2.5 \text{ miles}} = 1280 \text{ ft/mi}$$

When calculating slope gradients from topographic maps, it may be easiest to use the graphic map scale to measure out a set distance on the map (for example, 2 miles), and then determine the elevation change over that distance.

EXERCISE 29 PROBLEMS—PART I

In the following problems you will compute the gradients of Mauna Loa in Hawaii, Mount Vsevidof in Alaska, and SP Mountain in Arizona.

1. Using Map T-1, the "Hawaii, Hawaii," topographic map (scale 1:250,000; contour interval 200 feet), calculate the gradient of Mauna Loa along line AB, from the 5000' contour (near Point A) toward the summit. Measure out a distance of 10 miles using the graphic map scale inside the front cover of the Lab Manual, and then determine the elevation change over that distance.

$$\underset{\text{(Elevation Change)}}{\underline{\hspace{3cm}}} \text{feet} \div \underset{\text{(Number of Miles)}}{\frac{10 \text{ miles}}{}} = \underset{\text{(Gradient)}}{\underline{\hspace{2cm}}} \text{feet/mile}$$

2. Using Map T-2, the "Umnak, Alaska," topographic map (scale 1:250,000; contour interval 200 feet), calculate the gradient of Mount Vsevidof along line CD, from the 1000' contour (near Point C) toward the summit. Measure out a distance of 2 miles using the graphic map scale inside the front cover of the Lab Manual, and then determine the elevation change over that distance.

$$\underset{\text{(Elevation Change)}}{\underline{\hspace{3cm}}} \text{feet} \div \underset{\text{(Number of Miles)}}{\frac{2 \text{ miles}}{}} = \underset{\text{(Gradient)}}{\underline{\hspace{2cm}}} \text{feet/mile}$$

3. Using Figure 29-5, the "SP Mountain, Arizona," quadrangle (scale 1:24,000; contour interval 40 feet), calculate the gradient of SP Mountain from the north base of the cone (at the 6200' contour) toward the crater rim. Measure out a distance of 0.2 miles using the graphic map scale inside the front cover of the Lab Manual, and then determine the elevation change over that distance.

$$\underset{\text{(Elevation Change)}}{\underline{\hspace{3cm}}} \text{feet} \div \underset{\text{(Number of Miles)}}{\frac{0.2 \text{ miles}}{}} = \underset{\text{(Gradient)}}{\underline{\hspace{2cm}}} \text{feet/mile}$$

4. (a)   Which of the three volcanoes has the steepest slope?   _____

    (b)   Which of the three volcanoes has the most gentle slope?   _____

EXERCISE 29 PROBLEMS—PART II

The following problems are based on Map T-1 and Map T-2. Both of these maps have a scale of 1:250,000. Using the graph at the right, construct topographic profiles between the appropriate lettered points. Vertical exaggeration of topographic profiles is approximately 2× (see explanation of vertical exaggeration in Exercise 25).

1. Construct a topographic profile of the Mauna Loa volcano in Hawaii (Map T-1) from Point A to Point B. Except for the area around the summit, you only need to plot index contours.

2. Construct a topographic profile of Mount Vsevidof (Map T-2) from Point C to Point D. Except for the area around the summit and around the base, you only need to plot index contours.

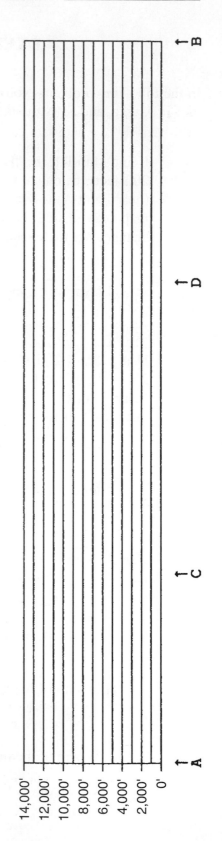

Name _____   Section _____

EXERCISE 29 PROBLEMS—PART III

The following questions are based on the portion of the "Mono Craters, California," quadrangle (scale 1:62,500; contour interval 80 feet) reproduced in Figure 29-3 and the stereogram of the same region shown in Figure 29-4. Note that north is toward the left side of the page. "Crater Mountain" is the highest peak in this chain of rhyolitic plug domes.

1. It is difficult to determine the exact number of plug domes shown on the map since they are irregular in shape and very close together. Look for roughly circular, steep-walled peaks. Some will have craters at the summit, while others will have nearly flat summits. Estimate the number of plug domes in the Mono Craters chain north (to the left) of the "Punch Bowl": _____

2. Contrast the general shape of Crater Mountain with that of Mount Vsevidof shown in Map T-2 and Figure 29-2. Especially note any differences in the summit areas of the volcanoes (symmetrical vs. irregular; summit crater vs. no summit crater; etc.):

3. Locate the rhyolite flow (below the words "Mono Craters Tunnel") in the southern part of the map. Approximately how thick is this flow under the word "Craters" in the label "Mono Craters Tunnel"? _____ feet

EXERCISE 29 PROBLEMS—PART IV

The following questions are based on Figure 29-5, a section of the "SP Mountain, Arizona," quadrangle (scale 1:24,000; contour interval 40 feet), and the stereogram of SP Mountain (Figure 29-6).

1. (a) Which occurred first, the large lava flow to the north of the cone, or the final formation of the SP Mountain cinder cone itself? _____

    (b) How do you know?

2. Approximately how thick is the lava flow west (to the left) of the word "lava" on the map? _____ feet

3. (a) The western base of SP Mountain touches another cinder cone. Is SP Mountain more likely to be younger or older than this other cone? _____

    (b) How can you tell?

EXERCISE 29 PROBLEMS—PART V—INTERNET

The following questions are based on Figures 29-7, 29-8, 29-9, and 29-10, photographs you can view on the Lab Manual Web site. Go to the McKnight and Hess textbook Web site *<http://www.prenhall.com/mcknight>*. Select "Lab Manual," then "Exercise 29."

1.　(a) Which of the four photographs shows a composite volcano?　　Figure 29-_____

　　(b) Describe the evidence you see in the photograph that supports your answer:

2.　(a) Which of the four photographs shows a shield volcano?　　Figure 29-_____

　　(b) Describe the evidence you see in the photograph that supports your answer:

3.　(a) Which of the four photographs shows a plug dome volcano?　　Figure 29-_____

　　(b) Describe the evidence you see in the photograph that supports your answer:

4.　(a) Which of the four photographs shows a cinder cone?　　Figure 29-_____

　　(b) Describe the evidence you see in the photograph that supports your answer:

EXERCISE 30
VOLCANIC CALDERAS

Objective:	To study the features of volcanic calderas.
Materials:	Lens stereoscope.
Reference:	McKnight and Hess, *Physical Geography*, 9th ed., pp. 437–439.

CALDERAS

While craters are found at the summit of many volcanoes, some composite and shield volcanoes have developed much larger depressions known as **calderas**. A caldera is a large, generally circular, basin-shaped depression that can be several kilometers across. Calderas form when the upper part of a volcano collapses, often catastrophically, during or following an eruption.

During a major eruption, the magma chamber below a volcano may be emptied, or nearly emptied, leaving an open cavity under the volcano. The volcano may then be unable to support its own weight, and so will collapse in on itself, leaving a wide, steep-walled caldera (Figure 30-1). After the formation of the caldera, volcanic activity may continue. It is common to see a series of small volcanic cones develop in and around a caldera.

The most famous caldera in North America is Crater Lake in Oregon. This caldera formed about 7700 years ago when one of the Cascade volcanoes (known as "Mount Mazama") collapsed. The caldera is now filled with water, forming a deep lake (Figure 30-2).

Although calderas may develop following major explosive eruptions of **composite volcanoes**, large **shield volcanoes** may develop calderas at their summits in a slightly different manner. Both Mauna Loa and Kilauea (Map T-1) have well-developed "summit" calderas. Calderas such as these develop when fluid lava is vented from rift zones along the flanks of the volcano. As the magma chamber empties, the summit area collapses and a caldera is formed.

OKMOK CALDERA

Okmok Caldera, on Umnak Island in the Aleutian Islands (Map T-2), formed from the catastrophic collapse of a large volcano. Figure 30-3 is a stereogram of the Okmok Caldera. The composition of Okmok varies, but is mostly basaltic. Although the structure is that of a collapsed shield volcano, there are interbedded layers of pyroclastic deposits as well.

The geologic history of the Okmok Caldera is complex, but evidently involved two caldera-forming eruptions. The first event, about 8250 years ago, formed the outer rim visible on the map, and deposited pyroclastic debris widely throughout the region. The second caldera-forming eruption occurred about 2400 years ago, and entailed the subsequent collapse of younger lava flows within the old caldera walls. The last significant activity in Okmok took place in 1997 when a lava flow was vented onto the caldera floor. An earthquake swarm was reported in 2001, and steam was rising from a small cone on the floor of the caldera in 2002.

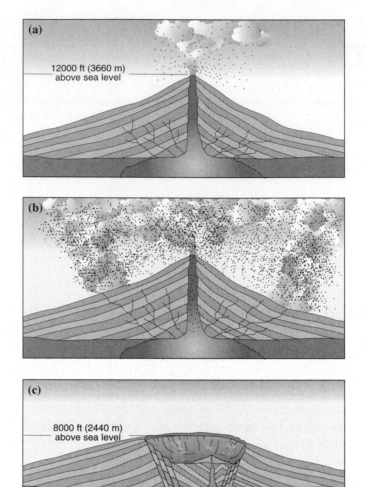

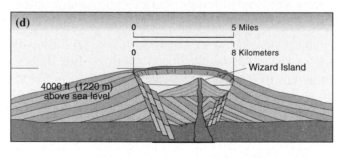

Figure 30-1: The formation of a caldera, based on Oregon's Crater Lake. (From McKnight and Hess, *Physical Geography*, 9th ed.)

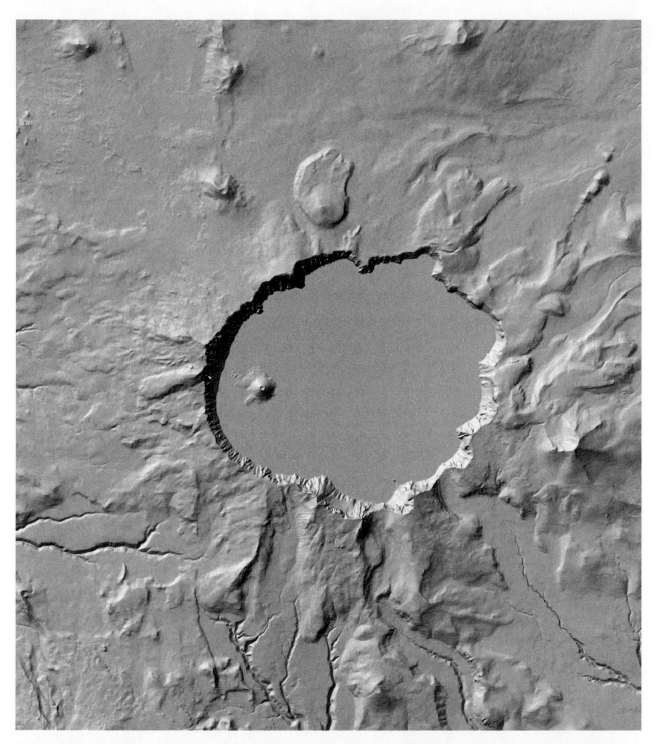

Figure 30-2: Digital shaded relief map of Crater Lake, Oregon. Wizard Island, on the western side of the lake, formed after the initial collapse of the caldera. (From U.S. Geological Survey; scale approximately 1:300,000; ↑N)

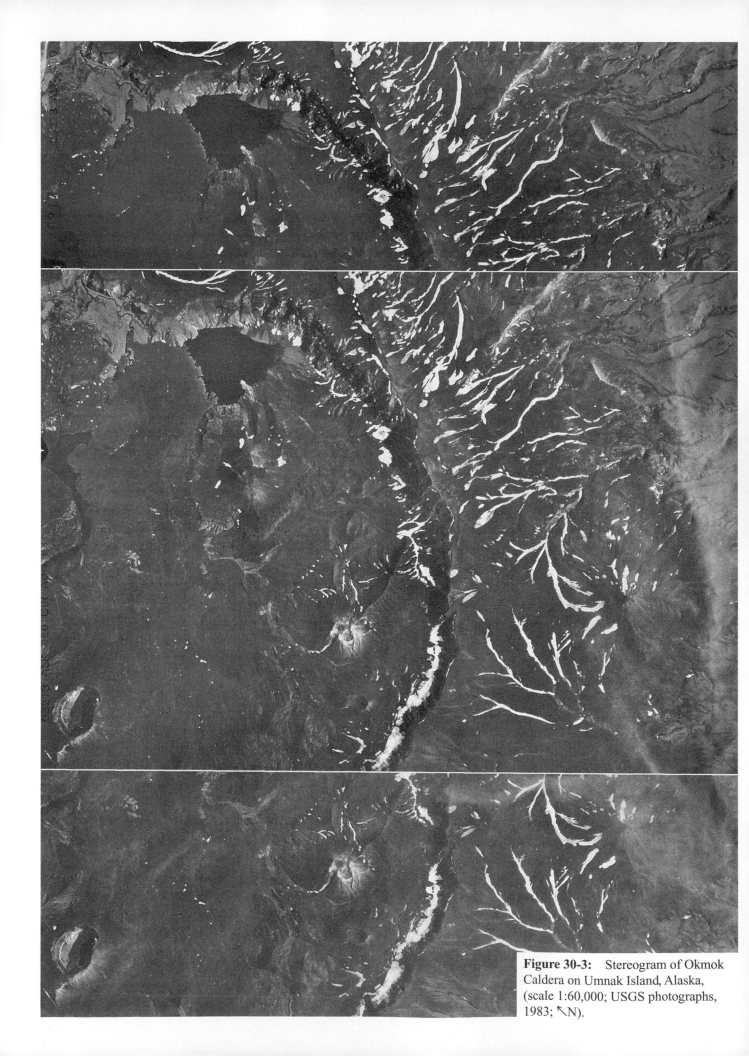

Figure 30-3: Stereogram of Okmok Caldera on Umnak Island, Alaska, (scale 1:60,000; USGS photographs, 1983; ↖N).

EXERCISE 30 PROBLEMS—PART I

The following questions are based on Map T-2, the "Umnak, Alaska," topographic map (scale 1:250,000; contour interval 200 feet), and Figure 30-3, a stereogram showing the Okmok Caldera on Umnak Island in the Aleutian Islands.

1. What is the approximate diameter of the rim of the Okmok Caldera?   _____ miles

2. What is the approximate depth of the caldera (from the rim
    down to the floor)?   _____ feet

3. A caldera similar to this one filled with water to become Crater Lake in Oregon (see Figure 30-2). Why isn't the Okmok Caldera presently filled with water?

4. What evidence from the map and stereogram suggests that further volcanic activity took place inside the caldera after the final collapse of the volcano? Be as specific as you can.

EXERCISE 30 PROBLEMS—PART II

The following questions are based on Map T-1, the "Hawaii, Hawaii," topographic map (scale 1:250,000; contour interval 200 feet).

1. Describe the dimensions of the following summit calderas:

Caldera (Volcano)	Width (miles)	Depth (feet)
Mokuaweoweo (Mauna Loa)		
Kilauea Crater (Kilauea)		

2. What is the apparent relationship between "Lua Hou" (a small depression near the summit of Mauna Loa) and the "Southwest Rift Zone"?

EXERCISE 30 PROBLEMS—PART III

The following questions are based on Map T-2, the "Umnak, Alaska," topographic map (scale 1:250,000; contour interval 200 feet). In this problem, you will estimate the height of the original Okmok volcano before the caldera was formed.

Gradients can be used to estimate an elevation increase over a given distance. (See Exercise 29 for a review of gradients.) For example, if a mountain has a gradient of 1000 feet per mile, we can estimate that over a horizontal distance of five miles, the elevation will increase by 5000 feet:

$$5 \text{ miles} \times 1000 \text{ ft/mi} = 5000 \text{ foot elevation increase over five miles}$$

1. Compute the gradient of the outer base of the Okmok Caldera along line EF. Use the coastline closest to Point E as the starting point for measuring horizontal distance, and the northwest rim of the caldera as the stopping point. It may be easiest to use the graphic map scale inside the front cover of the Lab Manual to measure out a distance of four or five miles, and then determine the elevation change over that distance.

    _____ feet ÷ _____ miles = _____ feet/mile
    Elevation Change   Number of Miles   Gradient

2. Estimate the height of the original volcano. Assume that the present gradient of the Okmok Caldera (calculated in Problem #1 above) is the same as that of the volcano before it collapsed. Given the complex history of the Okmok Caldera, this is a very simplistic assumption, but it can be used to provide a crude estimate of the volcano's previous height.

    (a) Following line EF, what is the horizontal distance from
         the coastline (closest to Point E) to the center of the caldera?   _____ miles

    (b) Multiply the horizontal distance (#2a above) by the
         gradient of the present caldera (#1 above). This is an
         estimate of the original elevation of the volcano
         before its collapse: _____ feet

    (c) Approximately how much higher was the original
         volcano than the present caldera rim?   _____ feet

EXERCISE 31
FAULTING

Objective:	To review the different kinds of faults, and to study a faulted landscape with a topographic map and a stereogram.
Materials:	Lens stereoscope.
Reference:	McKnight and Hess, *Physical Geography*, 9th ed., pp. 447–450.

TYPES OF FAULTS

Faulting occurs when stresses forcibly break apart and displace a rock structure. The displacement along a fault can be horizontal, vertical, or a combination of the two. Although there are many different kinds of faults, they all can be placed into four general categories.

Normal Faults: As shown in Figure 31-1, along a **normal fault** the movement is primarily vertical, exposing a steep fault plane. Normal faulting is the result of extension ("tension")—stresses working to stretch or pull apart the landscape (direction of stress shown with arrows).

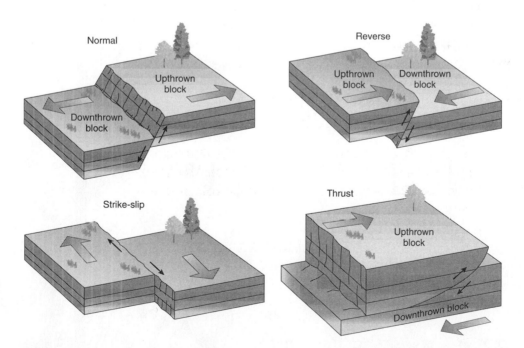

Figure 31-1: The principal types of faults. The large arrows show the direction of stress; the small arrows show the relative direction of displacement along the fault plane. (From McKnight and Hess, *Physical Geography*, 9th ed.)

213

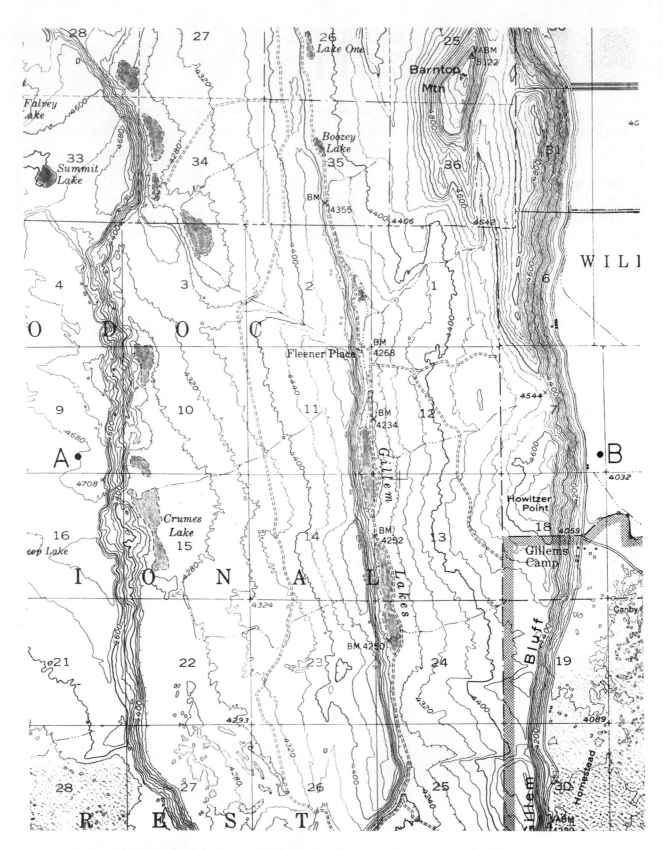

Figure 31-2: USGS "Mt. Dome, California," quadrangle (enlarged to scale 1:48,000; contour interval 40 feet; ↑N).

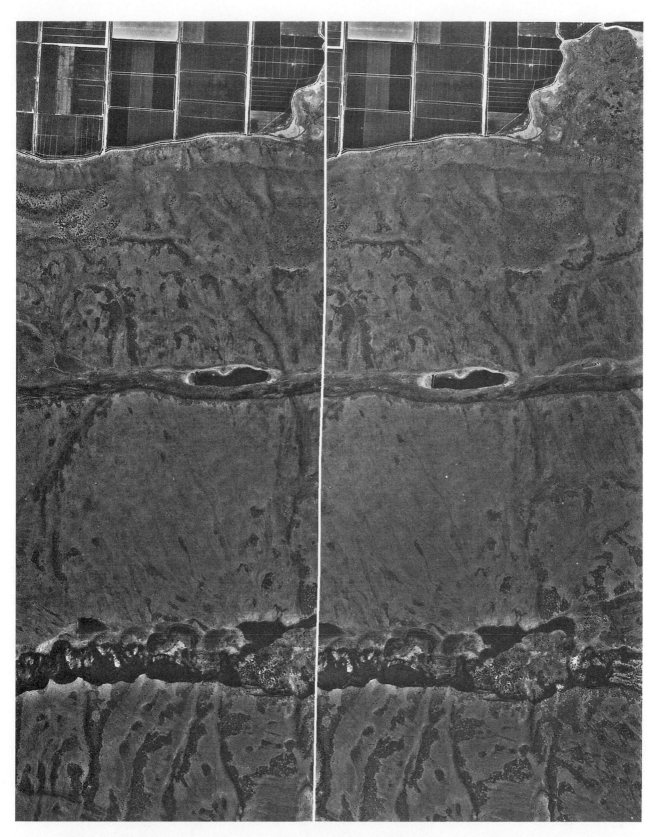

Figure 31-3: Stereogram of fault scarps near Mt. Dome, California. North is to left side of page (scale 1:40,000; USGS photographs, 1993; ← N).

Reverse and Thrust Faults: Movement along **reverse faults** (Figure 31-1) is also mainly vertical, but in this case compressional stresses have produced the fault displacement. **Thrust** (or "overthrust") faults also result from compression, but the upthrown block overrides the downthrown block at a low angle.

Strike-Slip Faults: The movement along a **strike-slip fault** (Figure 31-1) is primarily horizontal and is produced by shear stresses. Strike-slip faults are discussed in more detail in Exercise 32.

LANDFORMS PRODUCED BY FAULTING

There are many conspicuous landforms associated with faulting. For example, predominantly normal faulting throughout much of the Basin and Range province of the western United States has produced a series of fault-block mountains and down-dropped basins. Figures 31-2 and 31-3 show a faulted landscape in the Basin and Range province in northeastern California.

Tilted fault block mountains such as the Sierra Nevada (Figure 31-4) are produced by fault displacement along one side. When a block of land has been uplifted between two roughly parallel faults, a **horst** is formed (Figure 31-5). A down-dropped basin between two parallel faults is known as a **graben**.

Figure 31-4:   The Sierra Nevada is a tilted fault block mountain range. (From McKnight and Hess, *Physical Geography*, 9th ed.)

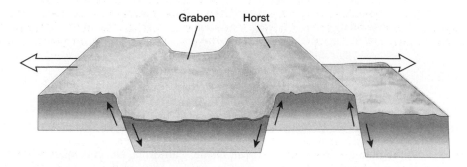

Figure 31-5:   Horst and graben. (From McKnight and Hess, *Physical Geography*, 9th ed.)

216

EXERCISE 31 PROBLEMS—PART I

The following question is based on the "Mt. Dome, California," quadrangle (Figure 31-2; enlarged to scale 1:48,000; contour interval 40 feet). Three prominent fault scarps can be seen running north to south across the map, and will be referred to as the "western" fault, the "central" fault, and the "eastern" fault. These faults scarps are the result of normal faulting. Figure 31-3 is a stereogram of the same region (in Figure 31-3, north is to the left side of the page).

Using the graph below, construct a topographic profile from Point "A" to Point "B." Plot the index contours, as well as the crest and bottom of the fault scarps. The vertical exaggeration of the profile is approximately 6.7×.

> Hint: Since the contour lines are very close together, it may be difficult to discern the elevation of the top and bottom of a scarp. To determine these elevations, find an index contour in the gently sloping area between two scarps, and then count the number of contour lines to the top or bottom of a scarp.

EXERCISE 31 PROBLEMS—PART II

The following questions are based on the "Mt. Dome, California," quadrangle (Figure 31-2; enlarged to scale 1:48,000; contour interval 40 feet) and the stereogram of the same region (Figure 31-3; north is to the left side of the page). Three prominent fault scarps can be seen running north to south across the map, and will be referred to as the "western" fault, the "central" fault, and the "eastern" fault. These fault scarps are the result of normal faulting.

1. Determine the approximate amount of vertical displacement along each of the three fault scarps at their intersection with line AB (when determining the amount of displacement, it may be easiest to count the number of contour lines shown on each scarp to determine the elevation change):

    (a) Western Fault: _____ feet

    (b) Central Fault: _____ feet

    (c) Eastern Fault: _____ feet

2. (a) Is the amount of vertical displacement along the "central fault" uniform from north to south?   _____

    (b) If not, describe the pattern of vertical displacement:

3. Explain the location and formation of "Crumes Lake" and the "Gillem Lakes."

EXERCISE 32
THE SAN ANDREAS FAULT

Objective:	To study features produced by strike-slip faults, and to examine the displacement of a stream by the San Andreas fault.
Materials:	Lens stereoscope.
Reference:	McKnight and Hess, *Physical Geography*, 9th ed., pp. 422–424 and 450.

STRIKE-SLIP FAULTS

In contrast to normal and reverse faults in which the dominant movement along the fault plane is vertical, displacement along **strike-slip faults** is predominantly lateral. Figure 32-1 is a block diagram showing the buildup of stress along a strike-slip fault, and finally the rupture and displacement along the fault. The fault shown in the diagram below is known as a "right-lateral" strike-slip fault. This means that the displacement, looking across the fault, is to the right. In other words, relative to our position on one side of the fault, things on the other side of the fault appear to have been offset to the right.

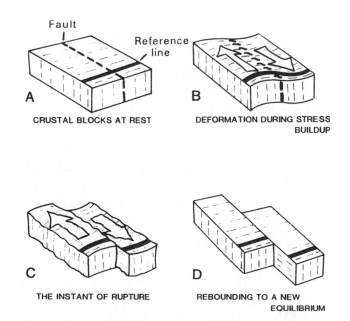

Figure 32-1: Movement along a strike-slip fault. (From U.S. Geological Survey Circular 1045)

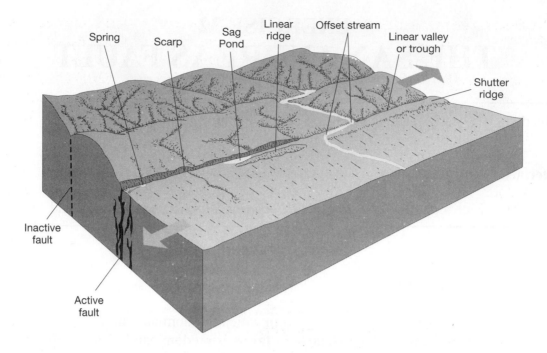

Figure 32-2: Common landforms produced by strike-slip faults. Diagram shows right-lateral offset (fault displacement shown with large arrows). (From McKnight and Hess, *Physical Geography*, 9th ed.; after U. S. Geological Survey Map I-575)

LANDFORMS PRODUCED BY STRIKE-SLIP FAULTS

Strike-slip faults can produce a wide variety of landforms (Figure 32-2). The trace of a large strike-slip fault may be expressed by a narrow **linear fault trough** or valley that can extend for many kilometers. Repeated movement along the fault crushes the rock in the fault zone, and this rock is more easily eroded, leaving a linear trough. Small depressions caused by the settling of small blocks with the fault zone also often develop and become filled with water to form **sag ponds**.

Linear features can develop along the trace of a strike-slip fault in a number of ways. Slight compressional stresses can squeeze up small linear ridges, parallel to the trace of the fault. In addition to the dominant lateral movement, many strike-slip faults also exhibit a limited amount of vertical movement ("dip-slip") that can produce **scarps** along the trace of the fault.

One of the most conspicuous landforms produced by a strike-slip fault is an **offset stream** or offset drainage channel. Through repeated fault movement, streams flowing across a fault gradually have their courses displaced.

THE SAN ANDREAS FAULT

The San Andreas fault is perhaps the most prominent strike-slip fault in the world. This right-lateral strike-slip fault extends for approximately 1300 kilometers (800 miles) from the Gulf of California, north in the Coast Ranges of California, and then finally out to sea.

220

Although commonly called the "plate boundary" between the North American Plate and the Pacific Plate, this is somewhat simplistic. The San Andreas fault system is the most important and most obvious component of this plate boundary, but it is likely that stresses associated with this boundary have resulted in more widespread faulting—possibly including faulting within the Basin and Range province of western North America (Figure 32-3). Perhaps only 60 percent of the approximately 5.6 centimeters (2.2 inches) per year of relative motion between the Pacific and North American Plates is released along the San Andreas fault itself.

The San Andreas fault is not a simple break. In places it has broken into strands, producing a fault zone several hundred meters wide. In addition, the fault system includes dozens of other mostly parallel right-lateral strike-slip faults, such as the Hayward and Calaveras faults in the San Francisco Bay Area, and the San Jacinto and Elsinore faults in southern California.

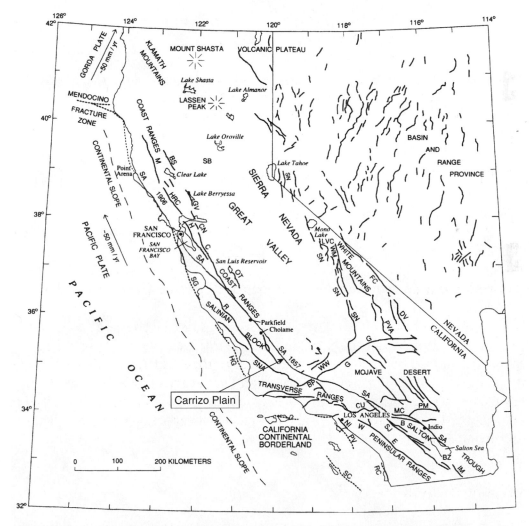

Figure 32-3: The San Andreas and other faults in California and Nevada. Labeled faults include C—Calaveras; E—Elsinore; H—Hayward; SA—San Andreas; SJ—San Jacinto. (From U.S. Geological Survey Professional Paper 1515)

THE SAN ANDREAS FAULT IN THE CARRIZO PLAIN

Figure 32-5 (on page 224) shows a portion of the "McKittrick Summit, California," quadrangle. A portion of this area is also shown in the stereogram in Figure 32-4. This quadrangle is located in the southern Coast Ranges of California, where the Temblor Range (northeast portion of map and stereogram) runs along the arid Carrizo Plain (southwest portion of map and stereogram). The San Andreas fault runs diagonally through this area, from the upper left corner to the lower right corner (approximately between the two arrows on the map). Ephemeral streams are shown as dashed and dotted lines on the map.

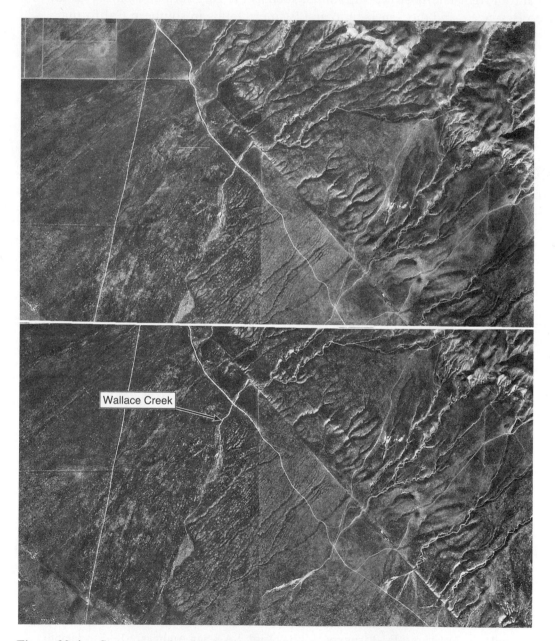

Figure 32-4: Stereogram showing San Andreas fault in the Carrizo Plain, California, (scale 1:40,000; USGS photographs, 1989; ↑N).

222

EXERCISE 32 PROBLEMS—PART I

The following questions are based on Figure 32-4, a stereogram of the San Andreas fault in the Carrizo Plain, and Figure 32-5, a portion of the "McKittrick Summit, California," quadrangle reproduced on the next page. The stereogram shows the area in the southern half of the topographic map.

1. One offset stream (known as "Wallace Creek") has been labeled for you on the map. On the map, use an arrow labeled "1" to identify another stream that has been offset by displacement along the fault. The contour pattern of dry gullies may also provide you with clues.

    Note: Several streams have had their courses deflected to the *left* rather than to the right. This can happen, for example, when a small **shutter ridge** is carried along one side of the fault, blocking a stream's course and causing it to flow along the trace of the fault (in this case, to the southeast) until it finds an outlet.

2. On the map, use an arrow labeled "2" to identify a small linear ridge running parallel to the trace of the fault. (Hint: look for tiny closed contour lines along the fault trace.) The stereogram may also be helpful in identifying ridges and scarps.

3. On the map, use an arrow labeled "3" to identify a sag or sag pond. The stereogram may be helpful in identifying sags and dry sag ponds.

4. What stream features, seen in the stereogram but not on the map, indicate the position of the fault? (Hint: look for small stream gullies that flow down toward the fault.)

5. Based on the topographic clues you have identified above, as well as the stereogram of the same region, use a colored pencil to sketch in the position of the San Andreas fault on the map.

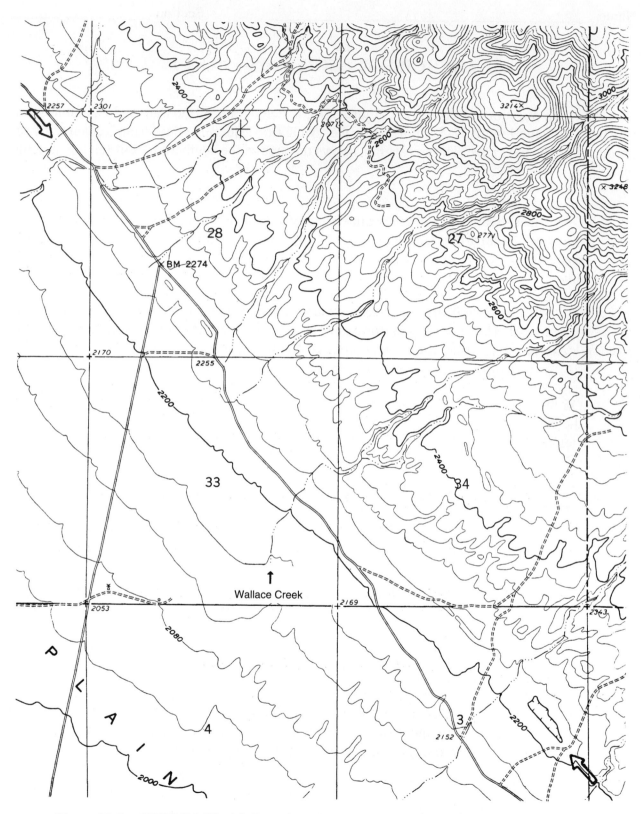

Figure 32-5: USGS "McKittrick Summit, California," quadrangle (scale 1:24,000; contour interval 40 feet; ↑N).

224

EXERCISE 32 PROBLEMS—PART II

The following questions are based on Figure 32-4, a stereogram of the San Andreas fault in the Carrizo Plain, and Figure 32-5, a portion of the "McKittrick Summit, California," quadrangle. "Wallace Creek" is an offset stream that has been labeled for you on Figure 32-5.

Most of the movement between the Pacific Plate side and the North American Plate side of the San Andreas fault is released abruptly after years of accumulating strain—at which time the fault ruptures with a displacement of several meters.

Further, it appears that different segments of the fault remain locked for different periods of time. In a general way, the size of an earthquake expected to occur along a segment of the fault system relates to the length of time the fault accumulates strain before rupturing. The longer the strain accumulates, the larger the earthquake when the fault finally ruptures.

1. Wallace Creek has been offset by 130.0 meters (430 feet) to the right along the fault. The age of stream deposits indicates that this offset began 3700 years ago. Based on these figures, calculate the average rate of movement along this segment of the fault in centimeters per year (or inches per year). Keep in mind that your answer is an estimate of the long-term average, *not* the expected movement *each* year:

    (a)   Total offset in centimeters (or inches): _____ centimeters (or inches)

    (b)   Average offset per year: _____ centimeters per year (or in./yr.)

2. The great Fort Tejon earthquake of January 9, 1857 (magnitude 7.8), ruptured a 360 kilometer (220 mile) segment of the San Andreas fault and produced 10.0 meters (33 feet) of offset in this area. Based on the average rate of fault movement calculated in Problem #1b above, estimate how many years of accumulated strain were released during that earthquake. (Note: this answer is based on a very simplistic assumption.)

                                                    _____ years of accumulated strain

3.   Assuming that this segment of the San Andreas fault ruptures at fairly regular intervals, and paleoseismic studies suggest that this may be true, estimate the year when the next great earthquake might occur along this section of the fault. (Note: this answer is also based on a very simplistic assumption.)

Approximate year of next great earthquake: _____

EXERCISE 33
MASS WASTING

Objective:	To study landform features produced by mass wasting.
Materials:	Lens stereoscope.
Resources:	Internet access (optional).
Reference:	McKnight and Hess, *Physical Geography*, 9th ed., pp. 469–478.

MASS WASTING

Mass wasting involves the relatively short distance, downslope movement of weathered rock, primarily under the influence of gravity. There are many types of mass wasting, each produced by a different combination of factors—such as the steepness of the slope, the coherency of the bedrock, and the amount of water present—and each leaving a different kind of mark in the landscape.

Rockfall: With **rockfall,** loose, weathered rock falls to the foot of a cliff or steep slope. The angular, largely unsorted material that accumulates is known as **talus** or **scree**, and over time may build up into a steeply sloping **talus cone** at the foot of the slope (Figure 33-1).

Landslide: **Landslides** involve the movement of masses of rock—occasionally coherent sections of a hillside—sliding downslope as a unit. A landslide leaves a prominent scar at its point of origin, as well as an irregular jumble of rock where it comes to rest (Figure 33-2). Landslides are frequently triggered by heavy rainfall, which adds mass to a hillside and makes it more susceptible to sliding. However, slides do not involve the flow of material in a mixture of water.

Figure 33-1: Talus cones accumulating from rockfall. (From McKnight and Hess, *Physical Geography*, 9th ed.)

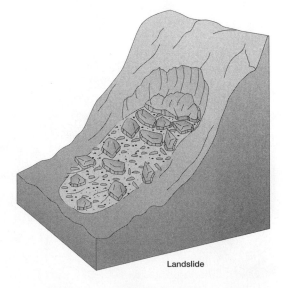

Figure 33-2: Landslide. (From McKnight and Hess, *Physical Geography*, 9th ed.)

227

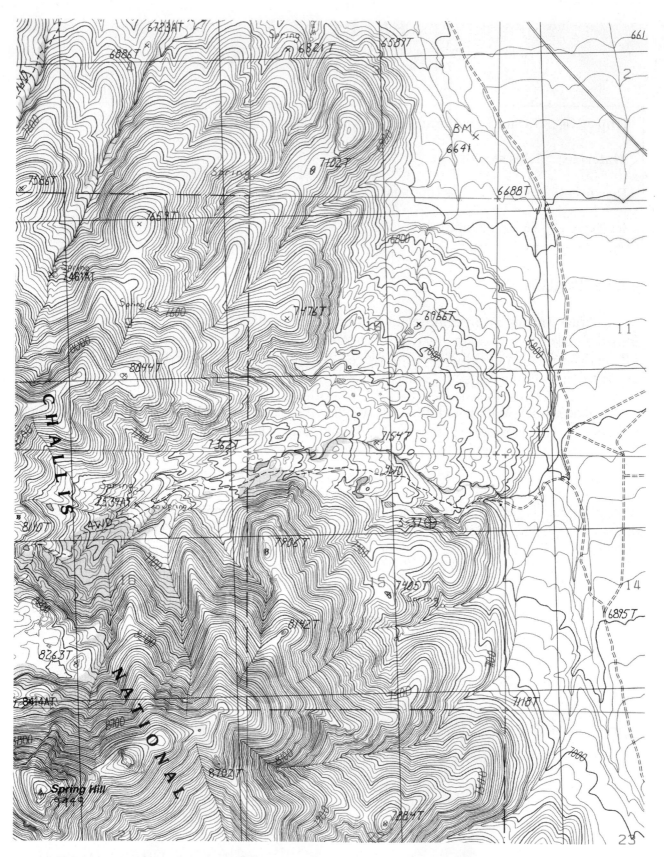

Figure 33-3: USGS "Spring Hill, Idaho," quadrangle (scale 1:24,000; contour interval 20 feet; ↑N).

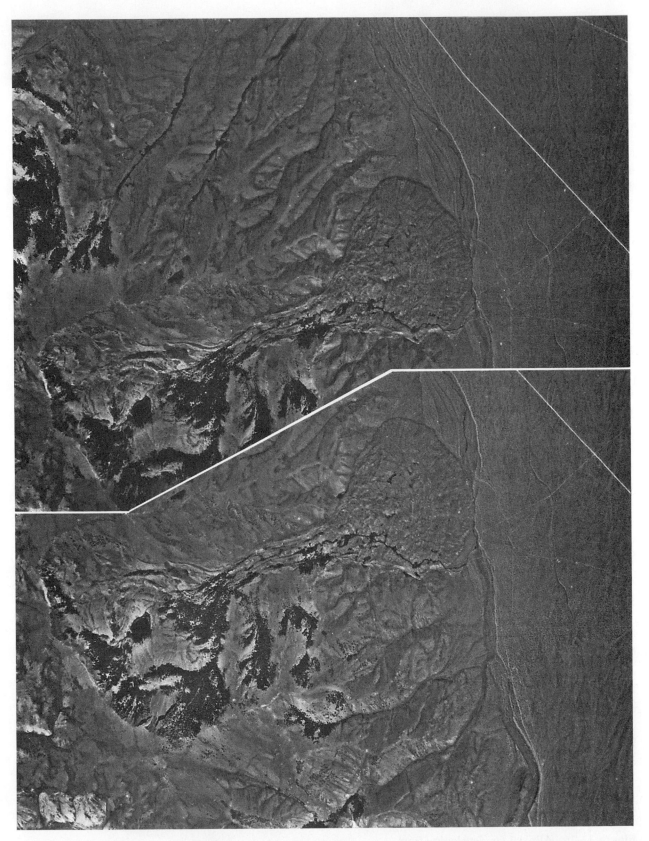

Figure 33-4: Stereogram of Pahsimeroi Mountains, near Spring Hill in Idaho (scale 1:40,000; USGS photographs, 1999; ↑N).

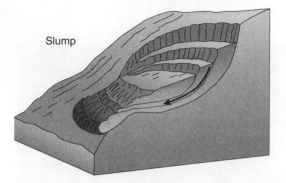

Figure 33-5: Slump. (From McKnight and Hess, *Physical Geography*, 9th ed.)

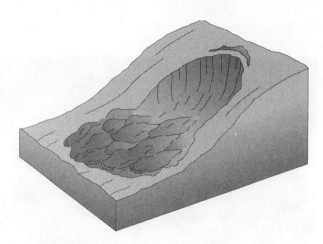

Figure 33-6: Earthflow. (From McKnight and Hess, *Physical Geography*, 9th ed.)

Slump:　A **slump** is a "rotational" slide that involves movement along a curved slide plane (Figure 33-5).

Earthflow:　When the quantity of water is great, a section of hillside consisting of loose or highly weathered material may begin to flow downhill as a waterlogged mass. Like a slide, an **earthflow** leaves a scar at its starting point, but in this case very wet material is flowing—rather than sliding—downslope (Figure 33-6).

Mudflow and Debris Flow:　A **mudflow** is a very wet mixture of water and rock that amasses in a stream valley, then flows down-valley with the consistency of wet concrete. When mudflows contain large boulders, they are often called **debris flows** (although the terms "debris flow" and "mudflow" are sometimes used interchangeably). Mudflows and debris flows are common in arid and semi-arid mountainous regions where a heavy rain can trigger a flashflood. The flashflood quickly moves down a dry canyon picking up loose weathered material, eventually depositing the mud and rock at the mouth of the canyon in an **alluvial fan** (Figure 33-7; additional discussion of alluvial fans is found in Exercise 40). Note that while landslides, slumps, and earthflows take place on hillsides, mudflows and debris flows develop in stream valleys.

Creep:　**Creep** or **soil creep** entails the very slow downslope movement of the surface layer of a hillside, often as the result of repeated freeze-thaw (or wetting and drying) cycles of the soil layer. Often the most visible signs of soil creep are fence posts or telephone poles that are leaning downhill (Figure 33-8).

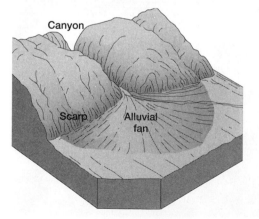

Figure 33-7:　Alluvial fan developing from mudflow and debris flow deposits at the mouth of a canyon. (From McKnight and Hess, *Physical Geography*, 9th ed.)

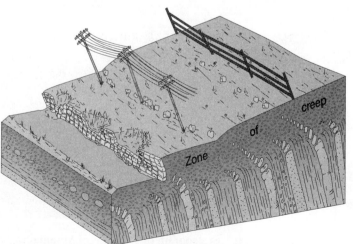

Figure 33-8:　Soil creep. (From McKnight and Hess, *Physical Geography*, 9th ed.)

EXERCISE 33 PROBLEMS—PART I

The following questions are based on Figure 33-3, a section of the USGS "Spring Hill, Idaho," quadrangle (scale 1:24,000; contour interval 20 feet), and Figure 33-4, a stereogram of the same region. The map and stereogram show a large mass wasting deposit at the foot of the Pahsimeroi Mountains in Idaho.

1.   What evidence shown on the map and stereogram suggests that the material in the deposit does not consist of coherent bedrock?

2.   (a)   Which kind of mass wasting most likely left this deposit,
             a type of *flow* or a type of *slide*?   _____

     (b)   What evidence shown on the map and stereogram supports your answer? (Hint:
             note the path taken by the material on its way downslope.)

EXERCISE 33 PROBLEMS—PART II

The following questions are based on Figure 33-3, a section of the USGS "Spring Hill, Idaho," quadrangle (scale 1:24,000; contour interval 20 feet). You are going to calculate the approximate volume of the mass wasting deposit shown at the foot of the Pahsimeroi Mountains.

1.   How thick is the deposit at the end (the "toe") of the deposit?
     (Take the 6,800' contour to be the top of the deposit):   _____ feet

2.   Although the deposit is somewhat irregular, assume that it is square or rectangular in
     shape. Estimate the length of the two sides of the deposit that are in contact with the
     mountain front (the northwest [NW] side and the southwest side [SW]), then calculate its
     surface area:

     _____ feet × _____ feet = _____ square feet
     (NW side length)   (SW side length)   (total surface area)

3.   Assuming that your answer to Question 1 above represents the uniform thickness of the
     deposit (a simplistic assumption), calculate the total volume of the deposit:

     _____ feet × _____ square feet = _____ cubic feet
     (deposit thickness)   (total surface area)   (approx. total volume)

231

Name _____   Section _____

EXERCISE 33 PROBLEMS—PART III—INTERNET

The following questions are based on Figures 33-10, 33-11, 33-12, and 33-13, photographs you can view on the Lab Manual Web site. Go to the McKnight and Hess textbook Web site *<http://www.prenhall.com/mcknight>*. Select "Lab Manual," then "Exercise 33."

1. (a)   Which of the four photographs shows the result of rockfall?   Figure 33-_____

   (b)   Describe the evidence you see in the photograph that supports your answer:

2. (a)   Which of the four photographs shows the result of landside or slump?
                                                              Figure 33-_____

   (b)   Describe the evidence you see in the photograph that supports your answer:

3. (a)   Which of the four photographs shows the result of earthflow?   Figure 33-_____

   (b)   Describe the evidence you see in the photograph that supports your answer:

4. (a)   Which of the four photographs shows the result of soil creep?   Figure 33-_____

   (b)   Describe the evidence you see in the photograph that supports your answer:

EXERCISE 33 PROBLEMS—PART IV

The following questions are based on Figure 33-9, a portion of the "Lucerne Valley, California," quadrangle (scale 1:62,500; contour interval 50 feet) shown on the following page. The map shows the result of a landslide that originated as an enormous rockfall off the summit of Blackhawk Mountain (marked by an arrow at the south end of the map). The slide moved north through Blackhawk Canyon, and then slid—perhaps on a cushion of compressed air—until it came to rest well beyond the mountain front (marked by an arrow at the north end of the map).

1. How far did this landslide move (begin measuring at the upper end
    of the steep slope just to the north of Blackhawk Mountain)?   _____ miles

2. How wide was the slide when it came to rest (estimate the width
    at the toe of the slide in Sections 20 and 21)?   _____ feet

3. Note the series of lateral ridges—beginning at the mouth of Blackhawk Canyon—that mark the edges of the slide after it moved down off the mountain. With a colored pencil, mark the east and west edges of the slide, from the mouth of Blackhawk Canyon to its toe in Sections 20 and 21.

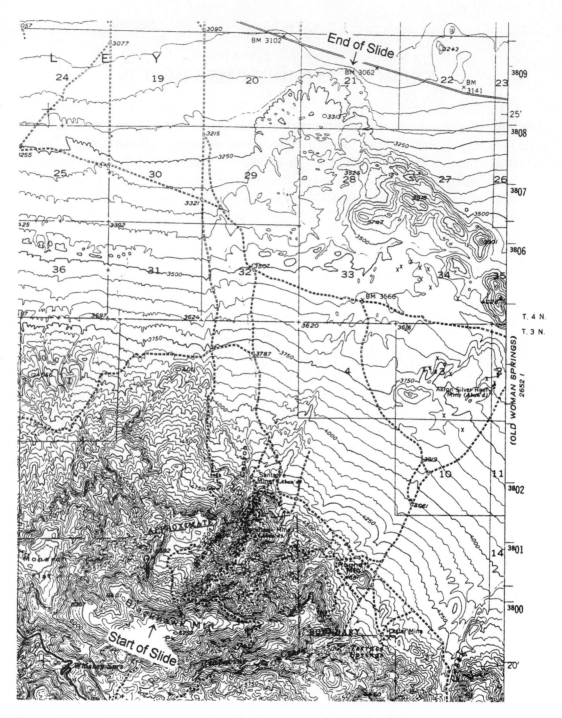

Figure 33-9: USGS "Lucerne Valley, California," quadrangle (scale 1:62,500; contour interval 50 feet; ↑N).

EXERCISE 34
DRAINAGE BASINS

Objective: To study stream drainage basins, stream order, and stream gradients.

Materials: Lens stereoscope.

Reference: McKnight and Hess, *Physical Geography*, 9th ed., pp. 481–483.

STREAM SYSTEMS

Running water is the most important agent of erosion on the Earth's land surface. Most of this fluvial erosion is accomplished by the action of **streams**. One important consideration in the study of fluvial geomorphology is the way in which streams come together as a system.

Several different characteristics of stream systems can be recognized. Tiny streams flow together to form larger streams, and these streams in turn join to become still larger streams. We see that within any river system there is a hierarchy of streams, and within this hierarchy we can see differences in the gradient, the length, the area of land being drained, and the amount of water being carried by a stream.

DRAINAGE BASINS

A **drainage basin**, or **watershed**, is an area within which all water flows toward a single stream. Figure 34-1 is a diagram showing the drainage basins of three adjacent streams. The dashed line represents the **drainage divide** that delimits the drainage basin of the middle stream from the drainage basins of the streams on either side. Drainage divides are typically the high ground that separates streams flowing into one drainage basin from streams flowing into another.

As shown in Figure 34-1, a drainage divide may also include an area of **interfluve**—the part of a landscape where water moves downslope as unchanneled **overland flow**, rather than as the channeled **streamflow** found in **valleys**. Figure 34-3 is a stereogram of the Eds Creek drainage basin near Deer Peak, Montana. Map T-3 is a color topographic map of the same region.

STREAM ORDERS

One way of analyzing patterns of tributaries within a stream system is with the concept of **stream order**. A "first-order" stream is the smallest stream in a stream system, and is defined as a stream without tributaries. Where two first-order streams join, a second-order stream is formed. Where two second-order streams join, a third-order stream is formed (Figure 34-2).

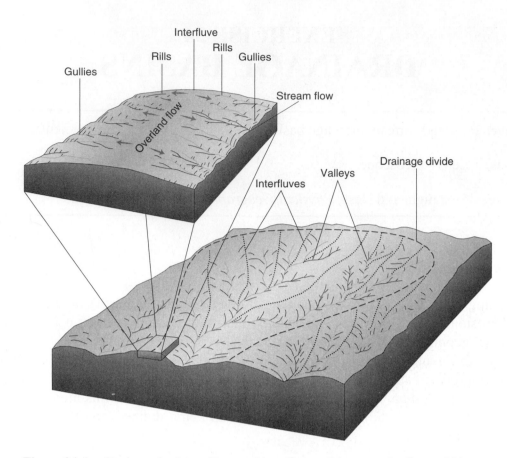

Figure 34-1: Drainage basins, valleys and interfluves. Streams and valleys within a drainage basin are enclosed by a surrounding drainage divide. (From McKnight and Hess, *Physical Geography*, 9th ed.)

Notice that when a first-order and second-order stream meet, a third-order stream is not formed. Two second-order streams are required to form a third-order stream, two third-order streams to form a fourth-order stream, and so on.

In most well-established stream systems, there will be more first-order streams than all other orders combined, and each successively higher order will contain fewer and fewer streams. Also, as stream order increases, stream length and stream drainage areas tend to increase, while the gradient of streams tends to decrease.

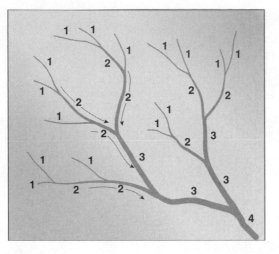

Figure 34-2: Stream orders. (From McKnight and Hess, *Physical Geography*, 9th ed.)

STREAM GRADIENT

The most common way to express the slope of a stream is by its **gradient**. If English measurement units are being used (as on the topographic maps in this exercise), the gradient of a stream is usually stated in feet of elevation change per mile. For example, if a stream drops 678 feet over a distance of 1.5 miles, the gradient is:

$$\text{Gradient} = \frac{\text{Elevation Change}}{\text{Number of Miles}} = \frac{678 \text{ feet}}{1.5 \text{ miles}} = 452 \text{ ft/mi}$$

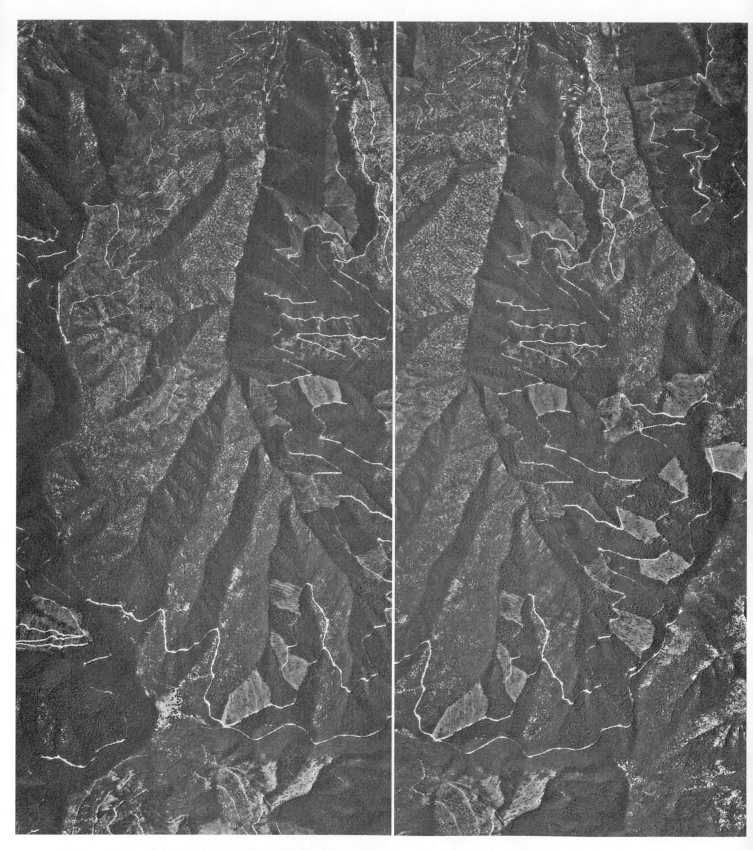

Figure 34-3: Stereogram of Eds Creek drainage basin near Deer Peak, Montana. North is to left side of page (scale 1:40,000; USGS photographs, 1995; ← N).

EXERCISE 34 PROBLEMS—PART I

The following questions are based on Map T-3, the "Deer Peak, Montana," quadrangle (scale 1:24,000; contour interval 40 feet), and Figure 34-3, a stereogram of the same area.

1. The unimproved dirt road (shown as a double dashed black line) looping around past Deer Peak roughly follows which natural feature associated with the Eds Creek drainage basin?   _____

2. The stream pattern within the drainage basin of Eds Creek on Map T-3 is reproduced at right at a smaller scale. On this small map, trace the length of all first-order streams with blue lines, the length of all second-order streams with red lines, and the length of Eds Creek (as a third-order stream) with a green line. If you don't have colored pencils, number each segment, 1, 2, or 3.

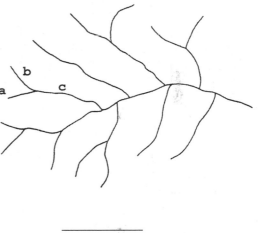

3. (a) How many first-order streams are shown?   _____

    (b) How many second-order streams are shown?   _____

4. Using Map T-3, determine the gradients of the two first-order streams labeled "a" and "b" on the map above, the second-order stream labeled "c" on the map above, as well as Eds Creek after it has become a third-order stream. Determine stream length to the nearest 1/10th mile (take your measurements from Map T-3, *not* the small map above). A graphic map scale is found inside the front cover of the Lab Manual.

Stream	Order	Elevation Drop (feet)	Length (miles)	Gradient (feet/mile)
a	1st			
b	1st			
c	2nd			
Eds Creek	3rd			

EXERCISE 34 PROBLEMS—PART II

Answer the following questions after completing the problems in Part I.

5.   The table below gives the gradients of 12 more 1st-order streams and 4 more 2nd-order streams in the Eds Creek drainage basin. Fill in the gradients of the streams calculated in Problem #4, Part I (streams "a" and "b" under 1st-order; stream "c" under 2nd-order; Eds Creek under 3rd-order):

1st-Order Stream Gradients		2nd-Order Stream Gradients	3rd-Order Stream Gradients
1680'/mi	1965'/mi	800'/mi	
1715'/mi	1485'/mi	680'/mi	
1225'/mi	1300'/mi	665'/mi	
1440'/mi	1335'/mi	800'/mi	
1200'/mi	1370'/mi		
1210'/mi	1355'/mi		
"a" _____ ft/mi		"c" _____ ft/mi	_____ ft/mi
"b" _____ ft/mi			(Eds Creek)

6.   Using the data from the table above, compute the following:

       (a)   Average gradient of 1st-order streams: _____ ft/mi

       (b)   Average gradient of 2nd-order streams: _____ ft/mi

7.   What generally happens to the gradients of
       streams as the stream order increases?   _____

8.   Describe the general width and shape (cross section) of the valley floors of first-order streams in the Eds Creek drainage basin:

9.   How is the valley floor of Eds Creek different from the valley floors of the first-order streams? (Hint: Look at the difference in valley width.)

Name _____   Section _____

EXERCISE 34 PROBLEMS—PART III

For the following questions, refer to Figure 34-4, a section of the USGS "Deer Peak, Montana," quadrangle reproduced below (scale 1:24,000; contour interval 40 feet):

1.   Use a red pencil to draw in the drainage divide separating the drainage basin of Beaver Slough Creek from the adjacent drainage basins.

2.   There are more small ephemeral streams in the Beaver Slough Creek drainage basin than are shown on the map with dashed lines. Using the pattern of the contour lines as your guide, with a blue pencil, draw in the courses of at least 10 more tributary streams within the Beaver Slough Creek system.

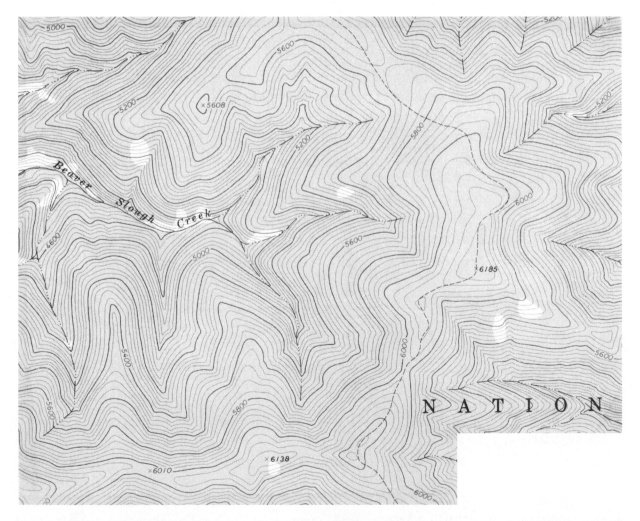

Figure 34-4:   Northwest corner of USGS "Deer Peak, Montana," quadrangle (scale 1:24,000; contour interval 40 feet; ↑N).

EXERCISE 34 PROBLEMS—PART IV

The following questions are based on Figure 34-5, a section of USGS "Dane Canyon, Arizona," quadrangle below, showing the southern edge of the Mogollon Mesa, formed by a nearly flat-lying layer of resistant rock.

1. Compute the gradient of any 1st-order stream north of the mesa edge and the gradient of any 1st-order stream south of the mesa edge. On the map label the northern stream "a" and the southern stream "b."

Stream	Elevation Drop (ft)	Length (miles)	Gradient (ft/mi)
(a) North			
(b) South			

2. If gradient were the only factor controlling the erosive power of these streams, what should happen to the position of the mesa edge with time?

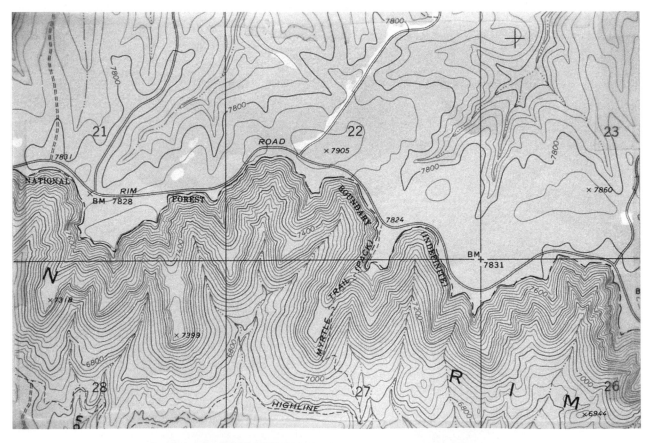

Figure 34-5:   USGS "Dane Canyon, Arizona," quadrangle (scale 1:24,000; contour interval 40 feet; ↑N).

EXERCISE 35
FLOODPLAINS

<table>
<tr><td>Objective:</td><td>To study the formation and characteristics of floodplain landforms.</td></tr>
<tr><td>Materials:</td><td>Lens stereoscope.</td></tr>
<tr><td>Reference:</td><td>McKnight and Hess, Physical Geography, 9th ed., pp. 501–504.</td></tr>
</table>

MEANDERING STREAMS

In the upper reaches of a typical river system, or in other places where the gradient of a stream is steep, erosion (often downcutting) is the most prominent fluvial process. In contrast, in the lower reaches of a typical river system, or in other places where a stream is flowing down a gentle slope, a stream will begin to meander and depositional features become much more common.

Over time, a stream will meander back and forth across its flat alluvial valley floor, known as a **floodplain**. Figure 35-1 illustrates how a **meandering stream** shifts its course through the process of lateral erosion.

Erosion is concentrated on the outside bank of a meander since the water is moving fastest here as it flows into the turn. At the same time, deposition takes place on the inside bank, where the water is moving most slowly. Through this process of lateral erosion on the outside bank, and deposition on the inside bank, the position of the stream channel gradually shifts back and forth across the floodplain.

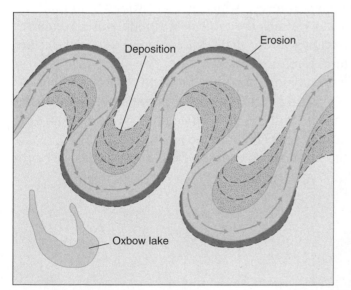

Figure 35-1: Lateral erosion and deposition of a meandering stream. (From McKnight and Hess, *Physical Geography*, 9th ed.; after Sheldon Judson, Marvin E. Kauffman, and L. Don Leet, *Physical Geology*, 7th ed. Englewood Cliffs, NJ: Prentice Hall, 1987, p. 264)

243

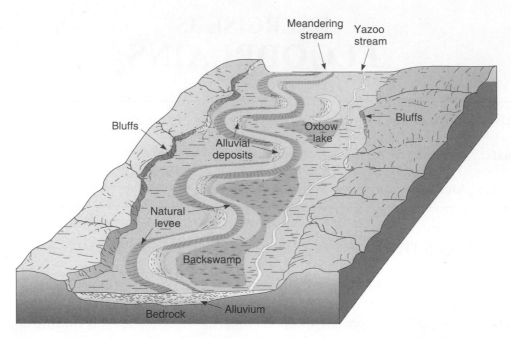

Figure 35-2: Common floodplain landforms. (From McKnight and Hess, *Physical Geography*, 9th ed.)

FLOODPLAIN LANDFORMS

The width of a major floodplain is often due, at least in part, to valley widening through lateral erosion, and floodplains are typically marked by low **bluffs** on both sides. However, most landforms found on a floodplain are largely the result of deposition. The floodplain itself is periodically inundated with flood waters. Along the course of the river, **natural levees** build up from the **alluvium** deposited along its banks during these floods (Figure 35-2).

Because of the nearly level terrain and natural levees which prevent water from draining back into the main river, poorly drained areas and swamps are typical of floodplains. Tributaries known as **yazoo streams** may run parallel to a main river for many kilometers. Yazoo streams are unable to enter because of the main river's natural levees.

When a stream is meandering tightly, it is common for one meander to cut into another, allowing the stream to take a shorter course. The resulting **cutoff meander** may be initially isolated as an **oxbow lake**. Eventually these cutoff meanders will fill up with sediment and dry out, first becoming a swamp, and then finally a dry **meander scar** (Figure 35-3).

Figure 35-4 is a stereogram showing the meandering course of the Souris River in North Dakota, and Map T-4 is a topographic map of the same region.

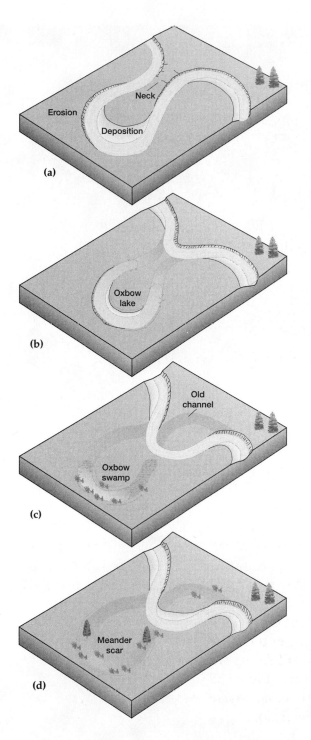

Figure 35-3: The formation of cutoff meanders on a floodplain. As the river cuts across the narrow neck of a meander, the cutoff river bend becomes an oxbow lake, which over time becomes an oxbow swamp, which in turn becomes a meander scar. (From McKnight and Hess, *Physical Geography,* 9th ed.)

MEANDERING RIVERS AS POLITICAL BOUNDARIES

Since meandering rivers often form political boundaries between states or counties, there is a need to fix these boundaries to avoid conflicts when the river shifts its course. For example, by the early 1900s, political boundaries had been permanently established along the Mississippi River. These boundaries remain fixed even if the river changes course. Today, boundaries often follow an old abandoned river channel rather than the present channel.

Figure 35-4: Stereogram of the Souris River near Voltaire, North Dakota (scale 1:40,000; USGS photographs, 1997; ↑N).

EXERCISE 35 PROBLEMS—PART I

The following questions are based on Map T-4, a portion of the "Voltaire, North Dakota," quadrangle (scale 1:24,000; contour interval 5 feet) and Figure 35-4, a stereogram of the same region.

1. (a)   In which direction is the Souris River flowing? From _____ to _____.

    (b)   How can you tell?

2. (a)   What is the approximate width of the Souris River channel?   _____ feet

    (b)   What is the approximate width of the Souris River floodplain?   _____ feet

    (c)   What evidence suggests that the river is widening its valley through lateral erosion?

3. Compare the present length of the meandering Souris River course shown on the map with the length of a river flowing down this valley if it were *not* meandering. (You can measure the distance with a piece of string, or your instructor can show you a more precise method.)

    (a)   Length of present meandering course: _____ miles

    (b)   Length of a straight course down the valley: _____ miles

4. Natural levees can be seen along the Souris River in the center portion of the map (north of Westgaard Cemetery). Approximately how high are the levees?

    _____ feet

EXERCISE 35 PROBLEMS—PART II

The following questions are based on Map T-4, a portion of the "Voltaire, North Dakota," quadrangle (scale 1:24,000; contour interval 5 feet) and Figure 35-4, a stereogram of the same region.

1.   (a)   Explain the formation of the narrow, triangle-shaped lake just to the east of Westgaard Cemetery (in the NE $\frac{1}{4}$ of Section 3). You may use a sketch to illustrate your answer.

     (b)   Describe the location of two more lakes, swamps, or topographic depressions along the Souris River that formed in a similar way. (You may refer to Public Land Survey township quarter sections to simplify your location description.)

2.   (a)   Describe a location where the formation of a new cutoff meander in the Souris River appears imminent.

     (b)   Sketch the current river course:

     (c)   Sketch the new river course after the cutoff:

EXERCISE 35 PROBLEMS—PART III

The following questions are based on Map T-5, a portion of the "Jackson, Mississippi-Louisiana," topographic map (scale 1:250,000; contour interval 50 feet; dashed lines are supplementary contours at 25-foot intervals). This map shows the Mississippi River near the town of Vicksburg, Mississippi. The eastern bluffs of the Mississippi River floodplain can be seen in the southeast corner of the map. The dashed black line along the Mississippi River shows the state boundary between Mississippi and Louisiana. Notice that the "boundary course" of the Mississippi River is quite different from the present course of the river. Some of the changes were natural, others were artificial. There is an extensive set of artificial levees along the course of the river (shown with closely spaced brown tick marks).

1. (a) Find "Willow Cut-off" and "Albemarle Lake" (an oxbow lake) in the center of the map. What natural features shown on the map suggest that a channel of the river once followed a course *between* the boundary course and the present course?

    (b) Name two other oxbow lakes shown on the map (either natural or artificially produced):

2. Compare the length (in miles) of the "boundary course" of the river with the main channel of the present course. (You can measure the distance with a piece of string, or your instructor may show you a more precise method.)

    (a) Length of present course: _____ miles

    (b) Length of "boundary course":   _____ miles

    (c) Amount of shortening: _____ miles

    (d) The present course length represents what percentage
         of the boundary course length? ("present" ÷ "boundary" × 100) _____ %

3. In general, how is the gradient of the present course
    different from the gradient of the boundary course?
    (In other words, is the present course steeper or less
    steep than the boundary course?)   _____

4. Compared to the "boundary course," why would the present course of the Mississippi River be an advantage to river traffic such as barges?

EXERCISE 35 PROBLEMS—PART IV

The following questions are based on Map T-5, a portion of the "Jackson, Mississippi-Louisiana," topographic map (scale 1:250,000; contour interval 50 feet; dashed lines are supplementary contours at 25-foot intervals). For reference, the dashed contour line on "Paw Paw Island" in the southern part of the map shows an elevation of 75 feet.

1. Approximately how high do the bluffs rise above the town of Blakely in the southeast (what is the local relief)?   _____ feet

2. How wide is the Mississippi River channel where it enters the map in the north?   _____ mile(s)

3. (a) To the west of Hollybrook, (south of Lake Providence along Highway 65), find the streams named "Otter Bayou" and "Swan Lake." What kind of floodplain landform explains the curved paths taken by these streams? (Hint: the landform is too low to be shown with this map's contour interval.)

    (b) Which human-built feature nearby appears to have been influenced by the same kind of landform?   _____

4. (a) Estimate the elevation of the town of Alsatia (west of the Mississippi River along Highway 65):   _____ feet

    (b) What is the approximate elevation of the Mississippi River near Alsatia?   _____ feet

    (c) Other than the levees, does there appear to be any land more than 25 feet higher than the river between Alsatia and the Mississippi River? (The dashed brown lines are 25-foot contours.)   _____

5. The Yazoo River (from which the geographic term "yazoo stream" was taken) flows into the Mississippi River just south of this portion of the map. Name another yazoo stream (or "creek," "bayou," etc.) shown on the map that parallels the Mississippi for at least 10 miles:

EXERCISE 36
STREAM DRAINAGE PATTERNS

Objective: To study different patterns of stream drainage.

Reference: McKnight and Hess, *Physical Geography*, 9th ed., pp. 491–493.

DRAINAGE PATTERNS

The overall drainage pattern of a stream system is often strongly influenced by the underlying geologic structure of a region. The most common stream drainage patterns are shown in Figure 36-1.

Dendritic Drainage: The common branching **dendritic** pattern indicates that the underlying structure is not exerting much influence on the courses of streams, and that all of the rock is more or less equally resistant to erosion.

Trellis Drainage: In contrast to dendritic drainage, with **trellis** drainage, the courses of streams are largely controlled by a pattern of alternating parallel ridges and valleys. Tributaries usually flow parallel to each other until one can cut across a low spot in the separating ridge and join another stream.

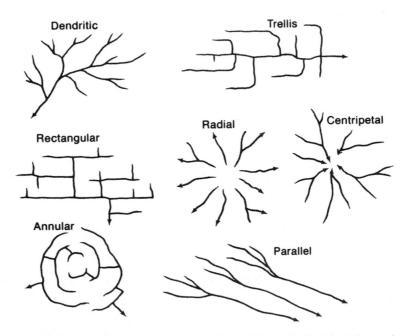

Figure 36-1: Common drainage patterns. (From McKnight, *Physical Geography*, 2nd ed.)

Radial and Centripetal Drainage: **Radial** patterns develop where streams flow down and away from a central high area. **Centripetal** drainage is the opposite of radial, and develops where streams converge as they flow down into a central basin.

Annular Drainage: An **annular** pattern may develop around an eroded dome or basin in which alternating bands of soft and resistant rock have been exposed.

Rectangular and Parallel Drainage: **Rectangular** patterns often indicate that streams are following a pronounced set of joints or faults. **Parallel** patterns can develop in a region with a uniform but usually gentle slope.

EXERCISE 36 PROBLEMS

The following questions are based on Map T-6, the "Johnson City, Tennessee-Virginia-Kentucky-North Carolina," topographic map (scale 1:250,000; contour interval 100 feet).

1.   (a)   Describe the general topography of the region between Clinch Mountain and Powell Mountain:

       (b)   What kind of stream drainage pattern has developed here? _____

       (c)   How has the road system been influenced by the topography?

2.   (a)   Describe the general topography in the region north of Poor Valley Ridge:

       (b)   What kind of stream drainage pattern has developed here? _____

       (c)   How has the road system been influenced by the topography?

3.   (a)   The Powell River has a meandering pattern.
                Is it flowing across a flat floodplain?   _____

       (b)   How do you know?

The following questions are based on Map T-2, the "Umnak, Alaska," topographic map (scale 1:250,000; contour interval 200 feet).

4.   What kind of drainage pattern has developed around the
       outside of the Okmok Caldera?   _____

5.   What kind of drainage pattern has developed inside the
       Okmok Caldera?   _____

EXERCISE 37
STREAM REJUVENATION

Objective: To study the consequences of stream rejuvenation.

Materials: Lens stereoscope.

Reference: McKnight and Hess, *Physical Geography*, 9th ed., pp. 506–508.

STREAM REJUVENATION

The tectonic history of a region can significantly influence the fluvial landscape. Rejuvenation occurs when a stream undergoes renewed downcutting. For example, the tectonic uplift of a region can result in **stream rejuvenation.** As the gradient is increased through uplift, the downcutting ability of a stream will also increase. There are several kinds of landforms that may result from rejuvenation.

Entrenched Meanders: Entrenched meanders (Figure 37-1) may develop when a region is uplifted. In this case, a stream downcuts a gorge into its old floodplain while maintaining its old meandering pattern. The resulting "meandering gorge" is quite striking since we normally expect to see a meandering river only on top of a flat floodplain.

Figure 37-2 and Figure 27-3 (on page 182) are stereograms showing the deeply entrenched meanders of the Green River in Utah. Map T-7 is a portion of the "Canyonlands National Park," topographic map showing this same region. Figure 37-3 is an oblique aerial photograph of this region.

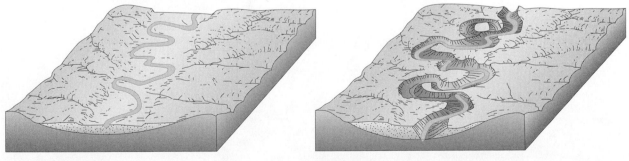

(a) Floodplain meanders

(b) Entrenched meanders

Figure 37-1: Formation of entrenched meanders. (a) Floodplain meanders before uplift and rejuvenation. (b) If the stream maintains its meandering pattern during uplift, renewed downcutting can produce entrenched meanders. (From McKnight and Hess, *Physical Geography,* 9th ed.)

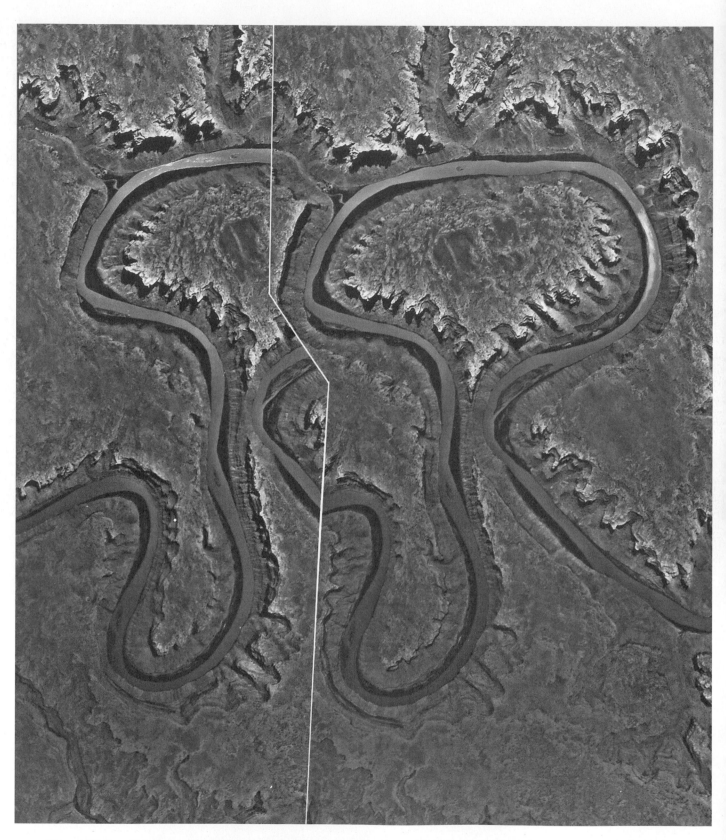

Figure 37-2: Stereogram of the entrenched meanders of the Green River in Utah. North is to the left side of the page (scale 1:40,000; USGS photographs, 1993; ← N).

Figure 37-3: Entrenched meanders of the Green River in Canyonlands National Park, Utah. (Tom L. McKnight photo from McKnight and Hess, *Physical Geography,* 9th ed.)

Stream Terraces: Stream terraces along a river represent old valley floors. During rejuvenation, a stream downcuts into its old floodplain floor, leaving portions of its old floodplain as terraces above the present level of the stream (Figure 37-4).

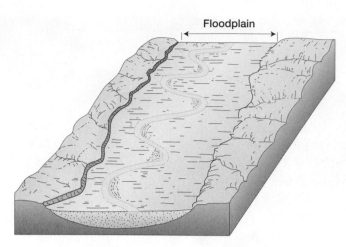

(a) Before uplift

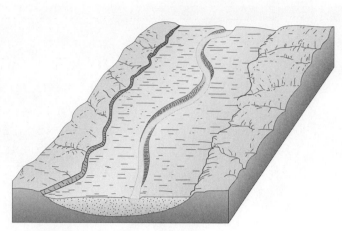

(b) Uplift

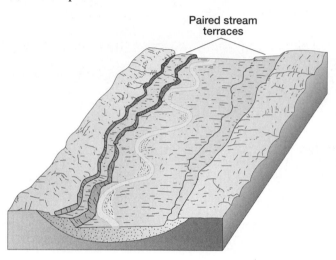

(c) After uplift

Figure 37-4: Formation of stream terraces. (a) Before uplift a stream meanders across an alluvial floodplain. (b) During a period of uplift, the stream begins to downcut into its original floodplain. (c) After uplift the stream again widens out a floodplain, leaving remnants of the original valley floor as a pair of stream terraces. (From McKnight and Hess, *Physical Geography,* 9th ed.)

EXERCISE 37 PROBLEMS—PART I

The following questions are based on Map T-7, the "Canyonlands National Park, Utah," topographic map (scale 1:62,500; contour interval 80 feet), Figures 27-3 and 37-2, stereograms of this region, and Figure 37-3, an oblique aerial photograph of this area. The map, stereograms, and photograph show the deeply entrenched meanders of the Green River in Canyonlands National Park, Utah.

1.   How deep is the gorge of the Green River? Use the top of the
land inside "Bowknot Bend" as your upper reference point.   _____ feet

2.   (a)   Describe where a cutoff meander developed in the past (describe the location relative to labeled places on the map):

(b)   Did the cutoff occur before or after the entrenchment began? _____

(c)   How do you know?

3.   (a)   Describe where another cutoff meander might develop in the future (describe the location relative to labeled places on the map):

(b)   How high is the land between the two loops of the river
at this point? (Determine the relief, not the elevation.)   _____ feet

4.   The gorge wall on the outside of some meander turns is noticeably steeper than the gorge walls on the inside of the meander turn. For example, see "Cottonwood Bottom" and the meander to the west of "Spring Canyon Point." What might explain this? (Hint: Consider the processes of erosion associated with both meandering and entrenchment; before entrenchment, was the stream course directly above its current location?)

EXERCISE 37 PROBLEMS—PART II

The following questions are based on Map T-4, the "Voltaire, North Dakota," topographic map (scale 1:24,000; contour interval 5 feet). You may also want to look at Figure 35-4 on page 246, a stereogram of this same area. The Souris River has downcut into the glacial outwash deposits along its course leaving stream terraces.

1.   Approximately how high are the stream terraces north of the
      Souris River in the SW$^{1}\!/_{4}$ of Section 33?   _____ feet

2.   (a)   Is the stream terrace north of the Souris River of uniform width? _____

      (b)   If not, describe the pattern:

EXERCISE 38
FLOOD RECURRENCE INTERVALS

Objective: To study flood recurrence intervals.

Reference: McKnight and Hess, *Physical Geography*, 9th ed., p. 486.

STREAMFLOW RECORDS

Although natural disasters such as floods seem to occur randomly, by analyzing long-term streamflow records it is possible to calculate the probabilities of floods of various sizes occurring each year.

The amount of water flowing through a stream is called its **discharge**, usually described in terms of cubic meters of water flow per second (cms). All streams vary in their discharge during a year, depending on such factors as seasonal precipitation and surface runoff conditions. In this exercise, we are interested in the annual peak discharge of a stream—the highest "flood flow" of a stream each year.

As stream discharge increases, the volume, speed, and height of a stream increase. With an increase in height during a flood, streams typically spill out of their channels and flood adjacent areas. For this reason the **gage height** at a monitoring station—which describes the height of a stream above its local level or **datum**—is one of the most common measures of flood size.

FLOOD RECURRENCE INTERVALS

In this exercise, we will study Cache Creek, a stream near Clear Lake in northern California, from 1980 to 2002 (a table with complete streamflow data is shown in Figure 38-2). The stretch of Cache Creek chosen for this exercise is in the upper reaches of the stream where its flow is not artificially regulated. These data represent only a 23-year period, so we must be careful about extrapolating beyond the data range, and about drawing conclusions about the actual probabilities of flooding along Cache Creek. A much longer period of study is required to make meaningful estimates of actual flood height and recurrence.

The first step in our analysis is to relate the discharge of Cache Creek to its gage height. This is shown with a **rating curve** (Figure 38-1). For each of the 23 years, the gage height in meters was plotted against its discharge in cms; a smooth line was added through the plot to more clearly show the relationship. (Note: because of the type of stream gage used to gather this data, when streamflow is less than about 30 cms gage height readings may not be accurate.) Notice that the "Peak Discharge" scale is logarithmic and so the rating curve line appears as a gentle curve. Using the rating curve, you can estimate the height of Cache Creek for any given discharge.

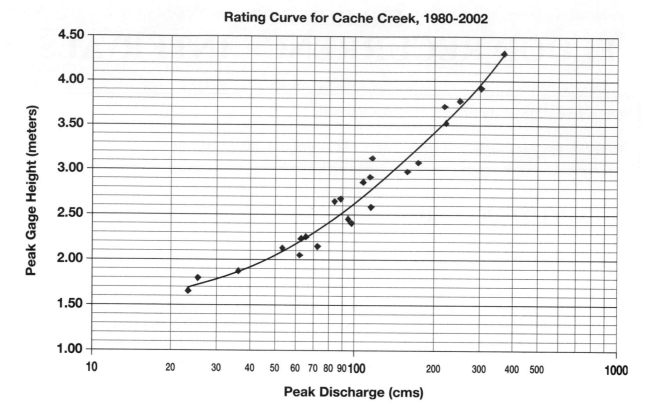

Figure 38-1: Rating curve for Cache Creek, California, 1980–2002. (U.S. Geological Survey stream-flow data)

The next step is to calculate the **recurrence interval** or **return period** of floods along Cache Creek. The recurrence interval is an estimate of the number of years between times a peak stream discharge is reached or exceeded. For example, a "5-year" flood refers to the highest gage height likely to be reached once every 5 years, and a "100-year" flood is the highest gage height likely to be reached once every 100 years. However, since these estimates are based on long-term averages, it is possible to have more than one 10-year flood in a decade, and for several decades to pass without such a flood. Further, because accurate long-term streamflow data are lacking for many streams, estimates of 100-year floods and 500-year floods may be somewhat misleading.

To use streamflow data to calculate the recurrence interval (RI) of a flood, we first rank the peak flood discharge of the stream for each year. For example, in the data set shown in Figure 38-2, 1997 had the highest peak flow with 370 cms, while 1986 was second with 302 cms. The rank of each year's peak discharge has been determined for you. We then use the following formula to calculate the recurrence interval:

$$RI = \frac{n + 1}{m}$$

In the formula "n" is the number of years in the data record (23 years in this case), and "m" is the rank of a given flood on the list of annual floods. For example, the recurrence interval for the 10th ranked flood (which took place in the year 2001) is $(23 + 1) \div 10 = 2.4$ years. This means that

262

a flood with a discharge of about 115 cms occurs on average once every 2.4 years along Cache Creek. The recurrence intervals for the years 1985 through 2002 have been calculated for you. You need to calculate the recurrence intervals for the years 1980 through 1984.

Once you have calculated the remaining recurrence intervals, plot the recurrence intervals against peak discharge on the chart in the exercise problem pages. Once your data points are plotted, draw a straight line through the data points, trying to get about half of the data points above this line, and half below—this is your **flood frequency curve**.

Year	Peak Gage Height in Meters	Peak Discharge in cms	Rank	Recurrence Interval (n + 1/m)
1980	2.98	159	7	
1981	2.05	62	19	
1982	2.58	116	9	
1983	3.08	174	6	
1984	2.40	97	12	
1985	2.15	73	16	1.5
1986	3.91	302	2	12.0
1987	2.23	63	18	1.3
1988	1.87	36	21	1.1
1989	2.25	66	17	1.4
1990	1.65	23	23	1.0
1991	2.45	95	13	1.8
1992	2.12	53	20	1.2
1993	3.52	222	4	6.0
1994	1.79	25	22	1.1
1995	3.77	250	3	8.0
1996	2.68	88	14	1.7
1997	4.31	370	1	24.0
1998	3.71	219	5	4.8
1999	3.13	117	8	3.0
2000	2.65	84	15	1.6
2001	2.92	115	10	2.4
2002	2.86	108	11	2.2

Figure 38-2: Streamflow data for Cache Creek at Hough Spring, California, 1980–2002. (U.S. Geological Survey streamflow data)

EXERCISE 38 PROBLEMS

The following questions are based on the rating curve and streamflow data for Cache Creek (Figure 38-1 and Figure 38-2):

1. Using the data in Figure 38-2, calculate the recurrence interval for Cache Creek's stream-flow for the years 1980–1984. Once you have calculated the recurrence intervals, fill in your answers below and in Figure 38-2 (round your answers to one decimal place):

    1980: _____ years   1981: _____ years   1982: _____ years

    1983: _____ years   1984: _____ years

2. Determine the Flood Frequency Curve for Cache Creek by plotting the "Recurrence Interval" against "Peak Discharge" on the chart below. Draw a straight line through the center of your plot, trying to have as many data points below the line as above.

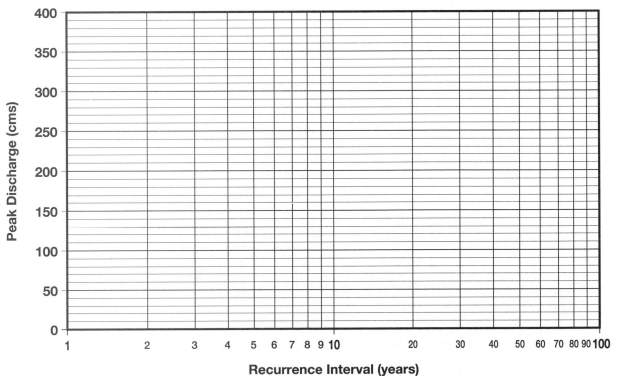

Flood Frequency Curve for Cache Creek, 1980-2002

3. Using the Rating Curve in Figure 38-1, estimate the gage height (to one decimal place) when Cache Creek has a discharge of:

   (a)   40 cms: _____ meters

   (b)   250 cms: _____ meters

4. Identify the approximate discharge of Cache Creek when it has a gage height of:

   (a)   2.0 meters: _____ cms

   (b)   3.5 meters: _____ cms

5. Using your Flood Frequency Curve , estimate the recurrence interval of a flood with a discharge of:

   (a)   100 cms: _____ years

   (b)   300 cms: _____ years

6. The discharge of the following floods will be:

   (a)   5-year flood: _____ cms

   (b)   10-year flood: _____ cms

7. In order to be above the water level of the 20-year flood, what is the minimum height above the stream level datum you should build a home?

                                            _____ meters

EXERCISE 39
KARST TOPOGRAPHY

Objective:	To study the landforms that develop in limestone regions.
Materials:	Lens stereoscope.
Reference:	McKnight and Hess, *Physical Geography*, 9th ed., pp. 517–521.

UNDERGROUND WATER

While the landscapes of most regions are strongly influenced by the work of running water on the surface, the action of water below the ground can also influence the surface topography. This is especially true in humid regions underlain by soluble rock such as limestone. Water beneath the surface moves slowly through the limestone structure. Through chemical action, this water can dissolve rock, transport this material, and eventually deposit it in new forms.

Limestone, and other rocks composed primarily of **calcium carbonate**, are easily altered by water. Rainwater becomes mildly acidic when it combines with carbon dioxide to form **carbonic acid**. Carbonic acid reacts with calcium carbonate to produce calcium bicarbonate, which is easily dissolved and transported in solution.

The chemical action of underground water is aided by the joints and bedding planes that are common in limestone. These openings allow greater movement of water through the underground structure. Eventually, underground cave networks, commonly called **caverns**, may develop. Within these caves the precipitation of dissolved calcium carbonate can produce striking features such as **stalactites** (columns hanging from the ceiling) and **stalagmites** (columns rising from the floor).

KARST TOPOGRAPHY

While most of the activity in limestone areas is taking place underground, there are also characteristic features that develop on the surface. This collection of landforms is known as **karst** topography (Figure 39-1). Karst regions in general are characterized by great local irregularities in topography, with many small hills and depressions.

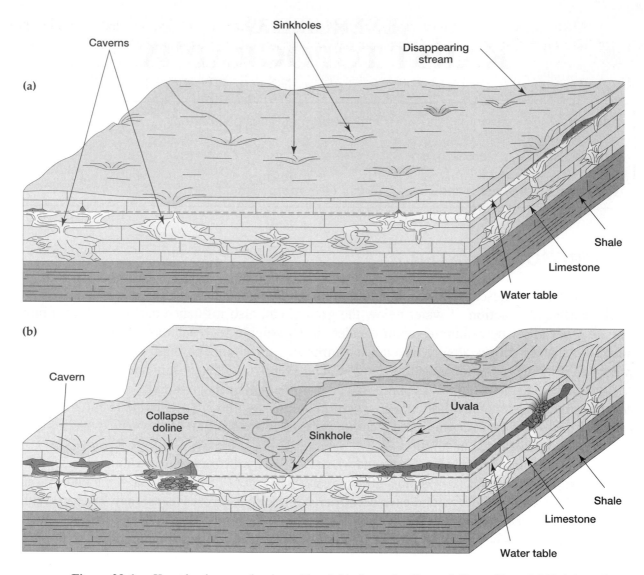

Figure 39-1: Karst landscapes dominated by sinkholes and collapse dolines. (From McKnight and Hess, *Physical Geography*, 9th ed.)

Often the most common surface feature in areas of karst is a rounded, steep-sided depression known as a **sinkhole** (or **doline**). Sinkholes develop when carbonate rocks are dissolved at the surface, often at a joint intersection. Sinkholes range in size from a few meters to several hundred meters across. A depression that results from the collapse of a subsurface cave is called a **collapse doline**. Where a series of sinkholes or collapse dolines coalesce, a karst valley known as an **uvala** develops.

One of the most distinctive characteristics of karst regions is the lack of a well-established surface drainage system. The surface drainage system has been largely replaced by a complex underground drainage system. Much of the water from precipitation simply seeps down below the surface through the joints and bedding planes.

Where surface streams do develop, they often do not flow very far. **Disappearing streams** result when a surface stream flows into the bottom of a sink, where it seeps into a crack or flows into a **swallow hole**—a direct opening into an underground channel.

Map T-9 shows an area of sinkhole karst topography near Park City, Kentucky. The boundary of Mammoth Cave National Park is just beyond the northern margin of the map. Figure 39-2 is a stereogram of the same area. The surface shown in the southern two-thirds of the map is predominately limestone, while in much of the northern third, a layer of sandstone caps the limestone.

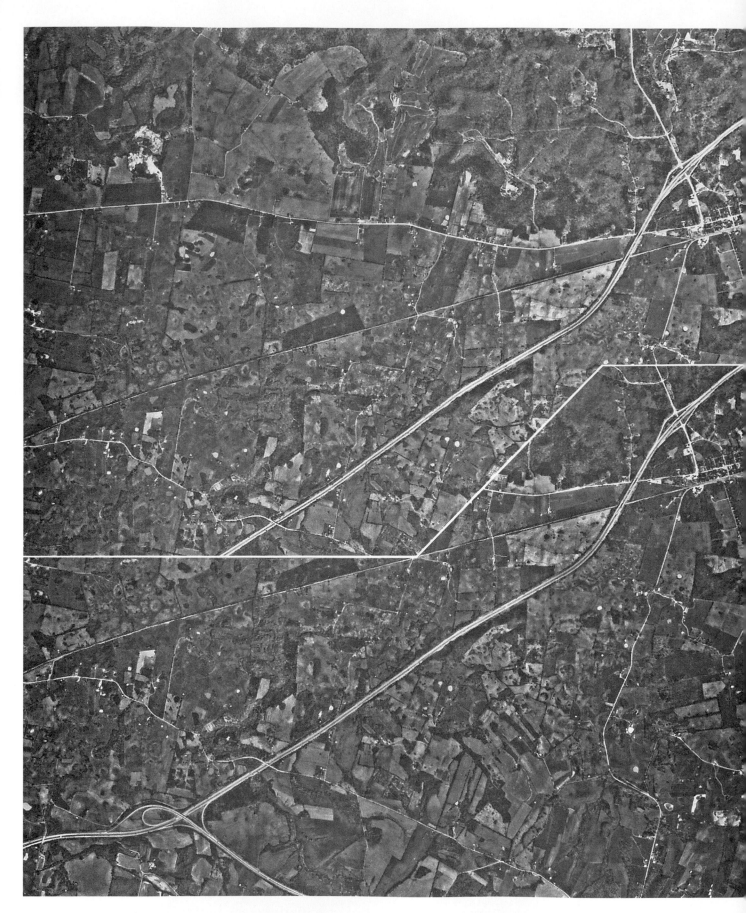

Figure 39-2: Stereogram of area near Park City, Kentucky (scale 1:40,000; USGS photographs, 1998; ↑N).

EXERCISE 39 PROBLEMS—PART I

The following questions are based on Map T-8, the "Putnam Hall, Florida," quadrangle (scale 1:24,000; contour interval 10 feet). This map shows a portion of northeastern Florida underlain by limestone. Here the water table (the upper level of ground water) is close to the surface.

1.   Describe the overall topography of this region:

2.   What is the approximate depth (from top to bottom) of the sinkhole
        containing a lake to the southwest of the Melrose Landing Airstrip?   _____ feet

3.   The elevation of the surface of a lake is a good indication of the level of the water table at
        that location. Assuming that the elevation of a lake is half a contour interval lower than the
        contour line closest to the shore, determine the elevations of the following lakes:

        (a)   Slipper Lake   _____ feet

        (b)   Lake Green Sills   _____ feet

        (c)   Whirlwind Lake   _____ feet

        (d)   Trotting Pond   _____ feet

        (e)   Lake Lucy   _____ feet

        (f)   Trout Lake   _____ feet

4.   Based on the lake levels in Problem #3 above, and noting the levels of other lakes and
        swamps, does it appear that the water table in this region is level or sloping? If sloping, in
        which direction?

5.   Why isn't a lake found in the bottom of the sinkhole 0.4 mile (0.6 km) south of the eastern
        Whirlwind Lake?

271

EXERCISE 39 PROBLEMS—PART II

The following questions are based on Map T-9, the "Park City, Kentucky," quadrangle (scale 1:24,000; contour interval 10 feet) and Figure 39-2, a stereogram of the same area. The boundary of Mammoth Cave National Park is just beyond the northern margin of the map. The surface shown in the southern two-thirds of the map is predominately limestone, while in much of the northern third, a layer of sandstone caps the limestone.

1. (a) Briefly contrast the general topography in the northern third of the map, with the topography in the southern two-thirds of the map. Consider such characteristics as the local relief and the number of sinkholes.

   (b) What might explain these differences?

2. The overlying layer of sandstone in the north is approximately 100 feet (30 meters) thick. What topographic evidence along the northern margin of the map helps confirm this?

3. Propose a reason why the hills in the northern part of the map are covered with vegetation, while those in the southern part have a much sparser cover.

4. In which direction does Gardner Creek flow?   From _____ to _____

5. What happens to all of the surface streams shown on the map?

EXERCISE 40
DESERT LANDFORMS

Objective: To study desert landforms of the Basin and Range province in the United States.

Materials: Lens stereoscope.

Reference: McKnight and Hess, *Physical Geography*, 9th ed. pp. 529–539 and 545–549.

SPECIAL CONDITIONS IN DESERTS

The landscapes of deserts tend to be quite different from the landscapes found in humid areas. There are a number of special conditions in arid areas that strongly influence landform development.

Perhaps surprisingly, running water is the most important process of erosion and deposition in deserts. There are a number of factors in deserts that compensate for the lack of regular precipitation and allow fluvial processes to be significant. First, deserts typically have a sparse cover of vegetation and soil. Without this mantle of protection, the bedrock of deserts is often directly exposed to the processes of weathering and erosion. Second, impermeable surface layers are common in deserts. These hard surface layers effectively increase the erosional potential of a rainstorm. Since the rainwater doesn't soak in easily, the runoff into stream channels is increased. Finally, while rainfall is infrequent in deserts, it often comes from an intense thunderstorm. Such short-lived downpours cause the dry streambeds to fill with water quickly and flow rapidly. These **flash floods** can result in a great deal of erosion in a short period of time.

Other conditions also influence the development of landforms in deserts. For example, **basins of interior drainage** are common. This means that ephemeral streams typically flow toward the bottom of a basin, where alluvium is deposited and the water evaporates. Although the work of wind may be more prominent in deserts than in humid areas, it mostly moves around loose sand. Desert sand dunes are discussed in Exercise 41.

COMMON DESERT LANDFORMS

While the landscapes of deserts vary greatly, the landforms in the Basin and Range province of the United States, (covering all of Nevada and portions of surrounding states), illustrate the results of the special conditions and processes operating in arid regions. Figure 40-1 is a diagram showing some of the common desert landforms found in the Basin and Range province.

In the Basin and Range province, the mountains and basins have been produced by block faulting. The mountain fronts are typically steep and rocky, and are dissected by V-shaped canyons. The basin floors are nearly flat, since they are slowly filling with alluvium washed down from the mountains.

Most of these basins have interior drainage, so at the lowest part of the basin, a dry lake bed known as a **playa** is found. A playa is an almost perfectly level expanse of dried mud, often covered with a thin crust of salt. At the bottom of a few basins, salts have accumulated to great thicknesses.

273

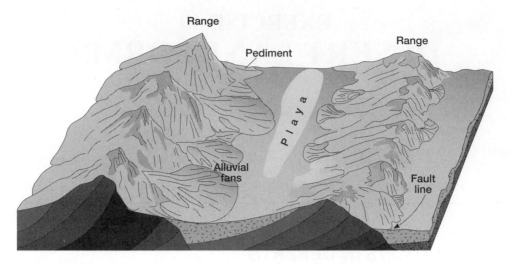

Figure 40-1: Typical Basin and Range landscape. (From McKnight and Hess, *Physical Geography*, 9th ed.)

At the foot of the mountains, in what is known as the **piedmont zone** (Figure 40-2), several prominent landforms may be found. In some piedmont zones a gently sloping bedrock platform called a **pediment** is visible. Pediments appear to be the remnants of the weathering and erosion of the mountain front. In most desert regions, the pediment is covered with a mantle of alluvium. Figure 40-3 is a portion of the "Antelope Peak, Arizona," quadrangle (scale 1:62,500; contour interval 25 feet). In the region shown on the map, the pediment has been mostly covered with a veneer of alluvium.

Probably the most prominent landforms in the piedmont zone are **alluvial fans**. As the ephemeral streams flow out of their steep canyons and reach the gentle slope of the basin floor, the water velocity decreases and alluvium is deposited. With time, the alluvium accumulates into a fan-shaped landform consisting of the mud, sand, gravel, and even boulders, brought down by flash floods and **debris flows** from the mountains (also see Figure 33-7 in Exercise 33).

In some cases, the alluvial fan from one canyon coalesces with the alluvial fan from an adjacent canyon. When alluvial fans join to form a continuous alluvial apron along a mountain front, the resulting landform is called a **bajada**. The stereogram and topographic map of the Stovepipe Wells region of Death Valley, California (Figures 40-4 and 40-5), show several alluvial fans that are coalescing to form a bajada.

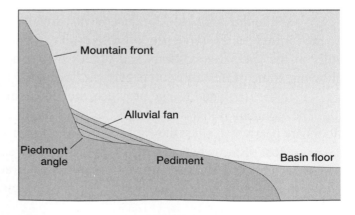

Figure 40-2: Idealized cross section of a desert piedmont zone. (From McKnight and Hess, *Physical Geography*, 9th ed.)

274

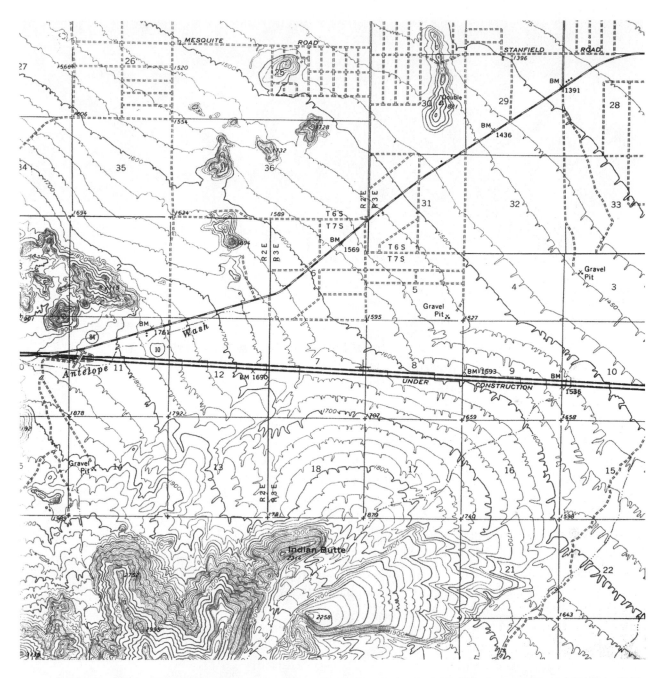

Figure 40-3: USGS "Antelope Peak, Arizona," quadrangle (scale 1:62,500; contour interval 25 feet; ↑N).

In many desert areas, isolated steep-sided landforms known as **inselbergs** are found. Inselbergs are the eroded remnants of mountain tops, and now stand out as hills or ridges rising out of the surrounding plains.

A striking feature in many deserts is a dark brown, shiny coating on exposed rock surfaces known as **desert varnish**. This coating of iron and manganese oxides seems to be a consequence of biochemical processes involving bacteria and wind-delivered clay. Desert varnish is an important dating tool for geomorphologists because the longer a rock surface has been exposed and undisturbed by fluvial erosion or deposition, the darker the coating of varnish.

275

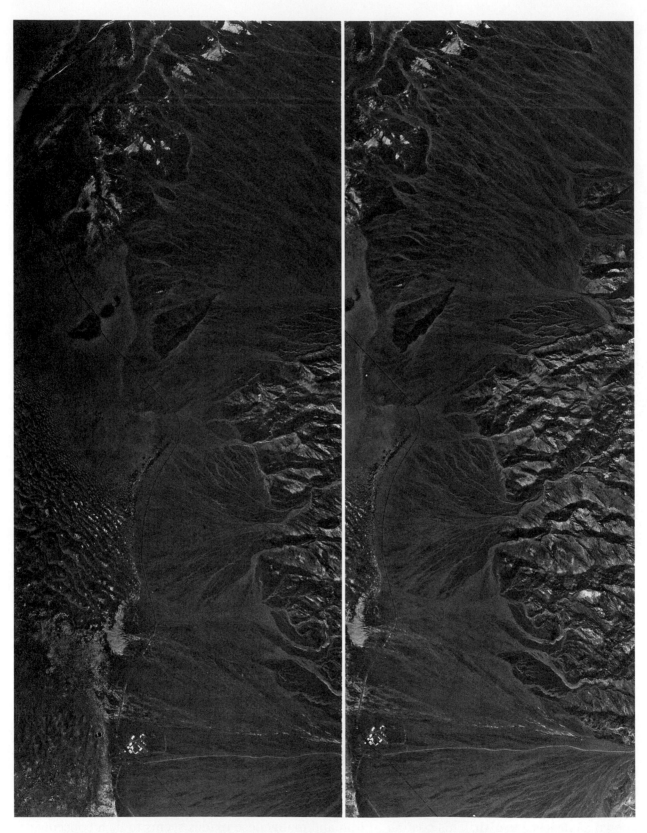

Figure 40-4: Stereogram of the Stovepipe Wells region of Death Valley, California. North is to the left side of the page (scale 1:40,000; USGS photographs, 1993; ← N).

EXERCISE 40 PROBLEMS—PART I

The questions on the following page are based on Figure 40-4, a stereogram of the Stovepipe Wells region of Death Valley, California, and Figure 40-5, a portion of the "Stovepipe Wells, California," quadrangle (scale 1:62,500; contour interval 80 feet), which shows the same region of Death Valley (north is to the left side of the stereogram and topographic map). Several large alluvial fans that come out of the Tucki Mountains are coalescing to form a bajada.

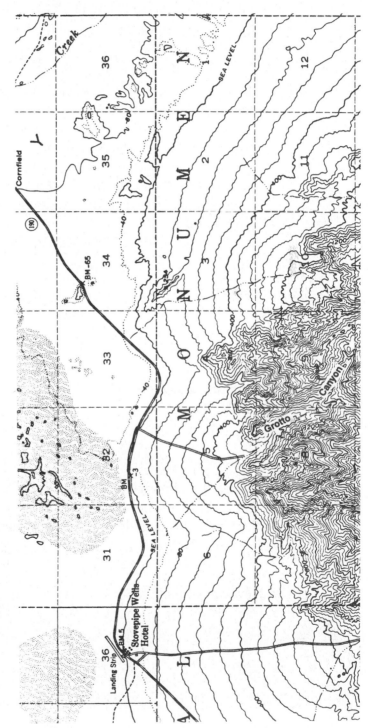

Figure 40-5: USGS "Stovepipe Wells, California," quadrangle. North is to the left side of the page (scale 1:62,500; contour interval 80 feet, dotted lines represent half-interval contours; ← N).

The following questions are based on Figure 40-4 and Figure 40-5, a stereogram and topographic map of the Stovepipe Wells region of Death Valley, California. North is to the left side of the stereogram and map.

1. What are the braided markings on the faces of the fans?

2. (a) Look at the upper portions and margins of the alluvial fans shown on the map and in the stereogram (especially the alluvial fan at the mouth of "Grotto Canyon"). In recent years does it appear that erosion or deposition has been more prominent at the tops of these fans? *(Hint: look carefully for evidence of either recent deposition or recent downcutting at the tops of the fans. For example, gullies cut into the tops of the fans are evidence of erosion; the presence or absence of desert varnish can also provide clues as to the location of recent activity on the fans.)*

    (b) How can you tell?

3. Suggest a reason and explain why the alluvial fans here vary so greatly in size:

4. (a) Locate the large triangle-shaped hill in the bajada, about 3 inches (8 cm) down from the top of the stereogram. Does it appear that alluvium brought down from the mountains is building up around this hill?

    (b) How can you tell?

EXERCISE 40 PROBLEMS—PART II

The following questions are based on Figure 40-3, a portion of the "Antelope Peak, Arizona," quadrangle (scale 1:62,500; contour interval 25 feet). In the northern portion of the map, a gently sloping pediment is visible.

1.   What evidence from the map suggests that the pediment has been covered with a mantle of alluvium?

2.   (a)   What kind of landform is illustrated by the cluster of small hills in the northern portion of the map?

      (b)   Explain their development.

3.   (a)   Describe the location of one clearly defined alluvial fan on the map.

      (b)   Which landform—the pediment or the alluvial fan—has a steeper slope?

EXERCISE 40 PROBLEMS—PART III

The following questions are based on Figure 40-6, a portion of the "Paymaster Ridge, Nevada," quadrangle (scale 1:24,000; contour interval 20 feet) reproduced on the following page. Several alluvial fans have developed along the northern and eastern mountain fronts shown on the map.

1.   With a red pencil, delineate at least two prominent alluvial fans shown on the map.

2.   Suggest a reason why the alluvial fans shown on this map vary so greatly in size.

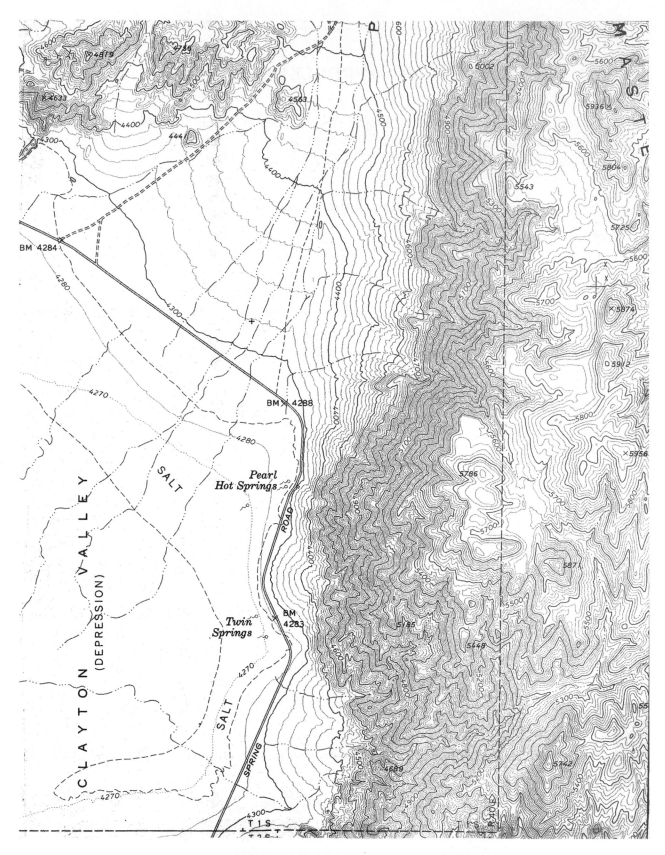

Figure 40-6: USGS "Paymaster Ridge, Nevada," quadrangle (scale 1:24,000; contour interval 20 feet; ↑N).

EXERCISE 40 PROBLEMS—PART IV

The following questions are based on Map T-10, the "Furnace Creek, California," quadrangle (scale 1:62,500; contour interval 80 feet; dotted lines represent 20-foot contours). This portion of the Furnace Creek quadrangle shows the Panamint Range and the western side of Death Valley. Several large alluvial fans can be seen along the eastern front of the Panamint Range. The basin floor here is called the Death Valley "salt pan," since salts have accumulated here in great thicknesses.

1.   (a)   What is the lowest elevation shown on the basin floor?   _____ feet

     (b)   What is the highest elevation shown in this
            part of the Panamint Range?   _____ feet

     (c)   What is the local relief shown on the map?   _____ feet

2.   What is the maximum change in elevation (either up or down)
you would experience along the basin floor traveling due
south, from Section 9 to the bottom of the map?
(Supplementary 20-foot contours are shown with dotted lines.)   _____ feet

3.   Why is it difficult to count the exact number of alluvial fans shown on the map?

4.   Find "Trail Canyon" coming out of the Panamint Range in the center of the map (a dirt road is shown coming down the fan of Trail Canyon). Why are the contours showing the Trail Canyon alluvial fan so irregular (many tiny zigzags)?

5.   How deep is the gully cut by the ephemeral stream (shown with a dashed blue line) that flows down the Trail Canyon alluvial fan where it crosses the "sea level" contour at the bottom of the fan? *(You can estimate the depth of a valley or gully on a slope by comparing the size of the "V" in the contour line to the overall spacing of contour lines on that slope. For example, if the V extends up to the position of the next higher contour line on the slope, the valley is about one contour interval deep; if it extends halfway to the next higher contour line, the valley is about one-half contour interval deep, and so on.)*

_____ feet deep

EXERCISE 40 PROBLEMS—PART V

The following questions are based on Map T-10, the "Furnace Creek, California," quadrangle (scale 1:62,500; contour interval 80 feet; dotted lines represent 20-foot contours).

1. Using the graph at right, construct a topographic profile from Point A in the Panamint Range, to Point B on the basin floor. Plot the index contours and any other contours needed to show key features along the profile.

2. On the topographic profile, label: (a) the basin floor; (b) the alluvial fan; and (c) the mountain front.

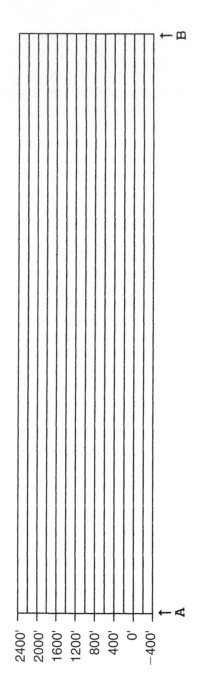

Topographic profile for line AB on the "Furnace Creek, California," quadrangle. Vertical exaggeration of the profile approximately 2.6×.

EXERCISE 41
SAND DUNES

Objective:	To study common types of desert sand dunes.
Materials:	Lens Stereoscope.
Reference:	McKnight and Hess, *Physical Geography*, 9th ed., pp. 540–542.

DESERT SAND DUNES

Sand dunes are the most conspicuous aeolian (wind produced) landform in many deserts (although few extensive desert regions are completely covered with sand dunes). Sand dunes can take on a variety of forms. The shape of a sand dune depends on the amount of sand available, the persistence and direction of the wind, and the presence of vegetation. Sand dunes with little vegetation cover may move in response to the local winds—grains of sand are blown up the gentle windward side of a dune (Figure 41-1) and then fall down the steep **slip face**. Three common kinds of desert sand dunes are shown in Figure 41-2.

Barchan: The best known kind of sand dune is the **barchan**. These are isolated, crescent-shaped dunes. The "horns" or "cusps" of the barchan point downwind. Barchans form in places where the supply of sand is limited and the winds consistently blow in one direction. A barchan dune migrates downwind over a mostly non-sandy surface.

Transverse: **Transverse** dunes are related to the barchans. Transverse dunes form in places where the supply of sand is greater. They maintain the generally crescent-shaped form of a barchan, but are much less uniform and tend to develop into interconnected ridges of sand. Figure 41-4 is a stereogram of transverse sand dunes in southeastern California. Figure 41-6 on page 288 is a topographic map of this same region.

Seif: **Seif** or longitudinal dunes are long parallel ridges of sand. It is thought that seif dunes develop in areas where there is a significant shift in wind direction for part of the year. Figure 41-3 is an aerial photograph of seif dunes in central Australia.

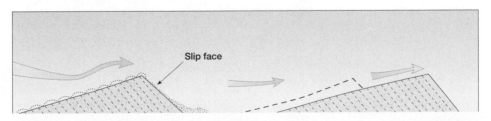

Figure 41-1:   Profile of desert sand dunes, with arrows showing wind direction. Sand dunes migrate downwind as sand grains move up the gentle windward slope and are deposited on the steep slip face. (From McKnight and Hess, *Physical Geography*, 9th ed.)

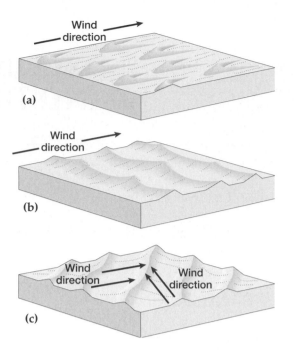

Figure 41-2: Common types of desert sand dunes: (a) barchans; (b) transverse dunes; (c) seifs. (From McKnight and Hess, *Physical Geography*, 9th ed.)

Figure 41-3: The parallel linearity of seif dunes is characteristic of some desert areas. This scene is from the Simpson Desert of central Australia. (Tom L. McKnight photo from McKnight and Hess, *Physical Geography*, 9th ed.)

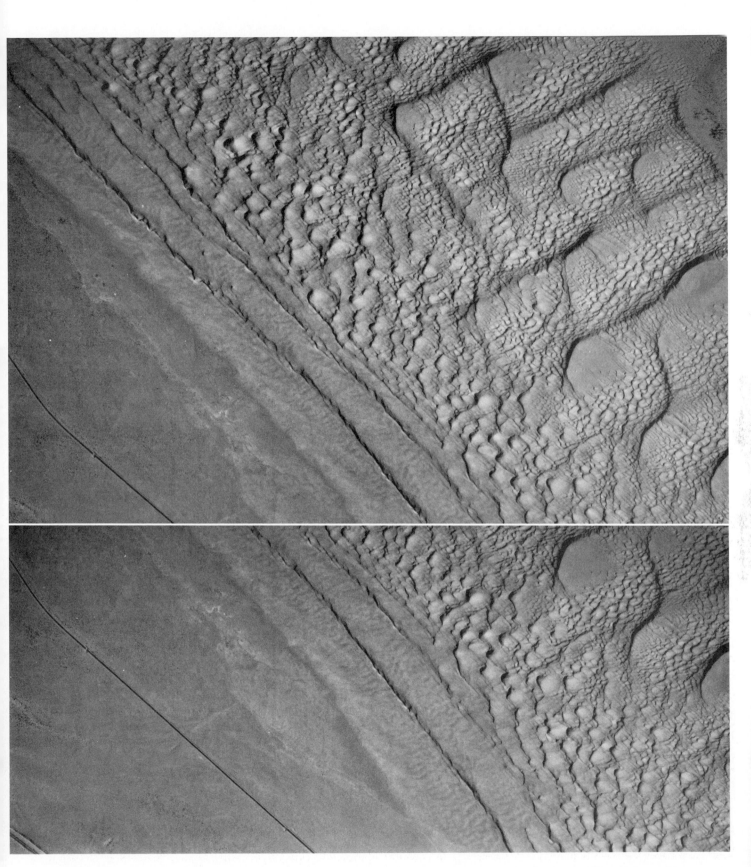

Figure 41-4: Stereogram of transverse sand dunes in southeastern California. (scale 1:40,000; USGS photographs, 2002; ↑N).

Figure 41-5 is a portion of the "Kane Spring NW, California," quadrangle, showing an active sand dune field near the Salton Sea in southern California.

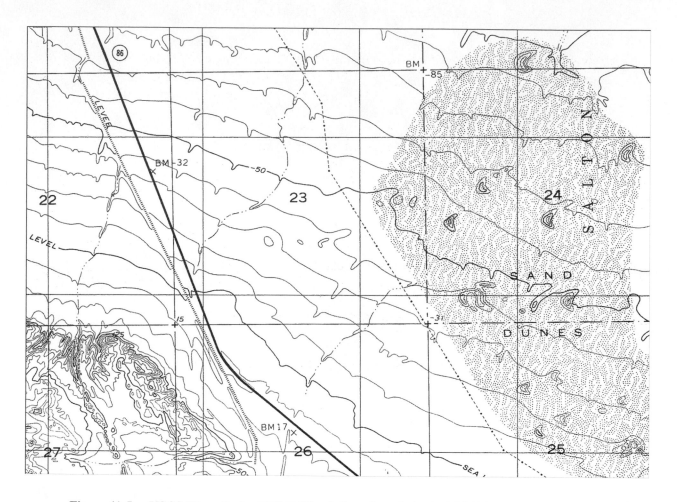

Figure 41-5: USGS "Kane Spring NW, California," quadrangle (scale 1:24,000; contour interval 10 feet; ↑N).

EXERCISE 41 PROBLEMS—PART I

The following questions are based on the portion of the "Kane Spring NW, California," quadrangle (scale 1:24,000; contour interval 10 feet) shown in Figure 41-5. These isolated dunes in the desert near the Salton Sea are moving over a surface that is only thinly covered with sand.

1.   (a)   What kind of sand dune appears to be most common in this dune field?

     (b)   How do you know?

2.   What is the height (the relief) of the tallest dune?   _____ feet

3.   What is the maximum width (or length) of the largest dune?   _____ feet

4.   (a)   From which direction does the prevailing wind blow? (The top of the map is north.)

                                                            From the _____

     (b)   How can you tell?

     (c)   If the prevailing wind direction remains the same, with time, in which direction
           will these dunes move?

                                    From _____ to _____

5.   Find the large dune just south of "24" in Section 24. Assume that this dune is moving at an
     average rate of 90 feet (27 meters) per year. Calculate how long will it take for this dune to
     migrate out of the area shown on this map (a graphic map scale is found inside the front
     cover of the Lab Manual).

     (a)   Distance to edge of map: _____ feet (or meters)

     (b)   Time to move to edge of map: _____ years

EXERCISE 41 PROBLEMS—PART II

The following questions are based on the "Glamis SE, California," quadrangle shown below (Figure 41-6); a stereogram of the same area is shown in Figure 41-4. The map shows a region of mostly transverse sand dunes in southeastern California. Note that many depression contours are used on this map, but they are difficult to read because of the sand stippling.

1.   With red lines, mark the location of at least five crescent-shaped dune crests.

2.   What is the maximum relief of the dune field? (Compare the height
of dune crests, with the bottom of the depression on the lee side.)   _____ feet

3.   What is the prevailing wind direction in this area?   From _____ to _____

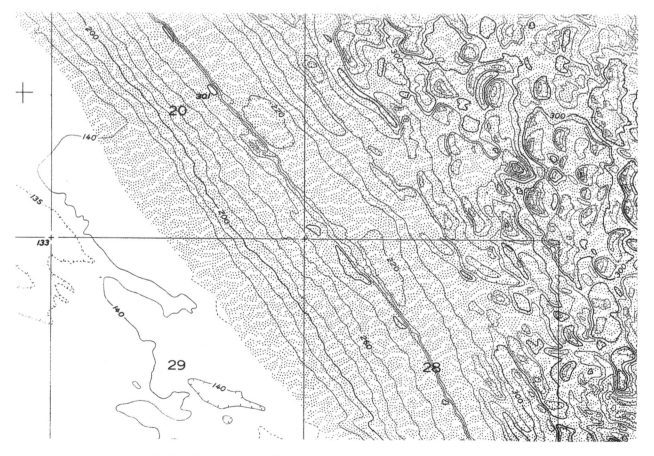

Figure 41-6:   USGS "Glamis SE, California," quadrangle (scale 1:24,000; contour interval 20 feet; dashed lines represent 5-foot contours; ↑N).

EXERCISE 42
CONTINENTAL GLACIATION

Objective:	To study landforms produced by continental glaciation.
Materials:	Lens stereoscope.
Reference:	McKnight and Hess, *Physical Geography*, 9th ed., pp. 555–562 and 565–575.

PLEISTOCENE GLACIATIONS

By the end of the **Pleistocene epoch**, 10,000 years ago, the Earth had undergone a series of extensive glaciations over a period of at least two million years. Most of this glaciation took place in the high latitudes of the Northern Hemisphere, and in the high mountain areas of the world. During the Pleistocene there was a series of glacial advances each followed by a period of melting and glacial retreat.

The continental and mountain (alpine) glaciers dramatically altered the preexisting landscape. Since the Pleistocene ended so recently (in terms of geologic time), the mark of these glaciations on the landscape is still very fresh in many parts of the world.

GLACIAL PROCESSES

The reshaping of the landscape by glaciers primarily takes place through three sets of processes:

Glacial Erosion: The direct force of the ice on the ground is enhanced by the abrasive action of the rocks being carried along the bottom of a glacier. **Glacial abrasion** often leaves a smooth, or striated surface.

Probably more important overall than abrasion in removing rock is **glacial plucking**. Meltwater trickles down into the cracks in the rocks below a glacier and refreezes, fracturing the rock through **frost wedging**. These "fingers" of ice extending down and around the rocks below the glacier help pull out material as the glacier moves on. Glacial plucking tends to leave a blocky or irregular surface.

Glacial Transportation and Deposition: When ice is under pressure, as inside a large glacier, it can flow slowly, conforming to the topography. Debris can be transported on top of a glacier, but also within the flowing ice of a glacier.

Drift is a general term for any material deposited by glacial action. Glacial drift that has been moved directly by the ice is known as **till**. Ridges of till can be deposited along the front and sides of a glacier, but till is also deposited in an unorganized fashion over the ground as a glacier retreats.

Glaciofluvial Processes: The **meltwater** from glaciers can also influence the landscape. **Glaciofluvial** deposits are often found many kilometers from the margin of the ice.

LANDFORMS PRODUCED BY CONTINENTAL GLACIATION

In the regions of the continents that were glaciated during the Pleistocene, ice sheets flowed out in all directions from their regions of accumulation, covering nearly the entire preexisting landscape. Continental ice sheets tended to flatten hills and reduce steep slopes. However, the ice sheets by no means produced a flat landscape. Areas that have experienced continental glaciation tend to be very irregular, but of low relief.

Typical landforms associated with the margin of a **continental ice sheet** are illustrated in Figure 42-1. The diagram shows the landscape both during and after glaciation.

Depositional Landforms: Landforms produced by deposition are often the most prominent ones in areas of continental glaciation. Some of the most conspicuous depositional features are

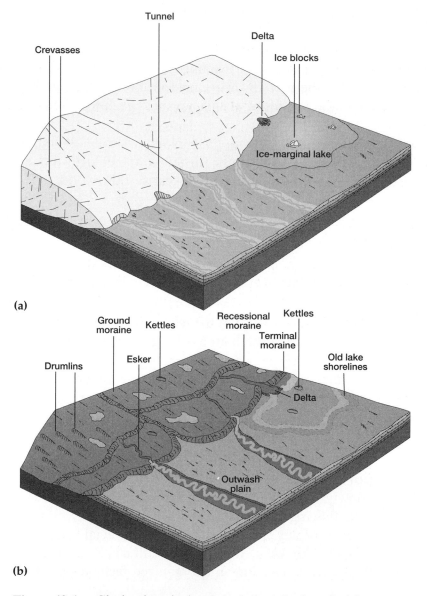

Figure 42-1:   Glacier-deposited and glaciofluvially deposited features of a landscape (a) covered by a continental ice sheet and (b) after the sheet has retreated. (From McKnight and Hess, *Physical Geography*, 9th ed.)

290

accumulations of till known as **moraines**. The **terminal moraine** (sometimes called the **end moraine**) marks the maximum advance of a glacier, while a series of **recessional moraines** often develop behind the terminal moraine as the glacier retreats.

Drumlins are elongated mounds of till that evidently have been reworked by a subsequent advance of the ice. The long axis of the drumlin is oriented parallel to the flow of the ice, with the blunt, steep end of the mound facing the direction from which the ice came. Map T-12 is a topographic map of a drumlin field in New York; Figure 42-3 is a stereogram of the same area.

Glaciofluvial Landforms: **Eskers** are glaciofluvial features that formed when streams flowing under an ice sheet became clogged with glacial meltwater debris. Today, eskers are seen as sinuous ridges of glacial sand and gravel that can run for many kilometers. Beyond the margin of the continental ice sheets, an **outwash plain** would develop. Outwash plains are often relatively flat areas covered with deposits of glacial sand and gravel. These outwash plains may extend well beyond the maximum advance of the ice. A **valley train** developed when glacial drift was washed down into a valley by meltwater. Today, these glaciofluvial deposits are seen along stream valleys, often great distances beyond the margin of the outwash plain.

Ice-Contact Deposits: Among the most varied features left by glaciers are those known as **ice-contact deposits** (Figure 42-2). These are the landforms that develop along the margin of the glacier, and include well-sorted sand and gravel, along with unorganized till. "Kame and kettle" topography often develops from ice-contact deposits.

A **kame** is a hill of debris that originally filled a hole in the ice. A **kettle** forms in the opposite manner, when a large piece of ice leaves a depression in the glacial drift. Today, many kettles are filled with water as small lakes.

Figure 42-2 shows landform development along the stagnant margin of an ice sheet. As a buried wedge of ice melts, the irregular topography of a **collapsed zone** develops in the outwash deposits.

Post-glacial Drainage Patterns: Areas that have experienced continental glaciation are generally characterized by poor drainage. There are many lakes and swamps in the depressions left by the glaciation. The previous stream system was often totally disrupted, leaving a rather chaotic or **deranged drainage pattern**. The Pleistocene glaciations took place so recently, in geologic terms, that there has not been enough time for a new drainage pattern to become well established.

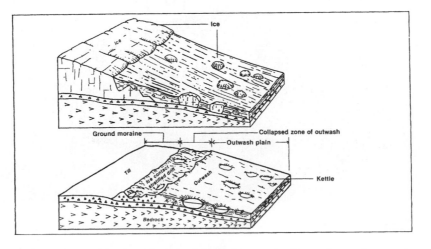

Figure 42-2:   The relationship of buried ice to a collapsed zone in an outwash plain. (From USGS, "Geologic History of Cape Cod, Massachusetts," 1992)

Figure 42-3: Stereogram of drumlin field near Sodus, New York, (scale 1:40,000; USGS photographs, 1995; ↑N).

EXERCISE 42 PROBLEMS—PART I

The following questions are based on Map T-11, the "Whitewater, Wisconsin," quadrangle (scale 1:62,500; contour interval 20 feet; dotted lines represent 10-foot contours). The irregular high ground of "Kettle Moraine State Forest," running diagonally from the lower left to the right center of the map, is a terminal moraine left by a Pleistocene ice sheet. The region northwest of the terminal moraine was once covered by the ice. The region in the southeast corner of the map is the edge of the glacial outwash plain.

1. Visualize a general topographic profile across this landscape, from the upper left corner to the lower right corner of the map, by determining the elevations of the following locations:

    (a)   McLery Cemetery: _____ feet

    (b)   Pumping Stations near Scuppernong: _____ feet

    (c)   Blue Spring Lake: _____ feet

    (d)   Crest of the terminal moraine about 0.5
          mile (0.8 km) south of Blue Spring Lake: _____ feet

    (e)   Round Prairie Cemetery: _____ feet

2. Estimate the minimum thickness of the ice at the terminal moraine in the area of Blue Spring Lake. Assume that the ice extended up at least to the highest point on the moraine. (Determine the thickness of the ice, not its elevation.)

                                                                                    _____ feet

3. Suggest one reason why the elevation of the outwash plain in the southeast is higher than the ground that was below the ice, northwest of the terminal moraine.

4. Briefly describe the current extent of drainage system development around the terminal moraine and in the glacial outwash plain to the southeast.

EXERCISE 42 PROBLEMS—PART II

The following questions are based on Map T-11, the "Whitewater, Wisconsin," quadrangle (scale 1:62,500; contour interval 20 feet; dotted lines represent 10-foot contours). The irregular high ground of "Kettle Moraine State Forest," running diagonally from the lower left to the right center of the map, is a terminal moraine left by a Pleistocene ice sheet. The region northwest of the terminal moraine was once covered by the ice. The region in the southeast corner of the map is the edge of the glacial outwash plain.

1. (a)   What are the landforms shown as a series of small hills near the upper left corner of the map?

    (b)   How did they form?

2. (a)   From which direction did the ice sheet advance toward what is now the terminal moraine? Be specific.

        From _____ to _____

    (b)   What evidence on the map led you to your answer?

3. Provide one explanation of the formation of the cluster of small lakes about 1 mile (1.6 km) northeast of La Grange (near the southern margin of the map).

4. (a)   The straight blue lines are artificial channels being used to drain swampy areas. Suggest one explanation of the formation of these swamps.

    (b)   What is the evidence that these drainage channels are having their intended result?

EXERCISE 42 PROBLEMS—PART III

The following questions are based on Map T-12, the "Sodus, New York," quadrangle (scale 1:24,000; contour interval 10 feet) and Figure 42-3, a stereogram of this same area. The map and stereogram show a number of drumlins, each with its long axis oriented approximately north-south.

1. Compare the dimensions of four of the drumlins on the map, identified below by their peak elevation. These drumlins are found from right to left on the map.

    "Drumlin Height" refers to the relief of the drumlin, not its elevation. Estimate the "length" of the drumlins from north to south (a graphic map scale is found inside the front cover of the Lab Manual). Finally, note whether the north-facing or south-facing side of the drumlin has the steepest slope.

Drumlin Peak Elevation	Drumlin Height	Length (in feet)	Steepest Slope (North or South Slope)
547 feet			
680 feet			
615 feet			
≈605 feet			

2. Most geomorphologists suggest that the long axis of a drumlin reflects the direction of ice flow, with the steepest end facing the direction from which the ice came.

    Based on this assumption, from which direction did the ice flow over this region?

    From _____ to _____

3. (a) Does it appear that these drumlins have been significantly altered by stream erosion?

   (b) Explain the reasons for your answer.

4. Briefly describe the current extent of drainage system development in this area.

5. To what extent have human features been influenced by the local topography?

EXERCISE 43
ALPINE GLACIATION

Objective:	To study the landforms produced by alpine glaciation, and to learn to recognize these landforms on topographic maps.
Materials:	Lens stereoscope.
Resources:	Internet access (optional).
Reference:	McKnight and Hess, *Physical Geography*, 9th ed., pp. 563–565 and 575–583.

MOUNTAIN GLACIATION

During the Pleistocene, most of the high mountain areas of the world were glaciated. Many of these regions are still undergoing glaciation, although on a reduced scale.

Alpine glaciers are individual glaciers that develop high on a mountain and then flow downvalley some distance, while other mountain glaciers develop and flow out of **highland ice fields** that can be many kilometers across. The emphasis of this exercise will be primarily alpine glaciation. Alpine glaciers don't necessarily develop at the top of the highest mountain peaks. They generally need protected valleys, often below the summits of peaks, in order to accumulate enough snow to form glacier ice.

MOVEMENT OF GLACIERS

As with continental ice sheets, the size of an alpine glacier is a consequence of the balance between the **accumulation** of snow and ice and the annual wasting away of the ice through melting, evaporation and sublimation—collectively known as **ablation**.

As shown in Figure 43-1, in the upper portion of a glacier there is greater annual accumulation of ice than ablation, while in the lower portion of the glacier there is greater ablation than accumulation. The boundary between these two zones of a glacier is called the **annual snowline** or **firn limit**. Firn is partially compacted snow that has survived from a previous winter. The location of the firn limit can vary from year to year, depending on the amount of precipitation and temperature levels.

As a glacier flows down its valley beyond the firn limit, it increasingly ablates until it reaches its **terminus**, the point it can no longer advance. The terminus of a glacier is the location where the ice is melting as quickly as it is flowing in. It is important to note that when the terminus of a glacier is stationary (or even when it is retreating up a valley), the ice within a glacier continues to flow forward.

297

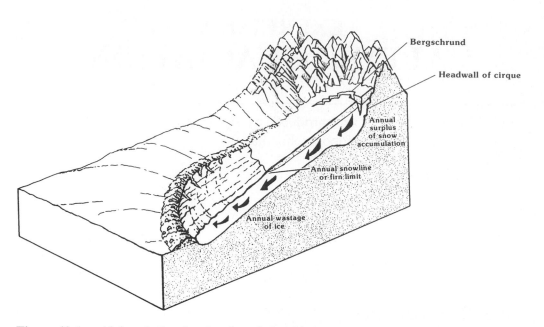

Figure 43-1: Alpine glacier showing the relationship between accumulation and ablation. (From U.S. Geological Survey Bulletin 1595)

EROSIONAL LANDFORMS FROM ALPINE GLACIATION

While depositional features tend to dominant the landscape once covered by continental ice sheets, erosional landforms are usually the most conspicuous features left by alpine glaciers.

The most basic of all alpine glacial landforms is the bowl or amphitheater-shaped valley head called a **cirque** (Figure 43-2b). The head and side walls of a cirque may be nearly vertical, while the floor has often been carved into a shallow basin (see the profile view in Figure 43-1).

Cirques grow through **glacial plucking** and **frost wedging** along the **headwall**. Especially in summer, a crevice at the head of the glacier, known as the **bergschrund** (shown at the top of the glacier in Figure 43-1) opens and exposes the headwall to the freeze–thaw cycle. When water seeps down into the cracks and joints of the rock and freezes, the expansion of the ice further pries apart the opening.

When cirques are being worn back into a ridge from opposite sides through glacial erosion and frost wedging, a jagged ridge crest called an **arête** is formed. If erosion from both sides continues enough to remove part of the arête itself, a sharp-crested pass known as a **col** is formed.

Horns are another prominent alpine glacial landform. A horn is a pyramid-shaped mountain peak that develops as cirques are worn into the peak from three or four sides.

Alpine glaciers alter the shape and profile of former stream valleys. Glaciers tend to deepen and steepen valleys, changing them from a V-shaped to a **glacial trough** with a U-shaped cross-section. In addition, glaciers may partially straighten the sinuous pattern typical of stream valleys.

In contrast, the downvalley profiles of glacial troughs are often somewhat irregular. Many glacial valleys have pronounced **glacial steps** (Figure 43-3) that evidently result from differences in the resistance of the valley floor rocks. The location of the upper edge of the ice, or "trimline," of a glacier is often clearly visible on the valley walls. Repeated cycles of frost wedging above the

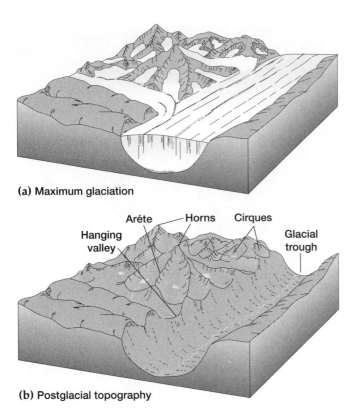

(a) Maximum glaciation

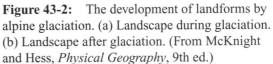

Aréte   Horns   Cirques

Hanging
valley   Glacial
                                         trough

(b) Postglacial topography

Figure 43-2:   The development of landforms by
alpine glaciation. (a) Landscape during glaciation.
(b) Landscape after glaciation. (From McKnight
and Hess, *Physical Geography*, 9th ed.)

glacier tend to leave a rather jagged landscape, while glacial erosion below the trimline tends to
leave a more smoothly sculpted landscape.

   Hanging valleys are left when tributary glaciers enter the main valley glacier. The smaller
tributary glaciers cannot deepen their valleys as much as the main trunk glacier, so after the ice is
gone, these tributary valleys are left entering high above the main valley floor (Figure 43-2a and b).

   Figure 43-4 is a stereogram showing Mt. Gibbs and the heavily glaciated eastern crest of
the Sierra Nevada in California. (This stereogram has been optimized for the area around Mt.
Gibbs—it does not show a clear stereo image of the landscape at lower elevations.) Map T-13, the
"Mono Craters, California," quadrangle (scale 1:62,500; contour interval 80 feet), shows this same
region of the Sierra.

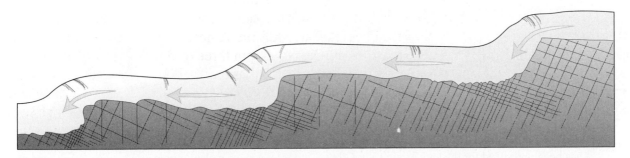

Figure 43-3:   A longitudinal cross section of a glaciated valley in mountainous terrain showing a sequence of
glacial steps. (From McKnight and Hess, *Physical Geography*, 9th ed.)

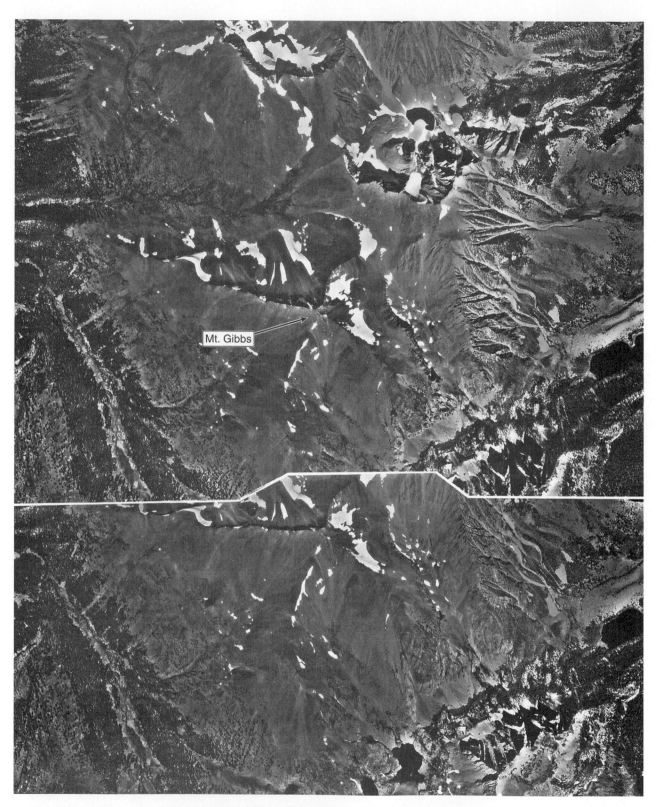

Figure 43-4: Stereogram of Mt. Gibbs and the glaciated eastern crest of the Sierra Nevada. This stereogram has been optimized for the area around Mt. Gibbs—it does not show a clear stereo image of the landscape at lower elevations (scale 1:40,000; USGS photographs, 1993; ↑N).

300

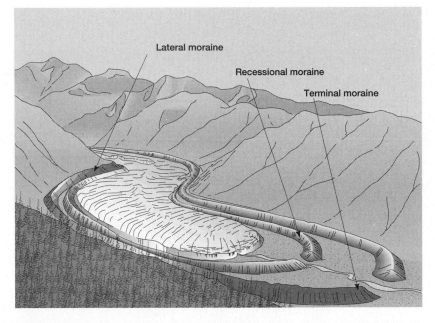

Figure 43-5: Moraines formed by an alpine glacier. (From McKnight and Hess, *Physical Geography*, 9th ed.)

DEPOSITIONAL LANDFORMS FROM ALPINE GLACIATION

While erosional landforms are usually the most prominent features left by alpine glaciers, a number of important depositional landforms may be seen as well.

The maximum advance of an alpine glacier may be marked by a **terminal moraine** (Figure 43-5), and pauses in the retreat of a glacier are marked by **recessional moraines**. Often, the most distinctive depositional features left by alpine glaciers are **lateral moraines**. These ridges—made of unsorted, angular rock debris known as **till**—accumulate along the sides of a valley glacier. Where two glaciers come together, their adjacent lateral moraines may join and continue down the middle of a glacier, forming a **medial moraine**.

Figure 43-6 is a stereogram showing Bloody Canyon and the eastern crest of the Sierra Nevada in California. Walker Lake lies between two sets of large lateral moraines (north is to the left side of the stereogram). Map T-13, the "Mono Craters, California," quadrangle (scale 1:62,500; contour interval 80 feet), shows this same region of the Sierra.

LAKES FROM ALPINE GLACIATION

Lakes are common in regions that have experienced alpine glaciation. A **tarn** is a lake that forms in the depression of a cirque. A chain of lakes may develop in a valley with glacial steps. Often each step will have a lake, connected to the lake on the step below by a stream. These chains of lakes are known as **paternoster lakes**, since they resemble the beads on a rosary. Finally, terminal or recessional moraines can act as dams to form lakes at the mouths of glacial valleys.

301

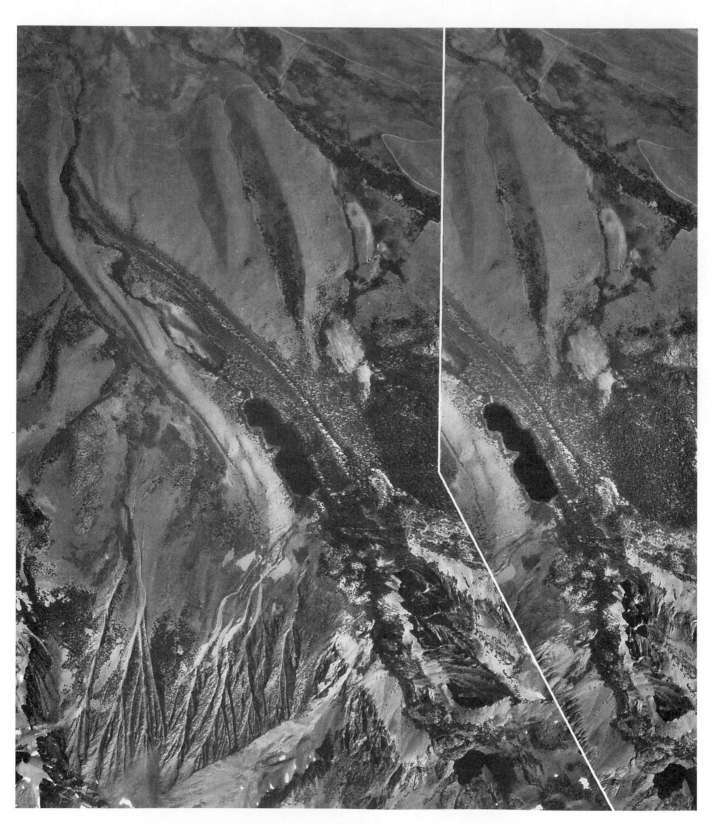

Figure 43-6: Stereogram of Bloody Canyon and Walker Lake along the eastern crest of the Sierra Nevada. North is to the left side of the page (scale 1:40,000; USGS photographs, 1993; ← N).

Name _____   Section _____

EXERCISE 43 PROBLEMS—PART I

The following questions are based on Map T-13, the "Mono Craters, California," quadrangle (scale 1:62,500; contour interval 80 feet), and Figures 43-4 and 43-6, stereograms of the same region. The heavily glaciated eastern crest of the Sierra Nevada is seen along the western sides of the map and stereograms. During the Pleistocene, glaciers in this region flowed down the valleys of the eastern slope of the Sierra toward the Mono Lake basin to the northeast. Large lateral moraines are found at the mouths of each canyon.

1. (a) A small glacier is located just north of the Dana Plateau (in the northwest section of the map). In what kind of glacial landform is this glacier found?   _____

    (b) What evidence suggests this feature was cut by a glacier that was larger than the present one?

2. (a) What is the name for the kind of glacial landform illustrated by Mt. Gibbs? (See Figure 43-4, a stereogram showing Mt. Gibbs.) _____

    (b) How did it form?

    (c) Find and name one more example of this same kind of landform: _____

3. (a) How many tributary glaciers clearly flowed into Bloody Canyon? _____

    (b) How can you tell?

4. Large lateral moraines can be seen at the mouth of Bloody Canyon (Walker Lake and Walker Creek are between these moraines). The glacier that left these moraines flowed down Bloody Canyon from near Mono Pass. Sawmill Canyon (just south of Bloody Canyon) consists of two large lateral moraines—these moraines were left by a glacier that at one time also flowed down Bloody Canyon.

    (a) Which set of moraines formed first: the Bloody Canyon moraines or the Sawmill Canyon moraines?   _____

    (b) How do you know?

EXERCISE 43 PROBLEMS—PART II

The following questions are based on Map T-13, the "Mono Craters, California," quadrangle (scale 1:62,500; contour interval 80 feet), and Figures 43-4 and 43-6, stereograms of the same region. The heavily glaciated eastern crest of the Sierra Nevada is seen along the western sides of the map and stereograms. During the Pleistocene, glaciers in this region flowed down the valleys of the eastern slope of the Sierra toward the Mono Lake basin to the northeast. Large lateral moraines are found at the mouths of each canyon.

1.   There are five small glaciers shown on this map (glaciers are shown as white patches with blue contour lines). Why can glaciers survive today in these locations but not in others?

2.   What evidence suggests that the edges of the Dana Plateau were extensively glaciated in the past?

3.   Find and describe the location of a hanging valley.

4.   (a)   Name one valley with glacial steps: _____

        (b)   How many steps?   _____

        (c)   How many lakes are found in the series of steps?   _____

5.   (a)   What is the name for the kind of glacial landform marked by the black dashed line halfway between Mt. Dana and Mt. Gibbs?

        (b)   How did it form?

6.   How thick was the ice in the glacier that flowed down Lee Vining canyon? You may assume that the top of a lateral moraine represents the upper level of the glacier. Measure the height of the lateral moraines south of the word "Creek" in "Lee Vining Creek."

                                                                    _____ feet

EXERCISE 43 PROBLEMS—PART III

Questions 1 and 2 on the following page are based on the section of the "Mt. Tom, California," quadrangle reproduced below (Figure 43-7). The map shows a pair of large lateral moraines at the mouth of Pine Creek coming down the eastern slope of the Sierra Nevada. A road (shown as a double black line) follows the course of Pine Creek out of the valley between the lateral moraines.

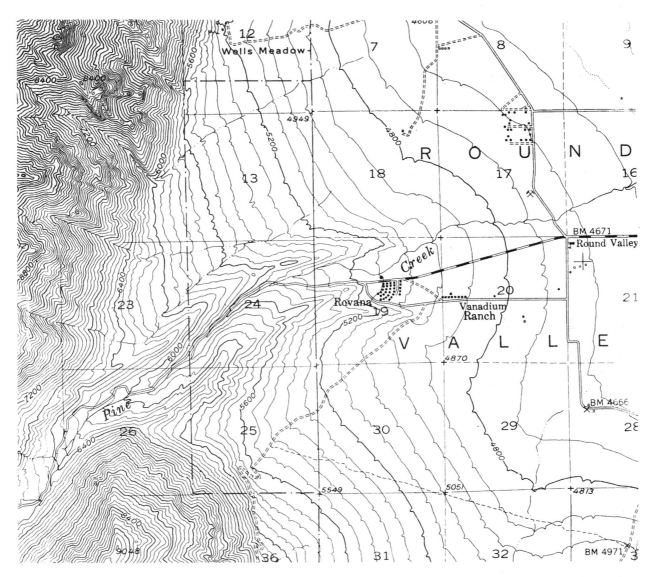

Figure 43-7: USGS "Mt. Tom, California," quadrangle (enlarged to scale 1:48,000; contour interval 80 feet; ↑N).

1. With a red pencil, mark the crests of each lateral moraine. Also mark the crests of any branches of these moraines.

2. From the pattern of moraines, describe the evidence of more than one glacial advance:

The following questions are based on Map T-13, the "Mono Craters, California," quadrangle (scale 1:62,500; contour interval 80 feet), and Figure 43-6, a stereogram showing Bloody Canyon and Walker Lake.

3. How high is the lateral moraine just south of the word "Lake" in "Walker Lake? (Determine the relief of the moraine, not its elevation.)

_____ feet

4. Based on the evidence you see in the map and in the stereogram, explain the formation of Walker Lake:

EXERCISE 43 PROBLEMS—PART IV

The following questions are based on Map T-14, the "Sumdum (D-4), Alaska," quadrangle (scale 1:63,360; contour interval 100 feet). The map shows two glaciers entering the "Tracy Arm." The Tracy Arm is a fjord just south of Juneau, Alaska (see Exercise 44 for a brief discussion of fjords). The "Sawyer Glacier" enters the Tracy Arm from the north, and the "South Sawyer Glacier" enters the Tracy Arm from the southeast.

1. What topographic evidence (other than the glaciers entering the water) suggests that the Tracy Arm is a fjord?

2. Find the tributary glacier that enters the South Sawyer Glacier from the south (the tributary enters just east of the word "Wilderness"):

    (a)   What are the brown stripes along the sides of the glacier (shown with brown stippling)? _____

    (b)   What are the brown stripes down the middle of the glacier?   _____

    (c)   Explain how these stripes came to be in the middle of the glacier:

3. Find the word "South" in the label for the "South Sawyer Glacier" (in the east central part of the map). Assume that the rate of movement of this glacier is 9 inches (22 cm) per day (a hypothetical rate). How long would it take the ice to move from the location marked by the "S" in the word "South," to the water of the Tracy Arm? It may be easiest if you determine the distance in inches or centimeters, rather than in feet, miles, or kilometers.

    (a)   Distance (from "S" to the water): $\dfrac{\rule{3cm}{0.4pt}}{\text{feet (or meters)}} = \dfrac{\rule{3cm}{0.4pt}}{\text{inches (or cm)}}$

    (b)   Time for ice to move to the Tracy Arm: _____ years

4. Describe a location where a horn has developed at the top of a mountain peak:

5. Describe the location where an arête is being formed:

6. Describe the location of a glacier that is currently confined to a cirque:

Name ______________________________________ Section ________________

EXERCISE 43 PROBLEMS—PART V—INTERNET

The following questions are based on Figures 43-8, 43-9, 43-10, 43-11, 43-12, and 43-13, photographs you can view on the Lab Manual Web site. Go to the McKnight and Hess textbook Web site, <***http://www.prenhall.com/mcknight***>. Select "Lab Manual," then "Exercise 43."

1. (a) Which of photograph—Figure 43-8 or Figure 43-9—shows a deposit of glacial till?

   Figure 43-__________

   (b) Describe the evidence you see in the photographs that supports your answer:

2. (a) Which of photograph—Figure 43-10 or Figure 43-11—shows a landscape predominately shaped by glacial erosion? Figure 43-__________

   (b) Describe the evidence you see in the photographs that supports your answer:

3. Look at Figure 43-12, a photograph showing a glaciated landscape on the eastern side of the Sierra Nevada mountains in California.

   (a) What erosional feature is marked by the letter "A"? ________________________

   (b) What erosional feature is marked by the letter "B"? ________________________

4. Look at Figure 43-13, a photograph showing the terminus of the Emmons Glacier on Mount Rainier in Washington. The end of the Emmons Glacier is heavily mantled with rock debris.

   (a) What kind of depositional feature is forming in the area marked with the letter "C"? ____________________________

   (b) What kind of depositional feature is marked by the letter "D"? ____________________________

   (c) Was the feature marked "D" formed by the present-day Emmons Glacier? ________

   (d) How do you know?

EXERCISE 44
COASTAL LANDFORMS

Objective: To study the special processes and landforms found along coastlines.

Materials: Lens stereoscope.

Reference: McKnight and Hess, *Physical Geography*, 9th ed., pp. 590–593 and 597–605.

SPECIAL COASTAL PROCESSES

Waves: Waves are by far the most important erosional force shaping coastlines. Wave erosion along a coastline is influenced by a phenomenon known as **wave refraction**. As illustrated in Figure 44-1, when a wave approaches shore, the segment of the wave to reach shallow water first begins to slow, while the segment of the wave in deeper water continues to move quickly. Because of wave refraction, waves typically strike parallel to shore, and tend to concentrate their erosive power on headlands.

Coastal Sediment Transport: Sediment is transported along a shoreline in two main ways (Figure 44-2). **Longshore currents** are commonly the key transportation mechanism of sediment along a shoreline. Longshore currents are set up by the action of the waves, and because most waves are generated by the wind, these currents generally flow downwind and parallel to the shore. Sediment also moves through **beach drifting** in a "zigzag" fashion through wave **swash** onto the beach, and **backwash** off the beach.

Changes in Sea Level: During the height of the Pleistocene glaciations, so much water was locked up on the continents as glacier ice that the level of the ocean dropped as much as

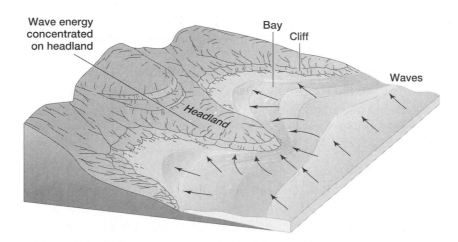

Figure 44-1: Wave refraction on an irregular coastline. (From McKnight and Hess, *Physical Geography*, 9th ed.)

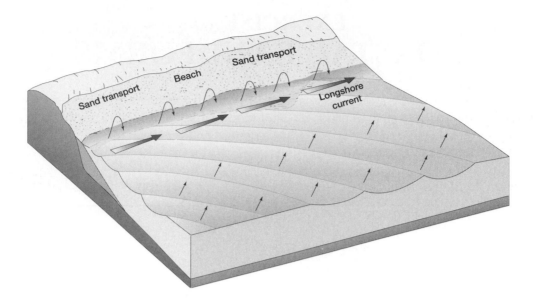

Figure 44-2: Coastal sediment transport. Beach drifting involves the zigzag movement of sand along a beach. Sand is brought obliquely onto the beach by the wave, and then is returned seaward by the backwash. Longshore currents develop just offshore and move sediment parallel to shore. Both beach drifting and longshore currents are set up by the action of waves striking a shoreline at a slight angle. (From McKnight and Hess, *Physical Geography*, 9th ed.)

100 meters (325 feet). At the end of the Pleistocene, 10,000 years ago, sea level rose and flooded many low-lying coastal areas. Evidence of this recent rise in sea level is visible along many coastlines around the world.

COMMON COASTAL LANDFORMS

While coastlines exhibit a great variety of landforms, there are several common coastal landform assemblages.

Shorelines of Submergence: Because of the recent rise in sea level at the end of the Pleistocene, many shorelines show evidence of being submerged. When stream-cut topography is submerged, it forms what is called a **ria coastline**. In ria coastlines, what were once stream valleys have now become inlets and bays, and what were once hilltops have now become islands. A **fjorded coast** develops when glacial valleys are flooded by the sea. Fjords are typically long, narrow inlets with steep valley walls leading up from the water.

Depositional Landforms: There are many different kinds of depositional features found along coastlines. In general, deposition takes place where the power of currents (especially longshore currents) or waves is diminished.

One of the most common depositional features is the **spit** (Figure 44-3). A spit typically forms where a longshore current (shown with an arrow) moves over deeper water, such as at the mouth of a bay. As the current moves out over deeper water, it loses some of its power, and deposition

310

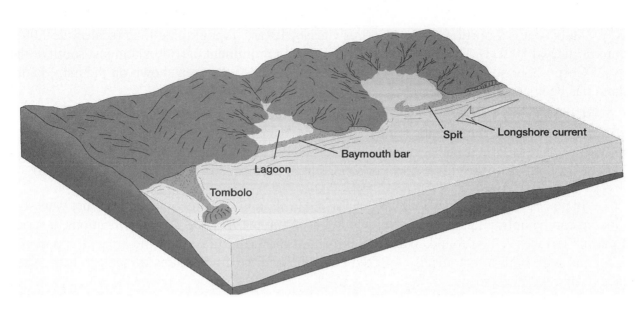

Figure 44-3: Common depositional landforms along a coastline. (From McKnight and Hess, *Physical Geography*, 9th ed.)

takes place. For this reason, a spit generally points down current. Some spits develop a "hook" when currents carry some sediment back toward shore. **Baymouth bars** develop where a spit extends across an inlet, closing off a **lagoon**. A **tombolo** is formed where waves converge from two directions, connecting an offshore island with the mainland.

      Barrier Islands: **Barrier islands** (also called **barrier bars** or **offshore bars**) are found on gently sloping, shallow coastal shelves, such as along much of the Gulf and Atlantic coast areas of the United States. Barrier bars are low-lying and generally run parallel to the mainland, although they are often found several kilometers offshore. Lagoons are commonly formed behind barrier bars (Figure 44-4). These lagoons will generally fill up with sediment over time. The formation of barrier bars is not completely understood. They evidently develop where waves break and deposit sediment some distance offshore, but the existence of some of the larger barrier islands appears to be associated with sea level changes during the Pleistocene.

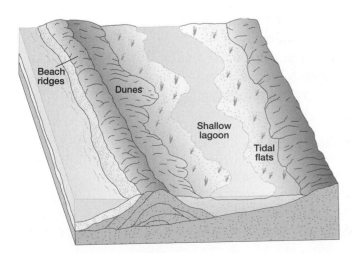

Figure 44-4: A typical relationship among the ocean, barrier island, and lagoon. (From McKnight and Hess, *Physical Geography*, 9th ed.)

Map T-16 is a portion of the "Corpus Christi, Texas," topographic map (scale 1:250,000; contour interval 50 feet). The map shows Padre Island, a prominent barrier island just south of the city of Corpus Christi along the gulf coast of Texas. South of the area shown on the map, Padre Island has been heavily developed.

Cliff/Marine Terrace: Figure 44-5 illustrates the combination of a cliff, wave-cut platform, and a marine terrace. The cliff tends to wear back through undercutting from wave action. At the same time, a wave-cut platform is being formed just below the surface of the water. As erosion proceeds, it is common for portions of the cliff to become isolated from the mainland as **sea stacks** (Figure 44-6).

In places where the coastline has been rising (a shoreline of emergence), a former wave-cut platform can be uplifted above sea level and left as a **marine terrace**. In some locations, a series of marine terraces can be found. The development of marine terraces in some areas is apparently associated with both a tectonically uplifted coastline and the fluctuations of sea level that took place during the Pleistocene.

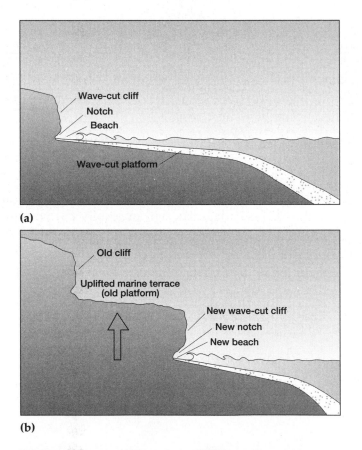

Figure 44-5:   A marine terrace develops when a wave-cut platform is tectonically uplifted above sea level. (From McKnight and Hess, *Physical Geography*, 9th ed.)

312

A series of marine terraces is shown in Figure 44-7, a stereogram showing the southwestern side of San Clemente Island in southern California. Figure 44-8 is a topographic map of the same region. Each gently sloping marine terrace level is separated from the next higher terrace level by a steep slope. The well-preserved lower terrace levels are the easiest ones to recognize in the stereogram.

Figure 44-6: Sea stacks and coastal cliffs in Port Campbell National Park, Victoria, Australia. (Tom L. McKnight photo from McKnight and Hess, *Physical Geography*, 9th ed.)

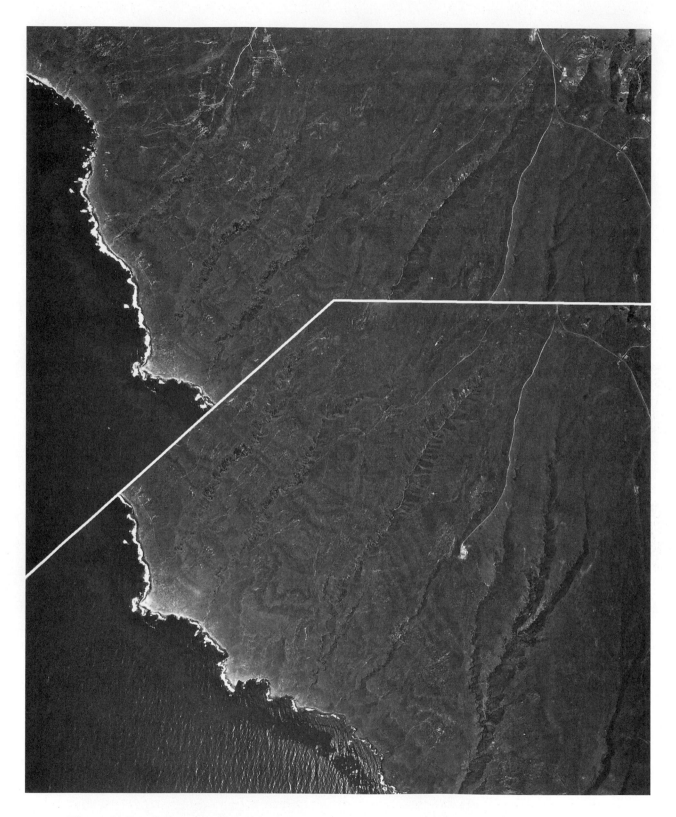

Figure 44-7: Stereogram of marine terraces on San Clemente Island, California (scale 1:40,000; USGS photographs, 1990; ↑N).

Name _____   Section _____

EXERCISE 44 PROBLEMS—PART I

The following questions are based on Map T-15, the "Point Reyes, California," quadrangle (scale 1:62,500; contour interval 80 feet).

1.   Explain the formation of Drakes Estero. Does it appear to be the feature of a shoreline of emergence or submergence?

2.   What suggests that Drakes Estero is quite shallow?

3.   (a)   Explain the formation of the hook-shaped lake southeast of "D Ranch."

      (b)   Explain the formation of the small pond and swamp just northwest of Drakes Beach.

4.   What is the dominant direction of the longshore current that produced Limantour Spit?

               From _____ to _____

5.   What evidence of wave erosion is visible along the shore of Drakes Bay between Drakes Beach and Point Reyes?

6.   Describe the general coastal topography along the south face of Point Reyes itself.

EXERCISE 44 PROBLEMS—PART II

The following questions are based on Map T-16, the "Corpus Christi, Texas," topographic map (scale 1:250,000; contour interval 50 feet; supplementary contours at 25-foot intervals). Padre Island is a prominent barrier island south of the city of Corpus Christi, Texas.

1.   (a)   How far offshore is the barrier island at the "P" in the words "Padre Island"?   _____ miles

      (b)   How wide is the island at this point?   _____ miles

      (c)   What is the highest elevation shown on Padre Island?   _____ feet

2.   (a)   On which side of Padre Island (east or west) does deposition seem most prominent?   _____

      (b)   Suggest a reason why.

3.   (a)   What is the most likely origin of Baffin Bay?

      (b)   What is the evidence for this?

4.   (a)   Does it appear that "Laguna Madre" (between Padre Island and the mainland) is filling with sediment?

      (b)   What is the evidence of this?

      (c)   What are the likely sources of this sediment?

Name _____   Section _____

EXERCISE 44 PROBLEMS—PART III

The following questions are based on Figure 44-8, a portion of the "San Clemente Island Central, California," quadrangle shown on the following page (scale 1:24,000; contour interval 25 feet; index contours drawn every fourth line), and the stereogram of San Clemente Island (Figure 44-7). The map and stereogram show a series of marine terraces on San Clemente Island in southern California. The terraces have been incised by streams in several places.

1. Using the graph below, construct a topographic profile from Point A to Point B. Plot index contours, and any intermediate contours necessary to accurately show significant changes in topography. The vertical exaggeration of the profile is 2×. The stereogram may be helpful in recognizing the extent of some terrace levels.

2. (a) How many marine terraces are shown on the profile?   _____

   (b) Number the terraces on your topographic profile (with the terrace closest to sea level as number "1").

   (c) With a blue pencil, number the terraces on the map in the same way.

3. Do all of the terraces shown on your topographic profile extend, without interruption, to the southeast and northwest along this side of the island?

4. Using the terraces shown on your topographic profile as a starting point, denote the extent of each terrace level across the entire map. Using a green pencil, outline the seaward lip of each terrace level shown on the map.

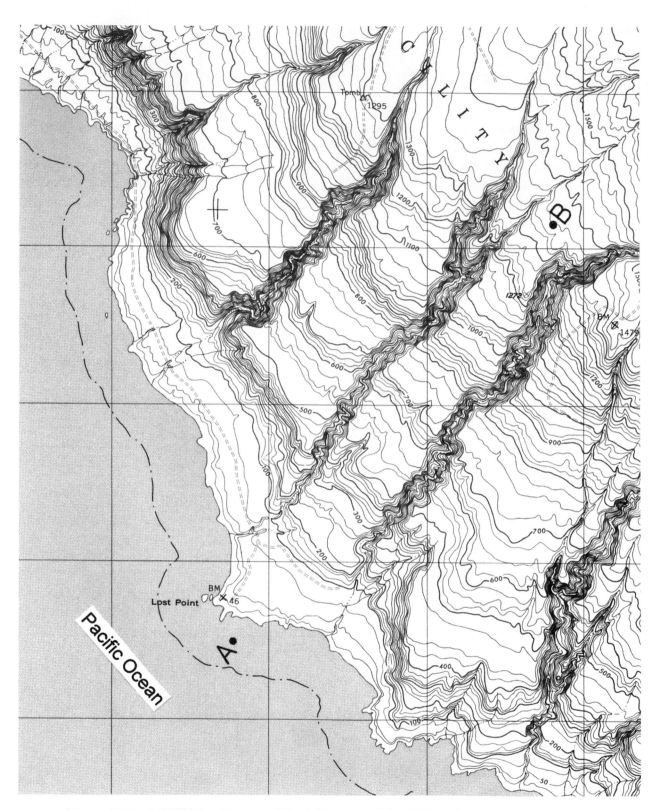

Figure 44-8: USGS "San Clemente Island Central, California," quadrangle (scale 1:24,000; contour interval 25 feet; note that the index contours on this map have been drawn every fourth line; ↑N).

APPENDIX I
WEATHER MAP SYMBOLS

The charts and diagrams on the following pages show the symbols and codes used on standard weather maps.

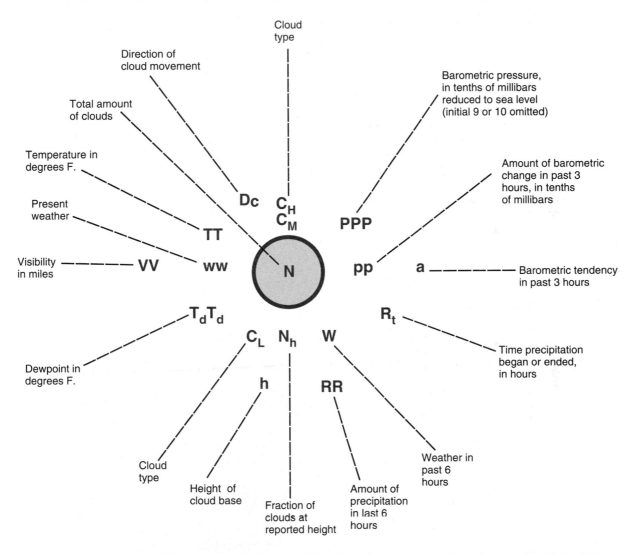

Figure I-1: Standard weather station model showing placement of codes. (From McKnight and Hess, *Physical Geography*, 9th ed.)

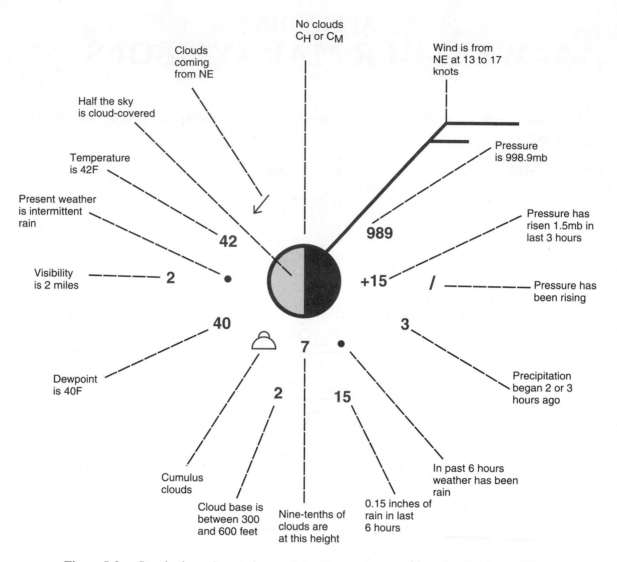

Figure I-2: Standard weather station model with sample data. (From McKnight and Hess, *Physical Geography*, 9th ed.)

00 Cloud development NOT observed or NOT observable during past hour.§	01 Clouds generally dissolving or becoming less developed during past hour.§	02 State of sky on the whole unchanged during past hour.§	03 Clouds generally forming or developing during past hour.§	04 Visibility reduced by smoke.	05 Dry haze.	06 Widespread dust in suspension in the air. Not raised by wind, at time of observation.	07 Dust or sand raised by the wind, at time of ob.	08 Well developed dust devil(s) within past hr.	09 Duststorm or sandstorm within sight of or at station during past hour.
10 Light fog.	11 Patches of shallow fog at station, NOT deeper than 6 feet on land.	12 More or less continuous shallow fog at station, NOT deeper than 6 feet on land.	13 Lightning visible, no thunder heard.	14 Precipitation within sight, but NOT reaching the ground at station.	15 Precipitation within sight, reaching the ground, but distant from station.	16 Precipitation within sight, reaching the ground, near to but Not at station.	17 Thunder heard, but no precipitation at the station.	18 Squall(s) within sight during past hour.	19 Funnel cloud(s) within sight during past hr.
20 Drizzle (NOT freezing and NOT falling as showers) during past hour, but NOT at time of ob.	21 Rain (NOT freezing and NOT falling as showers during past hr., but NOT at time of ob.	22 Snow (NOT falling as showers) during past hr., but NOT at time of ob.	23 Rain and snow (NOT falling as showers) during past hr., but NOT at time of ob.	24 Freezing drizzle or freezing rain (NOT falling as showers) during past hour, but Not at time of observation.	25 Showers or rain during past hour, but NOT at time of observation.	26 Showers of snow, or rain and snow, during past hour, but NOT at time of observation.	27 Showers of hail, or of hail and rain, during past hour, but NOT at time of observation.	28 Fog during past hour, but NOT at time of ob.	29 Thunderstorm (with or without precipitation) during past hour, but NOT at time of ob.
30 Slight or moderate duststorm or sandstorm, has decreased during past hour.	31 Slight or moderate duststorm or sandstorm, no appreciable change during past hour.	32 Slight or moderate duststorm or sandstorm, has increased during past hour.	33 Severe duststorm or sandstorm, has decreased during past hour.	34 Severe duststorm or sandstorm no appreciable change during past hour.	35 Severe duststorm or sandstorm, has increased during past hour.	36 Slight or moderate drifting snow, generally low.	37 Heavy drifting snow, generally low.	38 Slight or moderate drifting snow, generally high.	39 Heavy drifting snow, generally high.
40 Fog at distance at time of ob., but NOT at station during past hour.	41 Fog in patches.	42 Fog, sky discernible, has become thinner during past hour.	43 Fog, sky NOT discernible, has become thinner during past hour.	44 Fog, sky discernible, no appreciable change during past hour.	45 Fog, sky NOT discernible, no appreciable change during past hour.	46 Fog, sky discernible, has begun or become thicker during past hr.	47 Fog, sky NOT discernible, has begun or become thicker during past hour.	48 Fog, depositing time, sky discernible.	49 Fog, depositing time, sky NOT discernible.

50 Intermittent drizzle (NOT freezing) slight at time of observation.	51 Continuous drizzle (NOT freezing) slight at time of observation.	52 Intermittent drizzle (NOT freezing) moderate at time of ob.	53 Intermittent drizzle (NOT freezing) moderate at time of ob.	54 Intermittent drizzle (NOT freezing) thick at time of observation.	55 Continuous drizzle (NOT freezing) thick at time of observation.	56 Slight freezing drizzle.	57 Moderate or thick freezing drizzle.	58 Drizzle and rain slight.	59 Drizzle and rain, moderate or heavy.
60 Intermittent rain (NOT freezing), slight at time of observation.	61 Continuous rain (NOT freezing), slight at time of observation.	62 Intermittent rain (NOT freezing), moderate at time of ob.	63 Continuous rain (NOT freezing), moderate at time of observation.	64 Intermittent rain (NOT freezing), heavy at time of observation.	65 Continuous rain (NOT freezing), heavy at time of observation.	66 Slight freezing rain.	67 Moderate or heavy freezing rain.	68 Rain or drizzle and snow, slight.	69 Rain or drizzle and snow, mod, or heavy.
70 Intermittent fall of snow flakes, slight at time of observation.	71 Continuous fall of snowflakes, slight at time of observation.	72 Intermittent fall of snow flakes, moderate at time of observation.	73 Continuous fall of snowflakes, moderate at time of observation.	74 Intermittent fall of snow flakes, heavy at time of observation.	75 Continuous fall of snowflakes, heavy at time of observation.	76 Ice needles (with or without fog).	77 Granular snow (with or without fog).	78 Isolated starlite snow crystals (with or without fog).	79 Ice pellets (sleet, U.S. definition).
80 Slight rain showers.	81 Moderate or heavy rain shower(s).	82 Violent rain shower(s).	83 Slight shower(s) of rain and snow mixed.	84 Moderate or heavy shower(s) of rain and snow mixed.	85 Slight snow shower(s).	86 Moderate or heavy snow showers(s).	87 Slight showers(s) of soft or small hail with or without rain or rain and snow mixed.	88 Moderate or heavy shower(s) of soft or small hail with or without rain or rain and snow mixed.	89 Slight shower(s) of hail††, with or without rain or rain and snow mixed, not associated with thunder.
90 Moderate or heavy shower(s) of hail††. with or without rain or rain and snow mixed, not associated with thunder.	91 Slight rain at time of ob., thunderstorm during past hour, but NOT at time of observation.	92 Moderate or heavy rain at time of ob., thunderstorm during past hour, but NOT at time of observation.	93 Slight snow or rain and snow mixed or hail† at time of ob., thunderstorm during past hour, but not at time of ob.	94 Mod. or heavy snow, or rain and snow mixed or hail† at time of ob., thunderstorm during past hour, but NOT at time of ob.	95 Slight or mod. thunderstorm without hail†, but with rain and or snow at time of ob.	96 Slight or mod. thunderstorm with hail† at time of observation.	97 Heavy thunderstorm, without hail†, but with rain and or snow at time of observation.	98 Thunderstorm combined with duststorm or sandstorm at time of ob.	99 Heavy thunderstorm with hail† at time of ob.

Figure I-3: Standard weather station model symbols used to indicate "Present Weather" (ww). (From McKnight and Hess, *Physical Geography*, 9th ed.)

321

	C_L Clouds of type C_L	C_M Clouds of type C_M	C_H Clouds of type C_H	W Past Weather	N_h*	a Barometer characteristics
0	No Sc, St, Cu, or Cb clouds.	No Ac, As, Cu, or Ns clouds.	No Ci, Cc, or $\overline{Cs}$ clouds.	Clear or few clouds.	No clouds.	Rising then falling. Now higher than 3 hours ago.
1	Cu with little vertical development and seemingly flattened.	Thin As (entire cloud layer semitransparent).	Filaments of Ci, scattered and not increasing.	Partly cloudy (scattered) or variable sky.	Less than one-tenth or one-tenth.	Rising, then steady; or rising, then rising more slowly. Now higher than, as, 3 hours ago.
2	Cu of considerable development, generally towering, with or without other Cu or Sc; bases all at same level.	Thick As, or Ns.	Dense Ci in patches or twisted sheaves, usually not increasing.	Cloudy (broken or overcast).	Two- or three-tenths.	Rising steadily, or unsteady. Now higher than, 3 hours ago.
3	Cb with tops lacking clear-cut outlines, but distinctly not cirriform or anvil-shaped; with or without Cu, Sc or St.	Thin Ac; cloud elements not changing much and at a single level.	Ci, often anvil-shaped, derived from or associated with Cb.	Sandstorm, or dust-storm. or drifting or blowing snow.	Four-tenths.	Falling or steady, then rising; or rising, then rising more quickly, Now higher than, 3 hours ago.
4	So formed by spreading out of Cu; Cu often present also.	Thin Ac in patches; cloud elements and/ or occurring at more than one level.	Ci, often hook-shaped, gradually spreading over the sky and usually thickening as a whole.	Fog, or smoke, or thick dust haze.	Five-tenths.	Steady, Same as 3 hours ago.§
5	Sc not formed by spreading out of Cu.	Thin Ac in bands or in a layer gradually spreading over sky and usually thickening as a whole.	Ci and Cs, often in converging bands, or Cs alone; the continuous layer not reaching 45° altitude.	Drizzle.	Six-tenths.	Falling, then rising. Same or lower than 3 hours ago.
6	St or Fs or both, but not Fs of bad weather	Ac formed by the spreading out of Cu.	Ci. and Cs, often in converging bands, or Cs alone; the continuous layer exceeding 45° altitude.	Rain.	Seven- or eight-tenths.	Falling, then steady; or falling, then falling more slowly. Now lower than 3 hours ago.
7	Fs and /or Fc of bad weather (scud) usually under As and Ns.	Doubel-layered Ac or a thick layer of Ac, not increasing; or As and Ac both present at same or different levels.	Cs covering the entire sky.	Snow, or rain and snow mixed, or ice pellets (sleet)	Nine-tenths or overcast with openings.	Falling, steady, or unsteady. Now lower than 3 hours ago.
8	Cu and Sc (not formed by spreading out of Cu) with bases at different levels.	Ac in the form of Cu-shaped tufts or Ac with turrets.	Cs not increasing and not covering entire sky; Ci and Cc may be present.	Shower(s).	Completley overcast.	Steady or rising, then falling; or falling, then falling more quickly. Now lower than 3 hours ago.
9	Cb having a clearly fibrous (cirriform) top, often anvil-shaped, with or without Cu, Sc, St, or scud.	Ac of a chaotic sky, usually at different levels; patches of dense Ci are usually present also.	Cc alone or CC with some Ci or Cs, but the Cc being the main cirriform cloud present.	Thunderstorm, with or without precipitation.	Sky obscured.	

*Fraction representing how much of the total cloud cover is at the reported base height.

Figure I-4: Standard weather station model symbols for "Low Clouds" (C_L); "Middle Clouds" (C_M); "High Clouds" (C_H); "Past Weather" (W); "Total Cloud Cover" (N_h); "Barometric Tendency" (a). (From McKnight and Hess, *Physical Geography*, 9th ed.)

h (height of cloud base)	Approximate Cloud Height	
	Feet	Meters
0	0 – 149	0 – 49
1	150 – 299	50 – 99
2	300 – 599	100 – 199
3	600 – 999	200 – 299
4	1000 – 1999	300 – 599
5	2000 – 3499	600 – 999
6	3500 – 4999	1000 – 1499
7	5000 – 4699	1500 –1999
8	6500 – 7999	2000 – 2499
9	>8000 or no clouds	>2500 or no clouds

Figure I-5: Standard weather station model codes for "Height of Cloud Base" (h). (From McKnight and Hess, *Physical Geography*, 9th ed.)

R_t Code	Time of Precipitation
0	No precipitation
1	Less than one hour ago
2	1 to 2 hours ago
3	2 to 3 hours ago
4	3 to 4 hours ago
5	4 to 5 hours ago
6	5 to 6 hours ago
7	6 to 12 hours ago
8	More than 12 hours ago
9	Unknown

Figure I-6: Standard weather station model codes for "Time Precipitation Began or Ended" (R_t). (From McKnight and Hess, *Physical Geography*, 9th ed.)

Symbol	Wind Speed (knots)
	Calm
	1–2
	3–7
	8–12
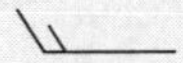	13–17
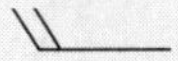	18–22
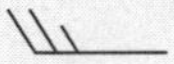	23–27
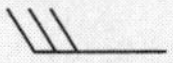	28–32
	33–37
	38–42
	43–47
	48–52
	53–57
	58–62
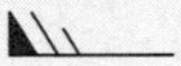	63–67
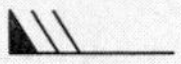	68–72
	73–77

Figure I-7: Standard weather station model symbols for "Wind Speed." (From McKnight and Hess, *Physical Geography*, 9th ed.)

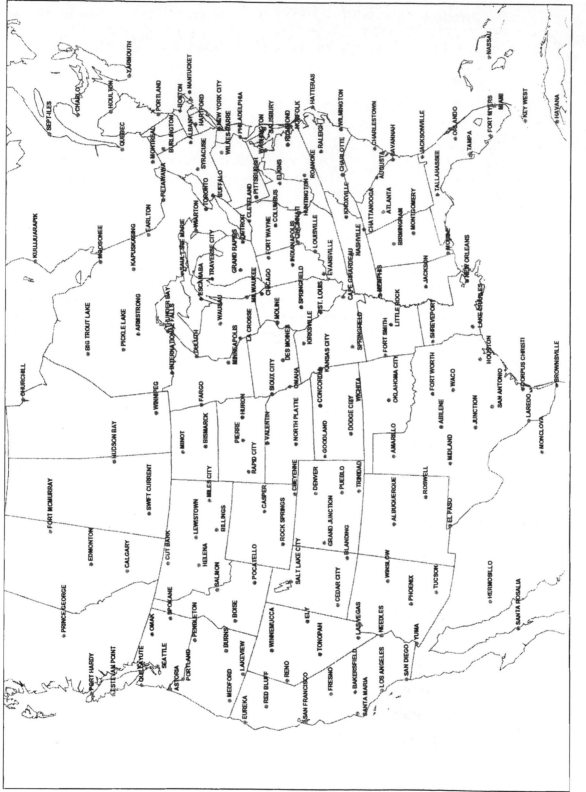

Figure I-8: Daily Weather Map station names and locations. (National Weather Service)

APPENDIX II
COLOR TOPOGRAPHIC MAPS

Sixteen topographic maps are reproduced in the back of the Lab Manual. On each map, the scale, contour interval, and a north arrow are provided. Graphic map scales for 1:24,000, 1:62,500, 1:63,360, and 1:250,000 can be found inside the front cover of the Lab Manual. The name, scale, contour interval, and date of publication (date of revisions in parentheses) for each of the 16 maps are shown below. The latitude and longitude of the southeast corner of each quadrangle appears on the following page.

Map	Quadrangle Name	Scale	Contour Interval	Date and (Revisions)
T-1	Hawaii, Hawaii	1:250,000	200'	1975
T-2	Umnak, Alaska	1:250,000	200'	1953 (1983)
T-3	Deer Peak, Montana	1:24,000	40'	1964
T-4	Voltaire, North Dakota	1:24,000	5'	1948
T-5	Jackson, Mississippi-Louisiana	1:250,000	50'	1955 (1973)
T-6	Johnson City, TN-VA-KY-NC	1:250,000	100'	1957 (1966)
T-7	Canyonlands National Park, Utah	1:62,500	80'	1968
T-8	Putnam Hall, Florida	1:24,000	10'	1993
T-9	Park City, Kentucky	1:24,000	10'	1973
T-10	Furnace Creek, California	1:62,500	80'	1952
T-11	Whitewater, Wisconsin	1:62,500	20'	1960
T-12	Sodus, New York	1:24,000	10'	1952 (1978)
T-13	Mono Craters, California	1:62,500	80'	1953
T-14	Sumdum (D-4), Alaska	1:63,360	100'	1960 (1984)
T-15	Point Reyes, California	1:62,500	80'	1954 (1968)
T-16	Corpus Christi, Texas	1:250,000	50'	1956

Map	Quadrangle Name	Quadrangle Location (southeast corner)	
		Latitude	Longitude
T-1	Hawaii, Hawaii	18°54' N	154°48' W
T-2	Umnak, Alaska	53°00' N	168°00' W
T-3	Deer Peak, Montana	46°52'30" N	114°30' W
T-4	Voltaire, North Dakota	48°00' N	100°45' W
T-5	Jackson, Mississippi-Louisiana	32°00' N	90°00' W
T-6	Johnson City, TN-VA-KY-NC	36°00' N	82°00' W
T-7	Canyonlands National Park, Utah	37°52'30" N	109°30' W
T-8	Putnam Hall, Florida	29°37'30" N	81°52'30" W
T-9	Park City, Kentucky	37°00' N	86°00' W
T-10	Furnace Creek, California	36°15' N	116°45' W
T-11	Whitewater, Wisconsin	42°45' N	88°30' W
T-12	Sodus, New York	43°07'30" N	77°00' W
T-13	Mono Craters, California	37°45' N	119°00' W
T-14	Sumdum (D-4), Alaska	57°45' N	133°00' W
T-15	Point Reyes, California	37°56' N	122°45' W
T-16	Corpus Christi, Texas	27°00' N	96°00' W

GLOSSARY

ablation Wastage of glacial ice through melting and sublimation.

absolute humidity A direct measure of the water vapor content of air, expressed as the mass of water vapor in a given volume of air, usually as grams of water per cubic meter of air.

accumulation (glacial ice accumulation) Addition of ice into a glacier by incorporation of snow.

adiabatic cooling Cooling by expansion, such as in rising air.

adiabatic warming Warming by compression, such as in descending air.

air mass An extensive body of air that has relatively uniform properties in the horizontal dimension and moves as an entity.

albedo The reflectivity of a surface. The fraction of total solar radiation that is reflected back, unchanged, into space.

alluvial fan A fan-shaped depositional feature of alluvium laid down by a stream issuing from a mountain canyon.

alluvium Any stream-deposited sedimentary material; frequently alluvial deposits consist of rounded, sorted, and stratified rock debris.

alpine glacier Individual glacier that develops near a mountain crest line and normally moves downvalley for some distance.

analemma A "figure-8" chart showing the declination of the Sun and the "equation of time" of the Sun throughout the year.

andesite A volcanic rock intermediate in silica content between basalt and rhyolite; composed largely of a distinctive mineral association of plagioclase feldspar.

angle of incidence The angle at which the Sun's rays strike Earth's surface.

annual snowline (firn limit) The elevation on a glacier above which winter snow is able to persist throughout the year; above the annual snowline, the accumulation of snow and ice exceeds ablation.

annular [drainage] pattern A network in which the major streams are arranged in a ringlike, concentric pattern in response to a structural dome or basin.

anticyclone A high-pressure center.

antitrade winds Tropical upper-air westerly winds that blow toward the northeast in the Northern Hemisphere and toward the southeast in the Southern Hemisphere.

aphelion The point in Earth's elliptical orbit at which the Earth is farthest from the Sun (about 152,171,500 kilometers or 94,555,000 miles).

arête A narrow, jagged, serrated spine of rock; remainder of a ridge crest after several glacial cirques have been cut back into an interfluve from opposite sides of a divide.

asthenosphere Plastic layer of the upper mantle that underlies the lithosphere. Its rock is very hot and therefore weak and easily deformed.

atmospheric window The range of wavelengths of infrared radiation to which the atmosphere is transparent (between approximately 8 and 12 micrometers).

average daily insolation Intensity of solar radiation received by a surface averaged over a 24-hour period.

average lapse rate The average rate of temperature decrease with height in the troposphere—about 6.5°C per 1000 meters (3.6°F per 1000 feet).

average monthly precipitation Average precipitation in each month of the year.

average monthly temperature Average temperature of each month of the year.

azimuth Description of direction in terms of the number of degrees clockwise from north.

backwash Water moving seaward after the momentum of the wave swash is overcome by gravity and friction.

bajada A continual alluvial surface that extends across the piedmont zone, slanting from the range toward the basin, in which it is difficult to distinguish between individual fans.

barchan dune A crescent-shaped sand dune with cusps of the crescent pointing downwind.

barrier island (barrier bar; offshore bar) Narrow offshore island composed of sediment; generally oriented parallel to shore.

basalt Fine-grained dark volcanic rock; low silica content.

base line Reference parallel from which townships are designated north or south in the Public Land Survey.

base reflectivity [radar image] Weather radar image showing the intensity of echoes very close to the horizon—usually about 0.5° above the horizon.

base velocity [radar image] Weather Doppler radar image showing the overall pattern of movement within a storm.

basin of interior drainage A topographic basin or valley that has no stream outlet leading to the ocean.

baymouth bar A spit that has become extended across the mouth of a bay to connect with a headland on the other side, transforming the bay into a lagoon.

beach drifting The zigzag movement of beach sediment in which the net result is a displacement parallel to the coast in a general downwind direction.

benchmark Metal disk embedded in rock or concrete that serves as reference marker for topographic maps; locations often labeled "BM" on topographic maps.

bergschrund The crevice at the head of an alpine glacier that forms in summer as the glacier pulls away from the headwall of a cirque.

biogeochemical cycles Planetwide cycles and flows of energy, chemicals, and nutrients into and out of ecosystems and biomes.

biome A large, recognizable assemblage of plants and animals in functional interaction with its environment.

bluff A relatively steep slope marking the outer edge of a floodplain.

broadleaf tree Tree with flat and expansive leaves.

calcium carbonate Chemical compound making up the mineral calcite; principal component of the rock limestone; $CaCO_3$.

caldera Large, steep-sided, roughly circular depression resulting from the explosion and/or collapse of a large volcano.

capacity (water vapor capacity) Maximum amount of water vapor that can be present in the air at a given temperature.

carbonic acid Mild acid formed when carbon dioxide dissolves in water; H_2CO_3.

cavern Large opening or cave, especially in limestone; often decorated with speleothems such as stalactites and stalagmites.

centripetal drainage pattern A basin structure in which the streams converge toward the center.

chaparral Shrubby vegetation of the mediterranean climatic region of North America.

circle of illumination The edge of the sunlit hemisphere that is a great circle separating Earth into a light half and a dark half.

cirque A broad amphitheater hollowed out at the head of a glacial valley by ice erosion.

climograph (climatic diagram) Chart showing the average monthly temperature and precipitation for a weather station.

col A pass or saddle through a ridge produced when two adjacent glacial cirques on opposite sides of a divide are cut back enough to remove part of the arête between them.

cold front The leading edge of a cool air mass actively displacing warm air.

collapse doline A sinkhole produced by the collapse of the roof of a subsurface cavern.

collapsed zone [of a glacier] Irregular topography resulting from the melting of ice blocks within the terminal moraine of a stagnant glacier.

composite reflectivity [radar image] Weather radar image displaying the strongest echo detected in each direction from the radar unit.

composite volcano (stratovolcano) Volcano with the classic symmetrical cone-shaped peak, produced by a mixture of lava outpouring and pyroclastic explosion.

condensation Process by which water vapor is converted to liquid water; a warming process because latent heat is released.

conditional instability A lapse rate somewhere between the dry and saturated adiabatic rates; rising air becomes unstable after condensation releases latent heat.

conic projection A family of maps in which one or more cones is set tangent to, or intersecting, a portion of the globe and the geographic grid is projected onto the cone(s).

conifer (gymnosperm) Seed-reproducing plants that carry their seeds in cones.

conformality The property of a map projection that maintains proper shapes of surface features.

conformal map [projection] A projection that maintains proper angular relationships over the entire map; over limited areas shows the correct shapes of features shown on a map.

continental ice sheet Large ice sheet covering a portion of a continental area.

continental rift valley Fault-produced valley resulting from spreading or rifting of continent.

contour interval Difference in elevation between two elevation contour lines.

contour line (elevation contour line) A line joining points of equal elevation.

Coriolis effect (Coriolis force) The apparent deflection of free-moving objects to the right in the Northern Hemisphere and to the left in the Southern Hemisphere, in response to the rotation of Earth.

creep (soil creep) The slowest and least perceptible form of mass wasting, which consists of a very gradual downhill movement of soil and regolith.

cumulonimbus [cloud] Cumuliform cloud of great vertical development, often associated with a thunderstorm.

cutoff meander A sweeping stream channel curve that is isolated from streamflow because the narrow meander neck has been cut through by stream erosion.

cyclone Low-pressure center.

cylindrical projection A family of maps derived from the concept of projection onto a paper cylinder that is tangential to, or intersecting with, a globe.

datum Elevation reference point for a map or stream gage.

Daylight-saving time Practice in many parts of the world to shift clocks ahead one hour for the spring, summer, and early fall, largely to conserve energy.

debris flow Streamlike flow of mud and water heavily laden with sediments of various sizes; a mudflow containing large boulders.

December solstice Day of the year when the vertical rays of the Sun strike the Tropic of Capricorn; on or about December 21.

deciduous tree A tree that experiences an annual period in which all leaves die and usually fall from the tree, due either to a cold season or a dry season.

declination arrow (declination diagram) Diagram on a map showing the relationships among true north, magnetic north, and grid north.

declination of the Sun Latitude receiving the vertical rays of the Sun.

dendritic [drainage] pattern A treelike, branching pattern that consists of a random merging of streams, with tributaries joining larger streams irregularly, but always at acute angles.

depression contour Elevation contour line with hachure marks pointing downslope into a depression.

deranged drainage pattern The chaotic stream drainage pattern resulting from the irregular topography found in recently glaciated landscapes.

desert varnish A dark shiny coating of iron and manganese oxides that forms on rock surfaces exposed to desert air for a long time.

dew point temperature (dew point) The critical air temperature at which water vapor saturation is reached.

disappearing stream Stream that abruptly disappears from the surface where it flows into an underground cavity; common in karst regions.

discharge (stream discharge) Volume of flow of a stream.

Doppler effect Shift in the frequency of a sound wave or an electromagnetic wave due to either the movement of the observer or the source of the waves.

drainage basin (watershed) An area that contributes overland flow and groundwater to a specific stream (also called a catchment).

drainage divide The line of separation between runoff that descends into two different drainage basins.

drift (glacial drift) All material carried and deposited by glaciers.

drumlin A low, elongated hill formed by ice-sheet deposition and erosion. The long axis is aligned parallel with the direction of ice movements, and the end of the drumlin that faces the direction from which the ice came is blunter and slightly steeper than the other end.

dry adiabatic rate (dry adiabatic lapse rate) The rate at which a parcel of unsaturated air cools as it rises and warms as it descends (10°C per 1000 meters [5.5°F per 1000 feet]).

dynamic high High pressure cell associated with prominently descending air.

dynamic low Low pressure cell associated with prominently rising air.

earthflow Mass wasting process in which a portion of a water-saturated slope moves a short distance downhill.

earthquake Vibrations generated by abrupt movement of Earth's crust.

easterly wave A long but weak migratory low-pressure trough in the tropics.

ecosystem The totality of interactions among organisms and the environment in the area of consideration.

entrenched meanders A winding, sinuous stream valley with abrupt sides; possible outcome of the rejuvenation of a meandering stream.

environmental lapse rate The observed vertical temperature gradient of the troposphere.

epicenter Location on the surface directly above the center of fault rupture during an earthquake.

epiphytes Plants that live above ground level out of contact with the soil, usually growing on trees or shrubs.

equal area projection See **equivalence.**

equivalence The property of a map projection that maintains equal areal relationships in all parts of the map. Such maps are also called equal area maps.

equivalent map [projection] A projection that maintains constant area (size) relationships over the entire map; also called an "equal area projection."

esker Long, sinuous ridge of stratified glacial drift composed largely of glaciofluvial gravel and formed by the choking of subglacial streams during a time of glacial stagnation.

evaporation Process by which liquid water is converted to gaseous water vapor; a cooling process because latent heat is stored.

evergreen A tree or shrub that sheds its leaves on a sporadic or successive basis but at any given time appears to be fully leaved.

eye [of tropical cyclone] The nonstormy center of a tropical cyclone, which has a diameter of 16 to 40 kilometers (10 to 25 miles) and is a singular area of calmness in the maelstrom that whirls around it.

fjord (fjorded coast) A glacial trough that has been partly drowned by the sea.

flash flood Sudden surge of flood water down a normally dry stream channel; commonly result from desert thunderstorms.

flood frequency curve Chart showing the relationship between a stream's peak discharge and its flood recurrence interval.

floodplain A flattish valley floor covered with stream-deposited sediments (alluvium) and subject to periodic or episodic inundation by overflow from the stream.

friction The force that impedes the relative motion of two objects in contact.

front A zone of discontinuity between unlike air masses.

frost wedging Fragmentation of rock due to expansion of water that freezes in rock openings.

gage height Height of stream above its local datum.

geostrophic wind A wind that moves parallel to the isobars as a result of the balance between the pressure gradient force and the Coriolis effect.

glacial abrasion The chipping and grinding effect of rock fragments embedded in the bottom of a glacier.

glacial plucking Action in which rock particles beneath the ice are grasped by the freezing of meltwater in joints and fractures and pried out and dragged along in the general flow of a glacier.

glacial steps Series of level or gently sloping bedrock benches alternating with steep drops in the down-valley profile of a glacial trough.

glacial trough A valley reshaped by an alpine glacier, usually U-shaped.

glaciofluvial deposition The action whereby much of the debris that is carried along by glaciers is eventually deposited or redeposited by glacial meltwater.

Global Positioning System (GPS) A satellite-based system for determining accurate positions on or near Earth's surface.

gnomonic map Maps on which a straight line represents a great circle.

GOES (Geostationary Operational Environmental Satellites) Weather satellites positioned over fixed locations on Earth to provide continuous multi-wavelength monitoring of the atmosphere and surface.

graben A block of land bounded by parallel faults in which the block has been downthrown, producing a structural valley with a straight, steep-sided fault scarp on both sides.

grassland Plant association dominated by grasses and forbs.

graticule The network of parallels and meridians on a map.

great circle Circle on a globe formed by the intersection of Earth's surface with any plane that passes through Earth's center. A path along a great circle represents the shortest distance between two points on a sphere.

Greenwich Mean Time (GMT) Time in the Greenwich time zone. Today more commonly called UTC or Universal Time Coordinated.

grid north (GN) North orientation on supplementary map grid system, such as the Universal Transverse Mercator grid.

Hadley cells Two complete vertical convective circulation cells between the equator, where warm air rises in the ITCZ, and 25° to 30° north and south latitude, where much of the air subsides into the subtropical highs.

hanging valley A tributary glacial trough, the bottom of which is considerably higher than the bottom of the principal trough that it joins.

headwall [of a cirque] The steep back wall of a glacial cirque.

highland ice field Largely unconfined ice sheet in high mountain area.

high pressure [cell] Area of relatively high atmospheric pressure.

horn A steep-sided, pyramidal rock pinnacle formed by expansive glacial plucking of the headwalls where three or more cirques intersect.

horst An uplifted block of land between two parallel faults.

humidity Water vapor in the air.

hurricane A tropical cyclone with wind speeds of 64 knots or greater affecting North or Central America.

ice-contact deposit Depositional features that develop along the active margin of a glacier.

inches of mercury Measure of atmospheric pressure based on the height of a column of mercury in a liquid barometer.

index contour Every fourth or fifth elevation contour line on most contour line maps; thicker than regular contour lines; usually marked with elevation.

infrared [radiation] Electromagnetic radiation in the wavelength range of about 0.7 to 1000 micrometers; wavelengths just longer than visible light.

inselberg ("island mountain") Isolated summit rising abruptly from a low-relief surface.

insolation Incoming solar radiation.

interfluve The higher land or ridge above the valley sides that separates adjacent valleys.

International Date Line The line marking a time difference of an entire day from one side of the line to the other. Generally, this line falls on the 180th meridian except where it deviates to avoid separating an island group.

intertropical convergence zone (ITCZ) The region near or on the equator where the northeast trades and the southeast trades converge; dominated by air rising in thunderstorm updrafts; associated with high rainfall.

island arc (volcanic island arc) Chain of volcanic islands associated with an oceanic plate–oceanic plate subduction zone.

isobar A line on a map joining points of equal atmospheric pressure.

isoline A line on a map connecting points that have the same quality or intensity of a given phenomenon.

isotherm A line on a map joining points of equal temperature.

jet stream A rapidly moving current of air concentrated along a quasi-horizontal axis in the upper troposphere or in the stratosphere, characterized by strong vertical and lateral wind shears.

June solstice Day of the year when the vertical rays of the Sun strike the Tropic of Cancer; on or about June 21.

kame A relatively steep-sided mound or conical hill composed of stratified drift found in areas of ice-sheet deposition and associated with meltwater deposition in close association with stagnant ice.

karst Topography developed as a consequence of subsurface solution.

kettle An irregular depression in a morainal surface created when blocks of stagnant ice eventually melt.

knot A unit of speed equal to 1 nautical mile, or 1.15 statute miles, per hour; 1.85 kilometers per hour.

Köppen climate classification system A climatic classification of the world devised by Wladimir Köppen.

lagoon A body of quiet salt or brackish water in an area between a barrier island or a barrier reef and the mainland.

landslide An abrupt and often catastrophic event in which a large mass of rock and earth slides bodily downslope in only a few seconds or minutes. An instantaneous collapse of a slope.

large-scale map A map with a scale that is a relatively large representative fraction and therefore portrays only a small portion of Earth's surface, but in considerable detail.

latent heat Energy stored or released when a substance changes state. For example, evaporation is a cooling process because latent heat is stored and condensation is a warming process because latent heat is released.

lateral moraine Well-defined ridge of unsorted debris (till) built up along the sides of valley glaciers, parallel to the valley walls.

latitude Location described as an angle measured north and south of the equator.

lava Molten magma that is extruded onto the surface of Earth, where it cools and solidifies.

lava dome (plug dome) Dome or bulge formed by the pushing up of viscous magma in a volcanic vent.

lens stereoscope Optical device for viewing stereograms.

lifting condensation level (LCL) The altitude at which rising air cools sufficiently to reach 100 percent relative humidity at the dew point temperature, and condensation begins.

linear fault trough Straight-line valley that marks the surface position of a fault, especially a strike-slip fault; formed by the erosion or settling of crushed rock along the trace of a fault.

lithospheric plates (lithosphere) Tectonic plates consisting of the crust and upper rigid mantle.

longitude Location described as an angle measured east and west from the prime meridian on Earth's surface.

longshore current A current in which water moves roughly parallel to the shoreline in a generally downwind direction; set up by the action of waves.

longwave radiation Wavelengths of thermal infrared radiation emitted by Earth and the atmosphere; also referred to as terrestrial radiation.

low pressure [cell] Area of relatively low atmospheric pressure.

magma Molten material below Earth's surface.

magnetic north (MN) For a given location, the compass direction toward the magnetic north pole.

mantle plume (hot spot) A location where molten mantle magma rises to, or almost to, Earth's surface; often found in the middle of a plate.

March equinox One of two days of the year when the vertical rays of the Sun strike the equator; every location on Earth has equal day and night; occurs on or about March 20th each year.

marine terrace A platform of marine erosion that has been uplifted above sea level.

mass wasting Relatively short distance, downslope movement of broken rock material primarily under the direct influence of gravity.

meandering stream (meandering stream channel) Highly twisting or looped stream channel pattern.

meander scar A former stream meander or stream channel through which the stream no longer flows.

medial moraine A dark band of rocky debris down the middle of a glacier created by the union of the lateral moraines of two adjacent glaciers.

meltwater (glacial meltwater) Water resulting from the melting of glacial ice.

meridian An imaginary line of longitude extending from pole to pole, crossing all parallels at right angles, and being aligned in true north–south directions.

meteogram Chart plotting hourly changes in weather conditions for a location over a one-day period.

midlatitude cyclone Large migratory low-pressure system that occurs within the middle latitudes and moves generally with the westerlies. Also known as extratropical cyclones and wave cyclones.

midocean ridge A lengthy system of deep-sea mountain ranges, generally located at some distance from any continent; formed by divergent plate boundaries on the ocean floor.

millibar A measure of atmospheric pressure, consisting of one-thousandth part of a bar, or 1000 dynes per square centimeter.

mixing ratio Description of the water vapor content of the air expressed as the mass of water in a given mass of dry air; usually as grams of water vapor per kilogram of dry air.

moraine The largest and generally most conspicuous landform feature produced by glacial deposition of till, which consists of irregular rolling topography that rises somewhat above the level of the surrounding terrain.

mudflow Down-valley movement of a rapidly moving mixture of soil and water.

natural levee An embankment of slightly higher ground fringing a stream channel in a floodplain; formed by deposition during floods.

normal fault The result of tension (extension) producing a steeply inclined fault plane, with the block of land on one side being pushed up, or upthrown, in relation to the block on the other side, which is downthrown.

occluded front A complex front formed when a cold front overtakes a warm front.

occlusion Process of a cold front overtaking a warm front to form an occluded front.

oceanic trench (deep oceanic trench) Deep linear depression in the ocean floor where subduction is taking place.

offset stream A stream course displaced by lateral movement along a fault.

one-hour precipitation [radar image] Weather radar image showing estimate of precipitation that has fallen over the last hour.

orthographic projection Map projection in which Earth appears as it would from space.

outwash plain Extensive glaciofluvial feature that is a relatively smooth, flattish alluvial apron deposited beyond recessional or terminal moraines by streams issuing from ice.

overland flow The general movement of unchanneled surface water down the slope of the land surface.

oxbow lake A cutoff meander that initially holds water.

paleomagnetism Past magnetic orientation.

parallel A circle resulting from a line connecting all points of equal latitude.

parallel [drainage] pattern A drainage pattern found in areas of pronounced regional slope, particularly if the gradient is gentle, with long streams flowing parallel to one another.

paternoster lakes A sequence of small lakes found in the shallow excavated depressions of glacial steps.

pediment A gently inclined bedrock platform that extends outward from a mountain front, usually in an arid region.

perihelion The point in its orbit at which a planet is nearest the Sun.

piedmont (piedmont zone) Zone at the "foot of the mountains."

plane of the ecliptic The imaginary plane that passes through the Sun and through Earth at every position in its orbit around the Sun; the orbital plane of Earth.

plane projection A family of maps derived by the perspective extension of the geographic grid from a globe to a plane that is tangent to the globe at some point.

plate tectonics A coherent theory of massive crustal rearrangement based on the movement of continent-sized lithospheric plates.

playa Dry lake bed in a basin of interior drainage.

Pleistocene epoch An epoch of the Cenozoic era between the Pliocene and the Holocene; from about 1.8 million to 10,000 years ago.

plutonic rock Igneous rock formed below ground from the cooling and solidification of magma.

polar front The zone of contact between unlike air masses in the westerlies and the polar easterlies; associated with the subpolar lows; typically found at about 55°–65° N and S latitude.

polarity (parallelism) [of rotation axis] A characteristic of Earth's axis wherein it always points toward Polaris (the North Star) at every position in Earth's orbit around the Sun.

potential evaporation The maximum amount of moisture that could be lost through evaporation if the water were available.

precipitation Drops of liquid or solid water falling from clouds.

pressure of air The force exerted by the atmosphere on a surface or walls of a container.

pressure gradient Change in atmospheric pressure over some horizontal distance.

pressure gradient force The propelling force exerted by a pressure gradient.

prime meridian The meridian passing through the Royal Observatory at Greenwich (England), just east of London, and from which longitude is measured.

principal meridian Reference meridian from which ranges are designated east or west in the Public Land Survey.

pseudocylindrical projection (elliptical projection) A family of map projections in which the entire world is displayed in an oval shape.

Public Land Survey (township grid) Land survey system used throughout most of the United States west of the Mississippi River that uses a rectangular grid with townships and ranges.

quadrangle Map (commonly a topographic map) delimited by lines of latitude and longitude on all four sides.

radar Radio detection and ranging.

radial [drainage] pattern Drainage pattern in which streams flow outward in all directions from a central dome or peak.

rating curve Chart showing the relationship between a stream's gage height and its discharge.

recessional moraine A glacial deposit of till formed during a pause in the retreat of the ice margin.

rectangular [drainage] pattern Pattern where streams follow sets of faults and/or joints, with prominent right-angled relationships.

recurrence interval (return period) [of a flood] Statistical estimate of the number of years between times when a given peak stream discharge will be reached or exceeded; for example, a "50-year flood" is the peak stream gage height likely to be reached once every 50 years.

relative humidity An expression of the amount of water vapor in the air in comparison with the total amount that could be there if the air were saturated. This is a ratio that is expressed as a percentage.

representative fraction (r.f.) The ratio that is an expression of a fractional map scale that compares map distance with ground distance.

reverse fault A fault produced from compression, with the upthrown block rising steeply above the downthrown block, so that the fault scarp would be severely oversteepened if erosion did not act to smooth the slope.

rhumb line (loxodrome) A true compass heading; a line of constant compass direction.

rhyolite Light colored volcanic rock that forms from magmas with high silica content.

ria coastline An embayed coast with numerous estuaries; formed by the flooding of stream valleys by the sea.

ridge [of high pressure] Linear or elongated area of relatively high atmospheric pressure.

rockfall (fall) Mass wasting process in which weathered rock drops to the foot of a cliff or steep slope.

sag pond A pond caused by the collection of water from springs and/or runoff into sunken ground, resulting from the crushing of rock in an area of fault movement.

saturated adiabatic rate (saturated adiabatic lapse rate) The diminished rate of cooling, averaging about 6°C per 1000 meters (3.3°F per 1000 feet) of rising air above the lifting condensation level.

saturation [with water vapor] Circumstance in which the air contains the maximum amount of water vapor for a given temperature; condensation typically will begin when the air reaches saturation.

saturation mixing ratio Mixing ratio of a saturated parcel of air; one expression of water vapor capacity.

scale [of a map] The relationship between length measured on a map and the actual distance represented on Earth.

scarp (fault scarp) A steep escarpment or nearly vertical cliff formed by fault movement.

sea stack Pillars or towers that form where coastal cliffs wear back leaving a remnant isolated from the mainland.

section Square tract of land, one mile to a side, in the Public Land Survey.

seif (longitudinal dune) Long, narrow desert dunes that usually occur in multiplicity and in parallel arrangement.

September equinox One of two days of the year when the vertical rays of the Sun strike the equator; every location on Earth has equal day and night; occurs on or about September 22nd each year.

shield volcano Volcanoes built up in a lengthy outpouring of very fluid basaltic lava. Shield volcanoes are broad mountains with gentle slopes.

shrub Woody, low-growing perennial plant.

silica Silicon dioxide (SiO_2) in any of several mineral forms.

sinkhole (doline) A small, rounded depression that is formed by the dissolution of surface limestone, typically at joint intersections.

sling psychrometer Instrument for measuring relative humidity consisting of a dry bulb and wet bulb thermometer mounted side-by-side; whirling promotes evaporation and cooling of the wet bulb.

slip face Steeper leeward side of a sand dune.

slump A slope collapse with a backward rotation; rotational slide.

small-scale map A map whose scale is a relatively small representative fraction and therefore shows a large portion of Earth's surface in limited detail.

solar altitude Angle of the Sun above the horizon.

solar constant The fairly constant amount of solar insolation received at the top of the atmosphere, about 1372 watts per square meter (W/m^2) or slightly less than 2 calories per square centimeter per minute, or 2 langleys per minute.

specific humidity A direct measure of water-vapor content expressed as the mass of water vapor in a given mass of air (grams of vapor/kilograms of air).

spit A linear deposit of marine sediment that is attached to the land at one or both ends.

stable [air] Air that rises only if forced.

stalactite A pendant structure hanging downward from a cavern's roof.

stalagmite A projecting structure growing upward from a cavern's floor.

standard time zones Global system of 24 time zones, each 15° of longitude wide, within which it is the same time; boundaries of most standard time zones have been manipulated for the convenience of the local population.

stationary front The common boundary between two air masses in a situation in which neither air mass displaces the other.

station model (weather map station model) Standardized system of data presentation used on weather maps to convey conditions at a weather station.

stereogram (stereopair; stereo aerial photographs) Matched set of vertical aerial photographs for viewing in three dimensions with a stereoscope.

storm relative motion [radar image] Weather Doppler radar image showing wind directions as if the storm were stationary.

storm total precipitation [radar image] Weather radar image that estimates the total amount of precipitation that has fallen since the last one-hour pause in rainfall.

stream Water flowing within a channel, typically along a valley bottom.

streamflow Channeled movement of water along a valley bottom.

stream order Concept that describes the hierarchy of a drainage network.

stream rejuvenation When a stream gains downcutting ability, usually through regional tectonic uplift.

stream terrace Remnant of a previous valley floodplain of a rejuvenated stream.

strike-slip fault A fault produced by shearing, with adjacent blocks being displaced laterally with respect to one another. The movement is entirely horizontal.

subduction Descent of the edge of an oceanic lithospheric plate under the edge of an adjoining plate.

subtropical high (STH) Large, semipermanent high-pressure cells centered at about 30° latitude over the oceans, which have average diameters of 3200 kilometers (2000 miles) and are usually elongated east–west; characterized by persistent dry weather.

succulents Plants that have fleshy stems that store water.

Sun time Local time based on the position of the Sun in the sky; local Sun time noon is when the Sun reaches its highest point in the sky.

swallow hole The distinct opening at the bottom of some sinks through which surface drainage can pour directly into an underground channel.

swash The cascading forward motion of a breaking wave that rushes up the beach.

Système International (SI) The international system of measurement, popularly known as the "metric system" of measurement.

talus (scree) Pieces of angular weathered rock, of various sizes, that fall directly downslope.

talus cone Sloping, cone-shaped heaps of dislodged talus.

tangent rays [of the Sun] Sun's rays that are just skimming past the Earth.

tarn Small lake in the shallow excavated depression of a cirque; sometimes used to describe any lake that forms on a glacial step.

temperature inversion A situation in which temperature increases with increasing altitude, the inverse of the normal condition.

terminal moraine A glacial deposit of till that builds up at the outermost extent of ice advance.

terminus [of a glacier] The end of a glacier, where ice is melting as quickly as it is flowing in.

thermal high High pressure cell associated with cold surface conditions.

thermal low Low pressure cell associated with warm surface conditions.

thrust fault (overthrust fault) A fault created by compression forcing the upthrown block to override the downthrown block at a relatively low angle.

till Rock debris that is deposited directly by moving or melting ice, with no meltwater flow or redeposition involved; typically consists of angular, unsorted, and unstratified rock debris.

tilted fault block mountain (fault-block mountain) An asymmetrical mountain formed by faulting on one side of a surface block without any faulting on the other side; results in a steep slope along the fault scarp and a relatively gentle slope on the other side.

tombolo A spit formed by sand deposition of waves converging in two directions on the landward side of a nearshore island, so that a spit connects the island to the land.

topographic map Large-scale map using elevation contour lines to depict the terrain.

topographic profile Side-view diagram showing elevation change along a line across a topographic map.

township 36-square-mile tract of land; township numbers refer to "tiers" north or south of a baseline in the Public Land Survey system.

trade winds The major easterly wind system of the tropics, issuing from the equatorward sides of the subtropical highs and diverging toward the west and toward the equator.

transverse dune A crescent-shaped sand dune that has convex sides facing the prevailing direction of wind and which occurs where the supply of sand is great. The crest is perpendicular to the wind and aligned in parallel waves across the land.

trellis drainage pattern A drainage pattern that is usually developed on alternating bands of hard and soft strata, with long parallel streams linked by short right-angled segments and joined by short tributaries.

tropical cyclone A migratory storm most significantly affecting the tropics and subtropics; consists of a prominent low-pressure center that is essentially circular in shape and has a steep pressure gradient outward from the center. When wind speed reaches 64 knots, they are called hurricanes in North America and the Caribbean.

troposphere The lowest thermal layer of the atmosphere, in which temperature decreases with height.

trough [of low pressure] Linear or elongated band of relatively low atmospheric pressure.

Universal Time Coordinated (UTC) or Coordinated Universal Time The world time standard reference; previously known as Greenwich Mean Time (GMT).

Universal Transverse Mercator grid (UTN) Supplementary rectangular grid system used on many topographic maps; marks off location in terms of the number of meters north or south of the equator, and east of a standard meridian.

unstable [air] Air that rises without being forced.

uvala A compound doline or chain of intersecting dolines.

valley That portion of the total terrain in which a drainage system is clearly established.

valley train A lengthy deposit of glaciofluvial alluvium confined to a valley bottom beyond the outwash plain.

vertical aerial photograph Aerial photograph taken with a camera pointing directly down toward the surface.

vertical exaggeration Exaggerated vertical scale of a topographic profile or raised-relief map; exaggerated steepness of slopes observed when viewing stereo aerial photographs.

vertical rays (of the Sun) Sun's rays that are striking perpendicular to the surface.

visible light Waves in the electromagnetic spectrum in the narrow band between about 0.4 and 0.7 micrometers in length; wavelengths of electromagnetic radiation to which the human eye is sensitive.

volcano A mountain or hill from which extrusive igneous material is ejected.

warm front The leading edge of an advancing warm air mass.

water vapor The gaseous state of moisture.

water vapor [satellite] images Weather satellite images showing the relative amount of water vapor in the mid-troposphere.

wave refraction Phenomenon whereby waves change their directional trend as they approach a shoreline.

westerlies The great wind system of the midlatitudes that flows basically from west to east around the world in the latitudinal zone between about 30° and 60° both north and south of the equator.

wind shear (vertical wind shear) Significant change in wind direction or speed in the vertical dimension.

yazoo stream A tributary unable to enter the main stream because of natural levees along the main stream.

Zulu time Universal Time Coordinated (UTC; Greenwich Mean Time [GMT]) expressed on a 24-hour clock; abbreviated "Z."

Additional Notes

Additional Notes

Additional Notes

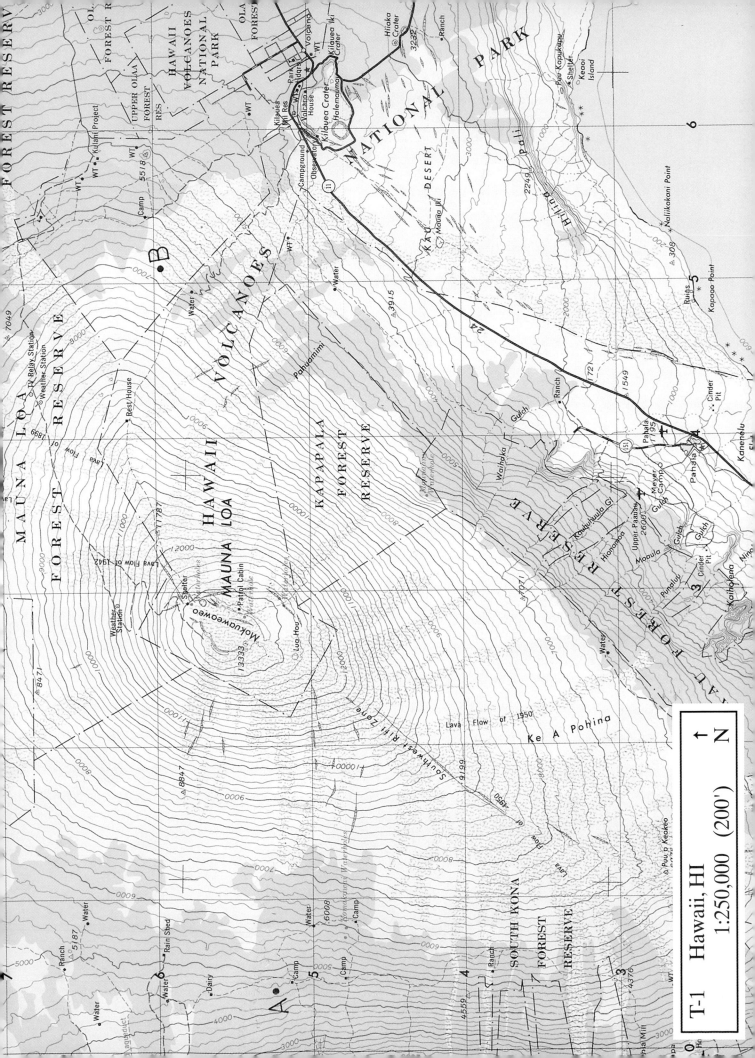

T-1   Hawaii, HI
1:250,000 (200')

N

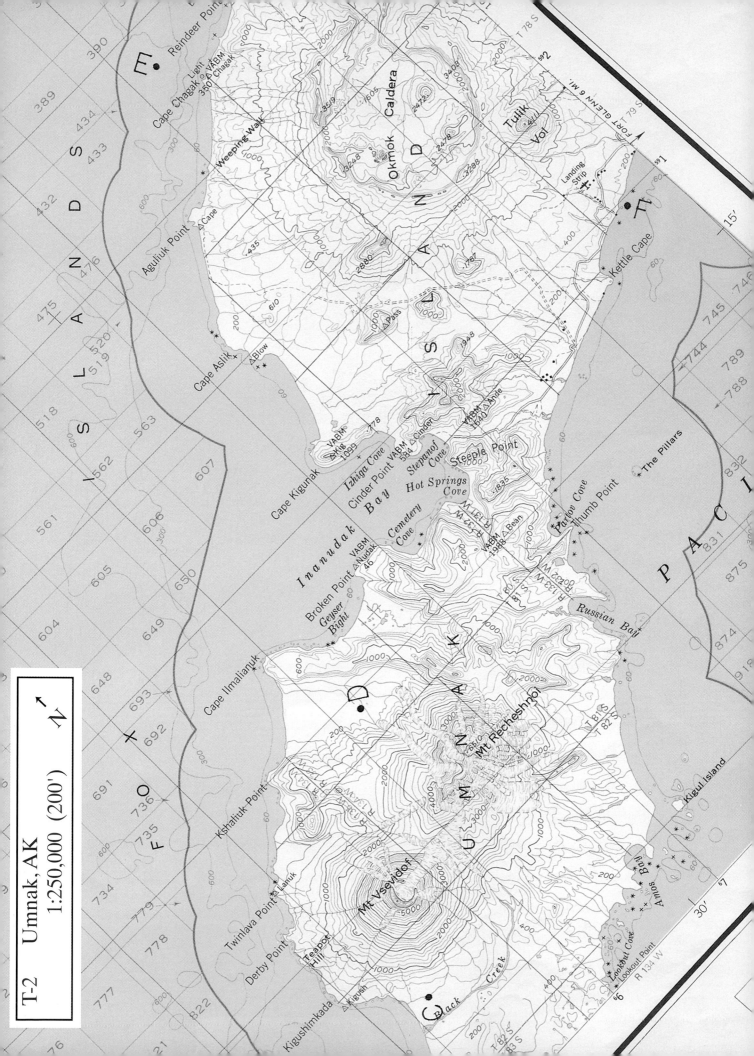

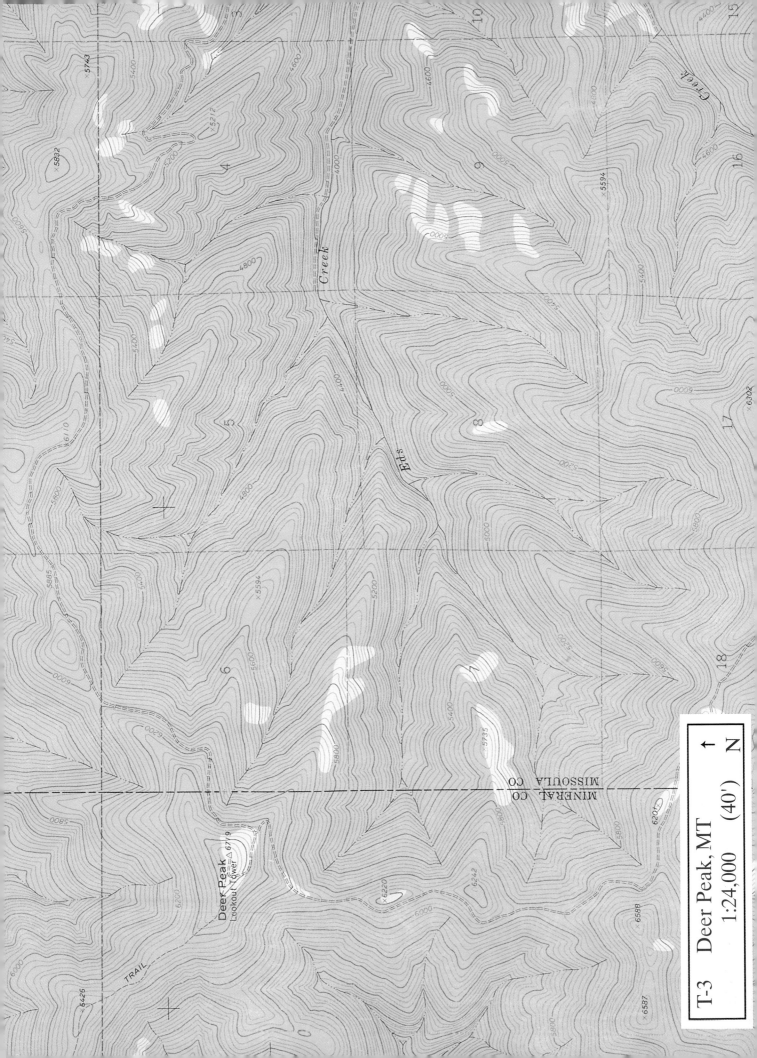

T-3   Deer Peak, MT
1:24,000   (40')

N

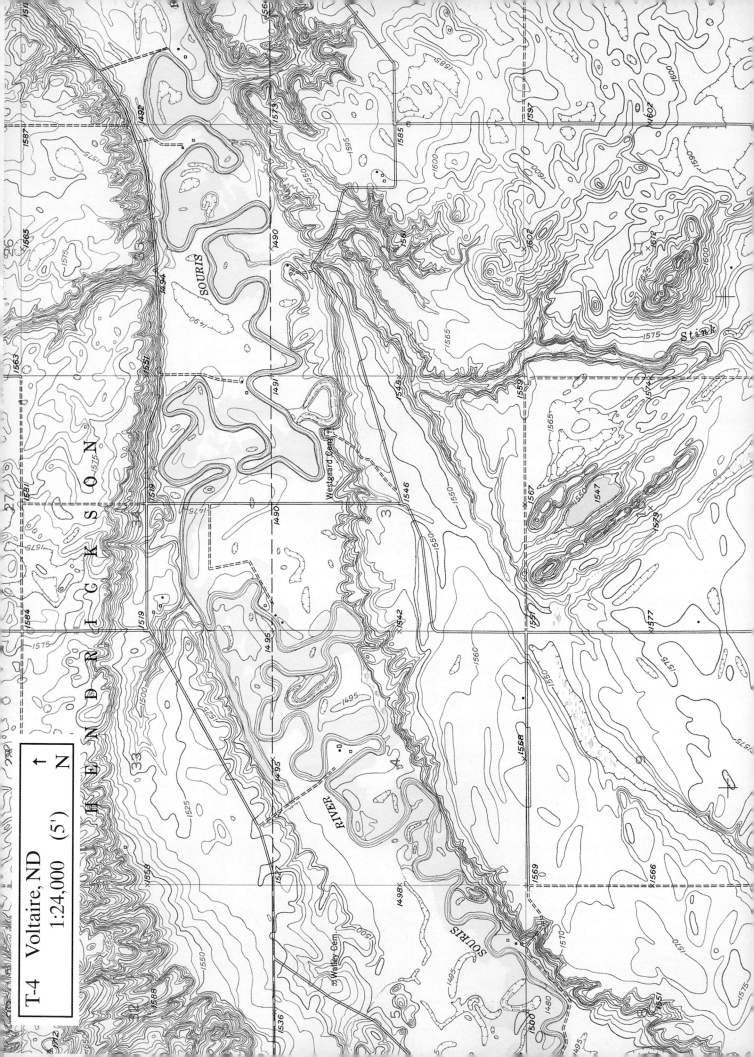

T-4   Voltaire, ND
1:24,000   (5')

N

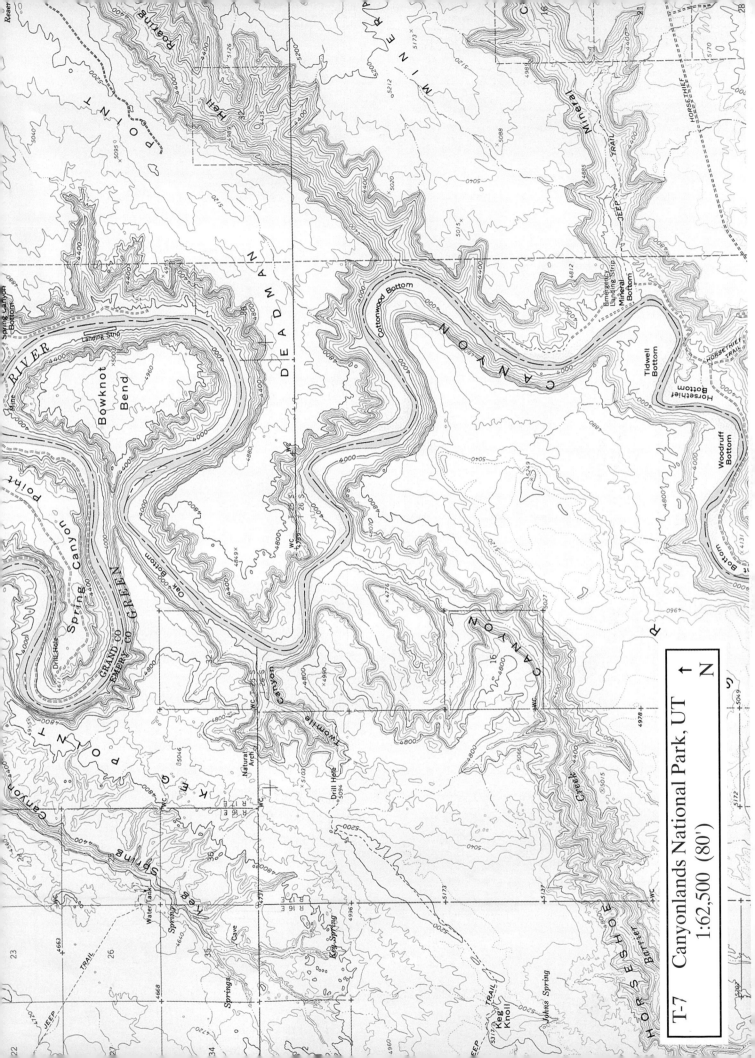

T-7 Canyonlands National Park, UT
1:62,500 (80')

T-8   Putnam Hall, FL

THE   KNOBS

Cave

Campground

Opossum Hol

Campground

Golf
Course

Hundred Dome
Cave

Jessie James
Cave
Gravel Slave Cave

Dome House
Cave

Bald
Knob

EDMONSON CO
BARREN CO

Oil
Well

Sewage Disposal
Pond

Oil
Well

Cem

577

Cem

Cem

578

585

31w

65

BM
615

NASHVILLE

BM
603

AND

620

BM
585

Oil
Well

LOUISVILLE

651

Gardner

550

Oil
Well

255

BM
618

Oil
Well

657

Oil Wells

610

650

Oil Wells

BM
645

Oil
Wells

BM637 Fairview
Ch

641

Oil Wells

Mt Vernor
Ch

EDMONSON CO
BARREN CO

700

Park City, KY

1:24,000   (10')

↑
N

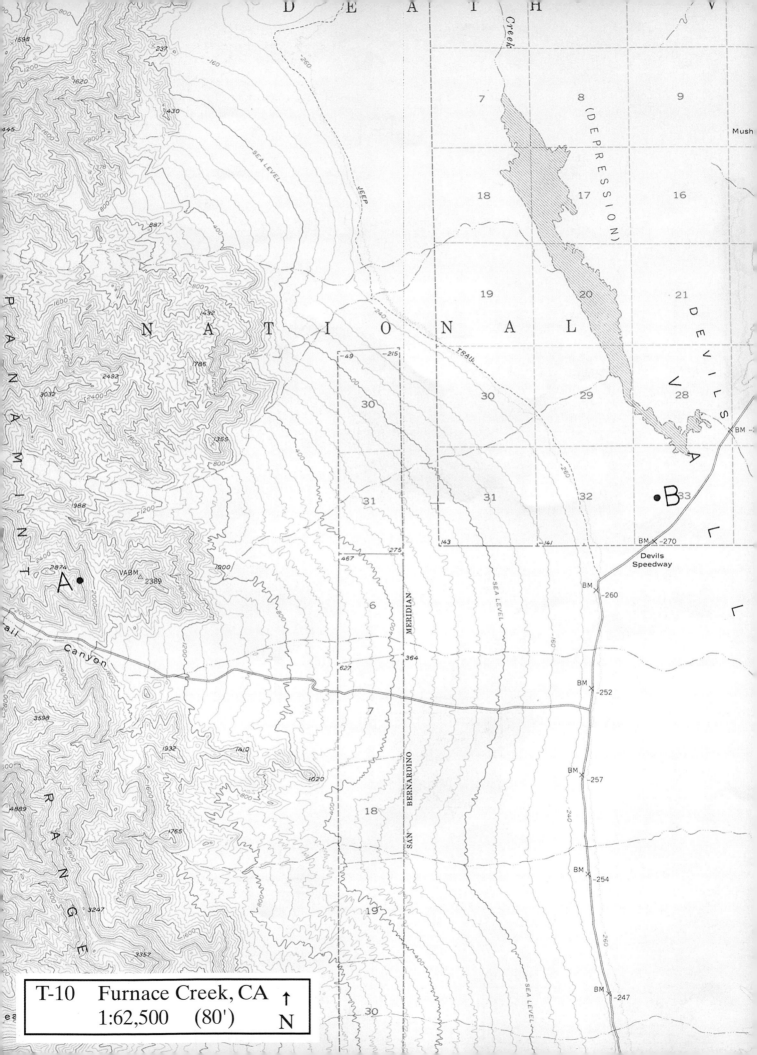

T-10   Furnace Creek, CA
1:62,500   (80')   N

T-12   Sodus, NY

1:24,000   (10')

↑
N

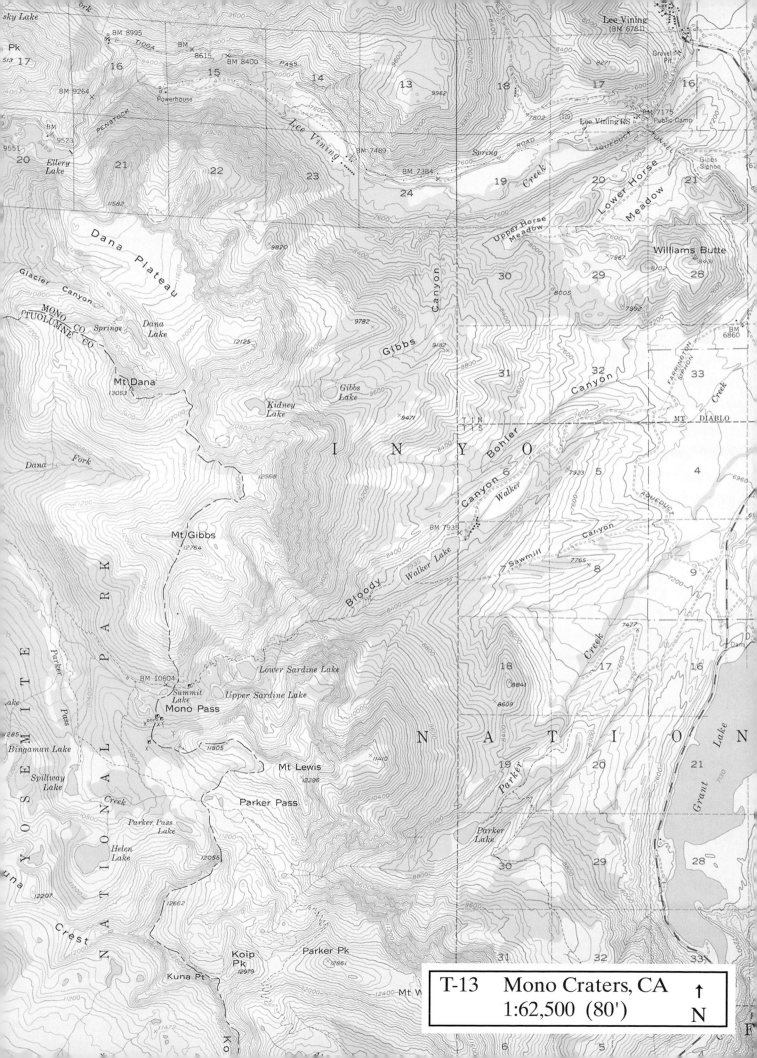

T-13   Mono Craters, CA

1:62,500 (80')

N

N A T I O N A L   F O R E S T

T R A C Y

A R M

TRACY ARM - FORDS TERROR

S O U T H

W I L D E R N E S S

T-14   Sumdum (D-4), AK

1:63,360   (100')

↑ N

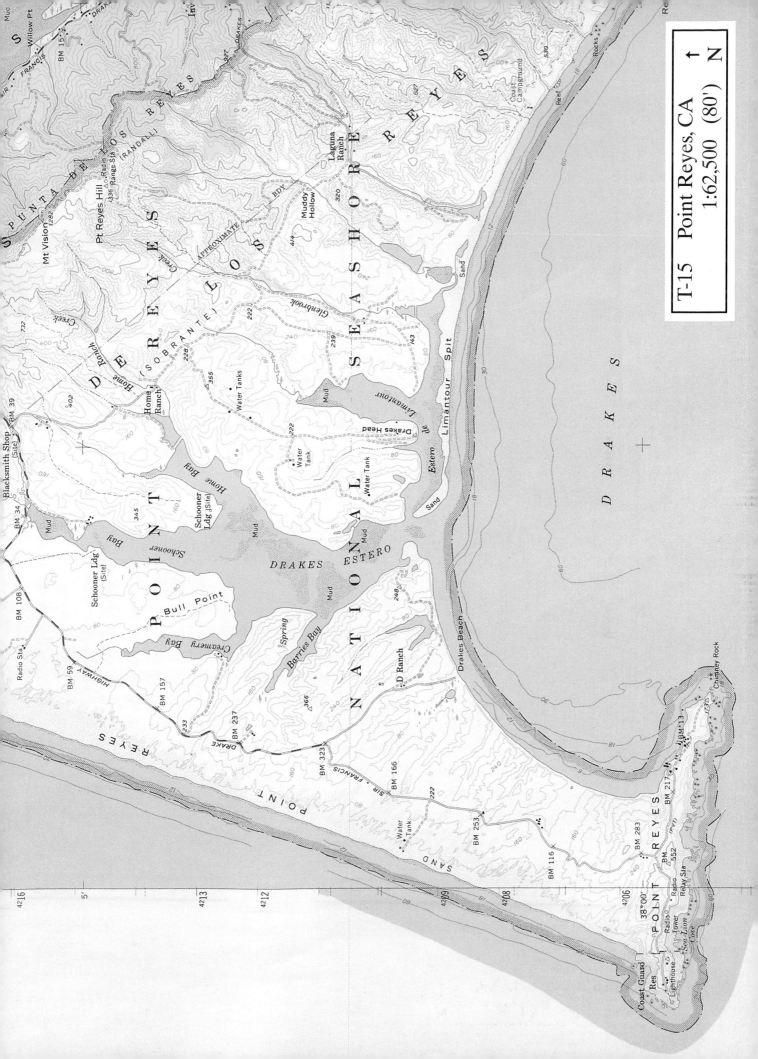

T-15　Point Reyes, CA
1:62,500　(80')　N

(286)

Laguna Vista

Pita Island

ENCINAL PENINSULA

24

NUECES CO

KLEBERG CO

Fo

Gin

19

Chapman Ranch

Cem

Tower

34

Gin

NUECES COUNTY
KLEBERG COUNTY

KINGSVILLE ROAD

ATION

Chiltipin Creek

Laureles Ranch

25

Bird Island
Oil Field

Sand
Mud

Channel

North
Bird
Island

Tunas Creek

LAGUNA LARGA

17

26

17

South
Bird
Island

BIG
HILL

42

Windmill

Ford

PADRE ISLAND

LITTLE DAGGER

9

Windmill

5

Windmill

KING RANCH

34

Windmill

25

Parra
Lake

Windmill

Madero
Lake

25

Jaboncillos Ranch

25

Alazan Mott

.13

Windmill

25

24

GREEN HILL
Shifting
sand
dunes

DAGGER
HILL

sand

Windmill

Drum
Point

Comitas
Lake

Sand
Mud

Compuerta

Sand
Mud

BIG
BALL
HILL

29

Sand
Mud

merous small int ponds

11

Oil

Point of Rocks

sand

tmannville

CAYO DEL GRULLO

ALAZAN BAY

Alazan Bay
Naval Range Station

Numerous small
intermittent ponds

Oil

Sandy
Hook

Tinhevallo

Sand Mud

BIG
BALL
HILL

Riviera
Oil
Field

Oil

Riviera Beach

Oil

Kleberg Point

Starvation
Point

Boggy Slough

Sand
Mud

LAGUNA
SALADO

Pie de Gallo

Negrohead
Point

KLEBERG COUNTY
KENEDY COUNTY

Griffins
Point

25

2

Black Bluff

BAFFIN BAY

Peñascal Rincon

Sand
Mud

Gas

Water

Oil

INTRACOASTAL WATERWAY

sand

Windmill

Channel

Yarborough Pass

Rocky Slough

sand

28

Water
27

Shifting
sand
dunes

Gaging
station

mud

MIDDLE
GROUND

ALTO DE LA CRUZ

8

Shifting
sand
dunes

Potrero de
los Caballos

Cuba I

sand

Oil

16

Shifting
sand
dunes

Shifting
sand
dunes

Potrero
Grande

Sand
Mud
Potrero
Cortado

LAGUNA MADRE

sand

mud
sand

Potrero de
las Canelas

30

mud

19

Potrero
Farías

60

15

Sand
Mud

mud